REVELATIONS 2012

Alexander James

Raider Publishing International

New York   London   Cape Town

Cover image photographed at the Museo de la Nacion in Lima, Peru by Jorge Mori

ISBN: 978-1-61667-126-6

Published By Raider Publishing International
www.RaiderPublishing.com
New York London Cape Town
Printed in the United States of America and the United Kingdom

REVELATIONS 2012

Alexander James

Prologue

Peru, South America. 1994

The Shadow Foreign Secretary stepped wearily out of the limousine. The long seventeen-hour flight from Heathrow to the Jorge Chavéz International Airport in Lima had been comfortable but tiring and during the thirty-minute drive into the capital he had struggled to keep his eyes open. Still, the welcoming ceremony was only scheduled for an hour, just enough time for the Peruvian President to pose with the most important visitor to his country for some years.

Alberto Fujimori wasn't the most popular leader the country had ever had despite being recently returned to power for a second term and security was tight due to the threat of terrorist attacks against him. (Most political observers agreed that a seventeen percent turn out at the polls hardly suggested overwhelming support.)

He was determined to use the visit as a propaganda tool to illustrate the progress made by his government in securing foreign investment for the country.

The second Henderson's feet touched the floor outside the car he was surrounded by several security men who bustled him quickly across the street towards a large, ornate building. There was only a small crowd, he noticed, on the opposite side of the road but they were contained behind barriers and the presence of a disproportionate number of military personnel leant a menacing feel to the scene.

On entering the building he felt the tension in the atmosphere ease immediately. The security men left his side and a small but very self-assured Japanese man approached him. He smiled, bowed his head and held out his hand for Henderson to shake. The grip was firm and warm and Henderson returned the smile.

After a few minutes shaking hands for the cameras and being introduced to members of the Peruvian government, the President led the way across the large hallway and through two enormous doors. The entourage of dignitaries, security men and press photographers followed behind at a respectable distance.

The room they entered was much smaller and darker than the one they'd just left and contained very little in the way of furniture; just three armchairs set in front of what appeared to be some kind of stone statue. Henderson and Fujimori sat down whilst more photographs were taken and the Prime minister made a short speech. Although he spoke in Spanish and Henderson was totally unaware of what was being said he smiled and nodded occasionally in what he hoped were the right places.

After a few minutes the small audience applauded and began to file out of the room. Only one of the men remained and the President beckoned him to sit in the third chair. He sat and introduced himself as Perez de Milas, the official interpreter. As Fujimori started speaking, Henderson smiled to disguise a yawn that threatened to reveal how tired he was. It was going to be a long thirty minutes.

Henderson was now once again in the great hallway sipping a glass of red wine and chatting to his opposite number in the Peruvian government. The man spoke only broken English so the conversation was restricted to pleasantries.

After a few minutes, Henderson politely excused himself and approached Perez de Milas to enquire about the whereabouts of the lavatory. He was directed back through the doors into the room where the meeting had taken place earlier.

As he made his way across the room, his attention was suddenly drawn to the stone statue that had provided the backdrop for the photographs. For a second he could have sworn he saw movement near the top of the stone.

He walked over to take a closer look and for the first time noticed the engravings on the stone.

The main figure was a man with huge circular eyes and two enormous fangs which protruded from thick, smiling lips. He wore a headdress made of feathers and in one hand he held a pointed staff. The man appeared to be watching a winged serpent that was trying to fly away. In its talons it held the writhing body of a woman.

Coiled around the woman's waist, preventing the serpent from rising, was the tail of a huge, snarling cat of some kind (*a jaguar?*)

Henderson wondered how old the stone was and made a mental note to ask the interpreter about it. He was about to turn away when again something caught his eye. There was something about the woman's face...

He leaned closer. *'Shit!'* Henderson's heart nearly stopped dead. The eyes opened and looked straight towards him. The pupils grew wider and he felt as though he were being drawn towards them ...into them.

He suddenly felt afraid. It was almost as if his very soul was being sucked into the stone. He tried to call out to the people in the hallway but his throat felt dry and constricted. He tried to avert his gaze from the huge black spheres that had now replaced the woman's pupils and then he saw the pinprick of light at their centres. It was growing steadily bigger and bigger...

1

Chavin de Huantar, Peru, August 5th 1888

"Jacques, over here, bring the specimen case!"

Jacques retrieved the brown, leather case from the forest floor and clambered through the undergrowth toward Professor Arnold.

Pushing aside a curtain of hanging vines he knelt down beside him.

"What is it, Professor?"

"*Chenopodium ambrosioides,*" whispered Arnold. "The tribesmen here use it to treat all forms of skin affliction. I believe it may provide a cure for the pox."

He leaned forward, and using a scalpel blade, deftly cut several of the small green shoots and placed them carefully between the sheets of brown paper inside the case.

Jacques studied the tanned face of the professor and once again thought how lucky he was to have been selected by one of the most eminent surgeons in Europe to assist in the collection of potentially life saving material. Since arriving from France six months ago to begin his doctorate at St. Martin's, Arnold, it seemed, had taken a shine to him and decided to take him under his wing so to speak.

"A fine day's work, Jacques; twenty-two specimens of which eight are presently unknown to medical science. Who knows what cures they might hold."

Arnold rose to his feet and patted Jacques on the back.

He looked up into the dense canopy of green vegetation high above their heads. "I fear the daylight will soon be gone, my boy. Let us head back and see what wonderful repast our dear chef has concocted for us this evening."

Jacques picked up the case and followed the old man through the forest toward the clearing.

Ten minutes later, the two men arrived at the camp. Jacques was amazed at how, in the space of a few hours, the clearing had been transformed from a dense thicket of undergrowth into a relatively comfortable place to spend the night. There were seven tents set in a circle round the periphery of the clearing, six for sleeping and one which housed the food and equipment. In front of the tents was a small communal area, at the centre of which, was a wooden shelter, housing a table which had been fashioned from leaves and vines. The guides they had hired in Arequipe had obviously been very busy. They had even laid the table with metal plates and cups in preparation for the evening meal. The fire was the central focal point of the camp and the large pot that hung over the flames bubbled gently. There was also a carcass impaled upon a spit suspended above the fire. The smell wafting across the camp made Jacques' mouth water as he approached. He hadn't realised until now just how hungry he was.

Several of the guides were sitting outside the tents playing cards whilst an enormous hairy man (the chef, judging by the blood stained vest he was wearing) was sharpening knives on a whet-stone. The professor stuck his machete into the ground and removed his backpack before wandering across to the pot and sampling some of the bubbling mixture. Having tasted it, he slapped the cook on the back and said something in Spanish which Jacques didn't understand but took to be a compliment.

The cook and the professor engaged in a short conversation at the end of which the cook put his index finger and thumb to his lips and drew them away as he kissed the air. The professor laughed and turned to Jacques. "No doubt you have tasted 'capybara' before Jacques? They seem to have tried cooking everything else that moves in your country."

"*Capybara?*" repeated Jacques. "It is not a dish that sounds familiar professor."

"It is not so much a dish as a rather large rodent," explained the professor enjoying the look of disgust that was now evident on Jacques' face.

"I think I shall complete my journal and take a wash before dinner," Jacques mumbled as he turned away.

The professor laughed at Jacques' apparent discomfort and slapped the cook on the back again as the Frenchman walked toward his tent.

The gentle patter of conversation round the camp and the cacophony of sound synonymous with the jungle after dark drifted towards the tent. Despite his earlier apprehensions about eating something that was closely related to a rat, Jacques had enjoyed his dinner immensely. He was now lying on his camp bed reading a medical journal. He was feeling very tired but before he could retire to his bed he needed to answer a call of nature.

He slipped from the tent and held the lighted torch in front of him. He trod carefully. He had been informed earlier, by one of the more experienced expedition members, how on a previous trip an undergraduate had had the misfortune to step on a small nocturnal spider; he had hardly flinched at the time. Two hours later he was dead.

He could still hear the animated voices and see the reassuring lick of the flames from the fire as he unbuttoned the fly on his trousers and began to urinate. Suddenly he felt something move at his shoulder and as he slowly turned his head he stared into two black reptilian eyes. Instinctively, he swung himself round and threw his body backwards in an attempt to rid himself of the snake. Struggling to maintain his balance, he reached out to grab hold of a vine. His fingers closed round the woody stem but immediately slid down and he felt himself begin to fall. He realised that he must have been standing at the top of the ravine because the ground beneath him gave way and he careered uncontrollably down.

The undergrowth tore at his skin and he felt a terrible stab of pain in his buttock. He put his hands up to protect his face as he fell further and further downwards....

Seconds later, he came to a jarring halt as he slammed into something hard and very solid. He reached up and felt at his head and the warm stickiness told him he was bleeding. He pulled a handkerchief from his jacket pocket and held it to his temple.

As he stood up he could hardly believe his luck. The torch had followed him down and somehow managed to remain alight. He gingerly bent down and picked it up. The dim glow of light revealed that the solid object that had halted his fall was some kind of wall. Jacques thought he must be concussed and shook his head. No, it really was wall. The huge stone slabs were covered in lush green moss, but the unmistakable pattern of the brickwork was clear. He picked up a stick and scraped the moss from a joint.

He knew that the Incas had built settlements all over this region but the maps they had used for the expedition made no reference to any in this area.

Could this, he wondered, be the ruins of an as yet undiscovered ancient Inca village? The archaeology department at St. Martin's would go wild when he told them about this!

Jacques tried to stifle his growing excitement and admonished himself for being so presumptuous, "Extremely unscientific, Jacques," he whispered out loud.

The sound of his own voice startled him and he peered round into the intense blackness of the forest.

He decided that despite the fact that he could no longer hear voices from the camp he had to find out more about the wall. Besides, he couldn't be more than a few hundred yards away from the tents.

He moved along it looking closely for any sign of entry. He held the torch as high as he could in an attempt to ascertain the wall's height but the slabs rose up as far as he could see.

He strode on for a minute or two and was about to give up, return to the camp, and come back in the morning when something caught his eye.

As he had stepped forward something had glinted in the torchlight.

He bent down and brought the torch down low. He propped it up against the wall and pushed his hands into the ferns, sweeping them aside. There in the undergrowth was what appeared to be a key of some sort.

Jacques picked it up carefully and examined it. It was about the size of a hip flask, with a pyramid shaped body and a curious stirrup shaped neck. It seemed to be made from some kind of metal. On one side was an engraving- a figure. He rubbed the moss away and revealed the figure to be of an animal of some kind. Jacques guessed from the round body marks and the fangs, which protruded from thick lips, that it represented a jaguar. He flipped the key over and found that the other side also had an engraved figure; this time of a naked girl. There was a distinct mark on the body, he noted, roughly in the position of the heart. Underneath the girl was a symbol of some sort. It resembled a half circle with six spikes emerging from the top.

The girl's oversized eyes were closed giving her a serene expression even though for some inexplicable reason, Jacques assumed she were dead rather than asleep.

At that moment, the torch began to flicker and he decided to make his way back to camp and return at first light. He turned to retrace his steps and as he did so, for the second time that night, he found himself staring into a pair of unearthly, black eyes.

2

Whitechapel, London, August 31st 1888

Jacques shivered again and poked the embers in an effort to glean some warmth from the almost dead fire. He wished now that he had taken up the invitation to dinner from Professor Arnold and his wife for that evening. No doubt their surroundings were slightly more salubrious than the rented flat that his allowance afforded him. There was no real reason why he should have turned it down. It was just that since their return from South America three weeks ago he hadn't been feeling too well. Maybe he had picked up a bug or something. After all, he must have been unconscious for several hours in the jungle before the search party found him almost face down in the stream. It was a mystery to this day how he had managed to stray so far from the camp.

The professor had sent out the search party the following morning when he realised no one had seen him since supper the night before. He had explained to the professor how he had fallen down a ravine in the darkness but beyond that he could remember nothing. The odd thing was that when he had fallen he could distinctly see the flames from the camp fire from where he was; yet he was found in a stream a mile and a half from the camp.

The other curious thing was the strange pyramid shaped key that he had found in his pocket. He had put it down to malaise at the time that he had not shown it to anyone but now as he looked at it sitting on the mantel above the hearth he knew that there was more to it than that. He had simply not wanted to show it to anyone.

Despite the cold, Jacques decided he needed a walk to clear his mind. He pulled on his overcoat and hat and made his way downstairs.

He stepped out into the fog that enshrouded the streets of London and set off at a brisk pace towards the park. He could just make out the glow from the oil lamps that illuminated the loading bays outside the abattoir.

He recalled the day he had arrived from Paris and had come to take a look at the lodgings the college had arranged for him, thinking how inappropriate it seemed for the same street to house both trainee surgeons *and* a slaughterhouse. Still, it was cheap and only a five-minute carriage ride to the college. His mother would not be impressed though, so in his correspondence he painted a slightly more generous picture than was really the case.

Despite the death of his father from tuberculosis when he was only ten years old, his mother had managed to earn enough money as a house maid to hire the services of a retired school master who gave him an hour's tuition a week. It wasn't much but by the time he was twelve, he could read and write and hold a reasonable conversation in both English and German.

A trust set up by a Parisian philanthropist who had visited England on many occasions and was very sympathetic towards the work of the Child Welfare Lobbyists enabled him, at the age of fifteen, to enter the hallowed halls of academia at the Université de Longchamps.

It was during his final year there that he developed his interest in medicine. Using money he had managed to save waiting tables at a café in the Latin Quarter and a small research grant from the Academy, he procured a place at St.

Martin's in London.

He had already made up his mind that when he had made his fortune, he would set up his own trust for underprivileged children like himself. It would be called *'The Elise Belfont Foundation Trust'* in honour of his mother.

A large black rat scurried out from an alley that ran behind the abattoir and brought an end to his reminiscences. He pulled his coat more tightly round himself and quickened his pace.

It was only after several minutes of walking that Jacques realised that he had been turning something over and over in his pocket. It was brought to his attention by a sudden sharp pain in his thumb.

He lifted the object from his pocket and brought it up close to his face so he could see what it was. The fog had become even thicker now and even though he held it close, it was still difficult to see. It was the scalpel from his medical kit. He had no recollection of putting it in his coat, nor any idea why he would put it there anyway; he always returned it to its case whenever he used it. Still, it was no use worrying about it now.

He wrapped a handkerchief tightly round his thumb and decided to finish his walk; he could stitch it later, if necessary, when he got back.

3

House of Commons, London, 1997

"... And to conclude, The Dome would represent all that was positive and progressive about our great nation. I strongly urge The House to add its support to the project. Thank you."

The Minister without Portfolio shuffled his papers and sat down.

Several members of the Opposition rose from their seats, including the Shadow Minister for Housing.

"Madame speaker, would it be too much to ask of Mr. Henderson to enlighten The House further as to the total cost of the project and also to give some indication of what he proposes to actually put in the Dome. As far as I can see, he is asking us to commit at least seven hundred and sixty five million pounds of tax payers' money to some ill thought out piece of propaganda aimed not at taking us into the next millennium, but at impressing the Government's bed-fellows in Europe. No doubt the contracts for the construction work will not go solely to the British work force but will be tendered out to all and sundry from across the Channel.

I would also like to ask him why the Dome should take precedent over other more pressing projects such as the ones initiated by myself and my party prior to the election, namely the regeneration of the inner city housing schemes and investment in skills and training for the unemployed."

The Opposition benches erupted. The applause and cries of support died down as Simon Henderson stood up to respond.

Henderson looked cool and poised as always when he spoke in public. His *Pierre Cardin* suit was creaseless despite three hours of intermittent standing and sitting. He was renowned for sartorial flair amongst his peers and had been recently voted among the country's 'Top Ten Best Dressed Men' in *'Vogue'* magazine.

He casually leaned one elbow on the bench and half twisted his body to indicate, with a wave of his arm, the party members behind him.

"We are the party which promised the electorate faithfully that we would take this country into the millennium ahead of the rest of Europe. We are already seen as a progressive nation, which values not only its own citizens but also those of all the other countries in the world. Our environmental policies are leading the way in setting new targets for decreases in atmospheric pollutants; our humanitarian policies have seen aid to developing countries increase threefold since we came to power and our commitment to the long-term nuclear disarmament programme is stronger than ever. We are respected around the world now and the strength of the pound bears testament to the economic growth that has taken place in the last twelve months."

There were howls of derision from the benches opposite and dozens of MPs were now on their feet hoping for a chance to respond to the Minister. Simon Henderson was, however, now in full flow and in no mood to relinquish the floor just yet.

"May I remind the house that in 1851 politicians said that *'The Great Exhibition'* was a waste of time and money. It took the commitment and vision of one individual, Prince

Albert, to ensure that the rest of the world became aware of the Industrial Revolution that had taken place in this country. Crystal Palace became the largest shop window in the world, without which, our nation would be all the poorer today."

The noise from the opposition benches was rapidly abating.

"May I also remind you that in the six months that it was open, 'The Exhibition' was visited by over six million people, half of whom were British. The fact that the population of our country at that time was less than twenty million makes that figure all the more remarkable. The Dome will do as much for Britain today as The Exhibition did in taking us firmly into the twentieth century. As for the funding, I can now reveal to The House that the seven hundred and sixty five million pounds my honourable friend referred to earlier will not come from the Treasury but will be raised from the private sector."

There was a minor attempt at laughing down the Minister but it soon fell flat. Most people were now intrigued to hear more. Henderson even had the confidence, or as some broadsheets reported it later, the arrogance, to pause for a drink of water before he continued.

"I can also reveal that at this point in time that two thirds of that figure is currently earning interest for its investors in 'The Millennium Fund', an account set up by the Bank of England on behalf of the Millennium Committee. Furthermore, the remaining two hundred and fifty million is having to be split into smaller investment units because the interest has been so overwhelming."

There was actually no more than a hum of noise inside The House now.

".... As for what the Dome will house; may I suggest to my honourable friend that he purchase a ticket and see for himself when it opens on New Year's Eve 1999...that is, of course, if there are any left *to* purchase."

Simon Henderson sat down with a smile on his face as big as his majority whilst the Shadow Minister for housing muttered something, which sounded indistinctly like 'smug, smart arse bastard' to the people who sat round him, although of course they couldn't be sure.

Later that evening, the Minister reflected upon how well the day in the House had gone. His principal speech had been received very positively on the whole. Apart from the odd predictable question about education and housing the response had been favourable.

He finished straightening his tie and studied himself in the mirror.

"Henderson, old boy, you are a fucking hero," he said to himself out loud.

The way in which he had side stepped the questions about what was going in the Dome and convinced the House that the Millennium Committee were right to keep it secret for as long as possible in order to maximise the impact of the exhibition was nothing short of rhetorical genius. In reality, even the Committee was not aware that he had already started negotiations with the Peruvian Government to bring the *'Lanzon Stone'* across the Atlantic. They would agree to it, of course, as it would form the centrepiece of the Dome Exhibition, a symbol of the Old World giving way to the technology of the new.

In the eyes of Alberto Fujimori, the Peruvian president, it would also be a tangible sign to the western world that Peru was back on its feet and ready to take its place in the New World Order.

Henderson had of course lubricated the cogs that drove this thinking by promising 'El Chinito', as Fujimori was affectionately known in South America, guaranteed British investment in Peru.

Henderson picked up the *Pyramidal Key* from its place

on the over mantel and felt its power run through him. He looked at the engraved figure closely. Apart from the slight opening of the eyes that he'd noticed in the last few weeks, there were no other changes in the appearance of the figure. He placed it carefully back on the shelf, walked toward the phone, and picked it up.

"Johnson, I'm ready. Have my car at the door in two minutes... Oh, and Johnson? Put a couple of bottles of champagne in the car refrigerator. I feel like celebrating."

He put on his overcoat and flicked the light switch off as he pulled the door shut behind him.

On the over mantel the key glowed brightly for a second. Then darkness returned to the room.

Johnson looked in his rear view mirror. His boss was relaxing in the back seat with a glass of the Dom Perignon he'd put in the cooler earlier. The smile hadn't left his face since they had left his apartment twenty minutes ago. He couldn't remember ever seeing the minister in such a buoyant mood

Henderson was actually thinking about his rise to power in the government. Ever since he had started at boarding school in Sussex at the age of twelve he had known exactly where his future lay. His father had been a very wealthy merchant banker and although they had never been very close, he had learned one very important lesson from him: 'It isn't what you know. It's to what purpose you put the knowledge that is important.' He thought about his baptism into the torrid waters of politics in the early seventies.

It was pure good fortune that he had discovered that Jack Spencer, the candidate for the constituency *he* was campaigning for, had a history of coronary problems. It was however less down to fate that the candidate had somehow managed to mislay his medication somewhere between the briefing meeting at Henderson's house and the particularly strenuous house-to-house calls to whip up support before the local elections that they'd planned for that day.

Henderson was campaign manager on that particular day and had been responsible for splitting the constituency up into sections and allocating them to party members.

He recalled how he had allocated Jack Spencer the area with the highest number of council flats per square mile on the basis that the 'common vote' was one of the most influential areas in local election and it was his face they needed to see at the chalk-face, so to speak. He had neglected to inform him that most of the council flats were four storey affairs, the vast majority of which, had lifts that were out of order.

It was also an indictment of the opposition party's policy of cutting services at local level (they were in office locally at that time) that the public phone box in the street where Jack finally succumbed to a massive heart attack was also out of order. By the time an ambulance was summoned it was too late.

Of course, Henderson was only too willing to step into the vacated candidacy even at such short notice. He romped to victory with a two thousand and fifty majority.

Johnson's voice brought him back to the present. "Miss Howarth –Jones' residence, Sir."

Henderson swallowed the remnants of his champagne, told Johnson to pick him up at eleven, and stepped out of the car.

As Henderson reached the top of the steps which led up to the house, the door opened and a hired-for-the-evening butler dressed in a black evening suit welcomed him inside. The party was already in full swing. He handed his coat and gloves to the butler and looked up just in time to see the hostess scurrying towards him. She planted a kiss in the air about an inch from his face.

"Simon, darling, delighted you could make it. I know

how busy you are these days. I've just been chatting to old Mikey Heselfinch; says you're doing a wonderful job sorting out that Domey thing down in Greenwich."

She leaned towards him conspiratorially. "I think it was awfully sweet of you to invite him to stay on the Committee. I know he still likes to feel useful."

Maisie Howarth-Jones was the ex wife of Sir Geoffrey Howarth-Jones, an ex Cabinet Minister in the last government. He had resigned from office when '*THE DAILY MIRROR*' ran a story about his apparent misuse of ministerial funds. The accompanying photographs of the minister in various states of undress, fondling his secretary on a beach in Buenos Aires had provided the Opposition with all the ammunition they needed to convince the electorate that the government was riddled with corruption and sleaze.

Maisie Howarth-Jones became a Westminster celebrity overnight when, far from defending her husband of seventeen years and standing solidly by his side as everyone expected, she gave an interview on national television explaining how he had had numerous affairs in the past, including one with the wife of the Chief Executive of the company now running the National Lottery. That particular affair, she explained, took place at about the time when the bids to run the Lottery were being considered by a committee being chaired by her husband.

"You know me, Maisie, I don't like to burn my bridges," confided the Minister. "You never know when you might need a favour yourself one day."

Maisie leaned forward again. "If it's favours you're looking for, darling..." she began.

Henderson didn't actually hear the rest of the sentence, although he had a fairly educated guess at what she was saying; he had seen someone he needed to talk to. In fact, it was his only reason for attending the party in the first place.

He made his excuses and wandered across the room, smiling and shaking hands with a variety of MPs and businessmen along the way.

He finally made it to the tall, dark haired man standing on the terrace overlooking the Thames.

"Did you get it?" he asked urgently.

The man raised his eyebrows. "It's nice to see you too, Minister," he said lighting a cigarette and not bothering to offer Henderson one.

"Did you get it?" he repeated through clenched teeth, taking a step closer.

The man suddenly felt threatened; he saw something in the Minister's eyes.

"No, not yet," he said hastily. He suddenly wanted the meeting to be over. "I know he's got it, though. I saw it on his table. He's allowed to keep it in his cell on account of personal religious beliefs. Apparently, he's converted to Buddhism while he's been inside and he's convinced them it's got something to do with his prayers. Load of bollocks, I reckon. It looks more like something out of a horror film. It's got a naked woman carved on it with blood coming from her chest."

Henderson shivered involuntarily, he knew he would find it. Now it was only a matter of time.

"Listen," he whispered. "Arrange another meeting. Convince him that you will publish an article explaining to your readers how Ian Brady, the most despised individual in criminal history, has become a changed character. How it was temporary insanity that possessed him all those years ago and that he is now ready to re-enter society. Tell him your article will go a long way to altering public opinion…
For fuck's sake, tell him anything you like as long as he gives you the key." Henderson's tone quickly changed, "…and Michael, if you manage to get it for Wednesday, there will be a small bonus for you. Let's say another

fifteen thousand?"

The reporter smiled and turned to go. Not since he'd faked those photographs of Sir Geoffrey in Buenos Aires with his secretary had he been offered this amount of cash for a deal.

4

Whitechapel, London, August 31st 1888

Jacques could feel the dampness of the cold London fog creeping up inside his coat, chilling him. He still didn't feel so good despite the fact that his head seemed to have cleared a little. He decided it was time to go back home.

He waited for a carriage to pass and crossed the road. As he stepped onto the pavement, a door suddenly opened in front of him and a dark shape tumbled onto the pavement at his feet.

"And don't show yer ugly face in 'ere again unless you've got a shillin ' in yer pocket to pay fer what yer drink."

The door slammed shut again. Jacques looked down at the figure on the floor and instinctively bent down to help him to his feet. The figure coughed, pushed Jacques roughly out of the way, and staggered off into the fog.

Jacques looked up at the sign above the door in front of him:

The Frying Pan Tavern'

He could hear the sound of music and raucous laughter coming from inside the public house and even though he had never taken a drink in his life, he felt an overwhelming compulsion to go inside. He pushed open the door and went inside.

There was an old piano in the corner. A man was playing whilst a woman sat on his knee. Several other men and women stood round joining in the singing and one or two seemed to be involved, as far as Jacques could make out, in varying degrees of sexual foreplay.

Standing at the bar were two or three men, who, judging by their blood stained clothes and spattered boots, had just finished a shift at the slaughterhouse.

A woman was propositioning them. She was draped across a stool and as she spoke she thrust her enormous breasts forward in what she obviously thought was a seductive pose.

"How about it, Billy?" she shrieked. "Tuppence fer a good time? What's a poor girl to do on such an 'orrible night? I'm practically givin' it away."

The man laughed, shaking his head apologetically, "Not tonight, Polly."

Jacques stepped forward to the bar.

"What can I get yer Guv?" the landlord asked, wiping imaginary dregs from the bar surface with a dirty rag.

Jacques was not sure what to ask for so he pointed to a bottle on a shelf. As the landlord poured the drink, Jacques felt something brush against his thigh. He turned to find the prostitute at his side.

"A whiskey man, eh?" said the prostitute now giving him the full benefit of her well-practised sales pitch; breasts and all.

Jacques turned to look at her and as he did he felt an incredible pain above his eyes and an image flashed into his mind. He saw the woman, lying in front of him. Her long hair was thrown across her face. Her naked body was opened up from the tip of her chin to below her navel and the glistening organs protruded through the gaping wound. He could see the heart clearly, still beating. Then, as quickly as it had come, the image was gone.

"Cat got yer tongue, Darlin'?" chirped the prostitute.

Jacques was unsure how to respond, Billy and his friends were now watching. They were stifling laughter, obviously amused by the scenario. The boy scarcely looked old enough to drink, let alone attract the attentions of a whore. He licked his lips nervously.

"I actually prefer champagne, mademoiselle. The whiskey is purely medicinal."

The prostitute's face lit up. "Mmm a Frenchie, eh? Listen, forget about the whiskey, if it's pepping up yer after I know just the thing."

She propped her leg up on a stool and lifted her skirt up in a mock gesture of adjusting her stockings. Jacques couldn't help but stare as her hands smoothed the black stockings and then rested for just a second longer than necessary on her thigh.

He could hear the muffled laughter again from behind him. "You must forgive me," he said. "I have a pressing appointment. Maybe another time."

Jacques strode quickly from the bar. The doors closed behind him and he stepped back outside and into the chill of the evening fog.

"Ain't yer got a 'ome to go to? Come on, I've a pan o' coals waiting fer me upstairs and they'll have gone cold before I get to me bed."

The landlord shoved Mary through the doors and shut them behind her.

She pulled her cardigan more tightly round her shoulders in a vain effort to keep out the cold. Her breath added to the fog that, if anything, had gotten thicker. Her head was spinning slightly. Despite having had no luck with the 'gentlemen, as she referred to them, she had still managed to procure a drink or two. At least she was warm on the inside.

She hummed a tune as she walked, wishing she'd left

with one of her friends earlier; she hadn't realised the fog was this bad. Her leather-heeled boots clicked loudly on the pavement as she walked. If it wasn't so cold she'd take them off, *'Never mind,'* she thought. *'Nearly home now.'*

She lived in a small, draughty room above a fish shop in Buck's Row which she rented from the owner. More often than not she paid her rent in favours, which suited her fine except the old bastard smelled like a halibut.

Still, it was easy to hold her breath for a minute, which was usually as long as he took.

She took the key from her purse and stepped into the ginnel where a flight of stairs led up to the room. Her foot touched the first step when she suddenly became aware of a dark shape standing a few feet further into the shadows. Her first thought was that it was the owner of the shop; she hadn't 'paid' him this week.

The figure stepped closer and she moved back wards up the steps automatically. She breathed a sigh of relief as she recognised the man.

"Cor Blimey yer don't half know how to frighten a girl. Change yer mind did yer?"

She put her arm through his. "Come on, we may as well use my place now were 'ere. It'll cost yer an extra sixpence though."

Inside, she removed her cardigan and sat on the edge of the dresser. She unbuttoned her dress at the top revealing a petticoat with a drawstring waist. She put her hands on her hips and smiled.

"I hope yer 'ands are warm luvvie the fog's fair chilled me through."

The man stepped forward and she grinned. She might even enjoy this; he was quite the most handsome client she'd ever had, even if he looked a bit young.

The man drew his hand from his pocket and reached up toward her face. She closed her eyes as she felt him lift her chin slightly. She was expecting to feel the warmth of his mouth on her neck and felt a tingle of excitement run through her. His other hand came up to her breasts and she suddenly felt her petticoat spring loose.

" 'Ere you're a fast worker," she said, opening her eyes.

It was only then that she saw the blade in his hand. There was a sort of gurgling sound as her intestines slid from her inside and slipped down onto her dress. Instinctively, she put her hands down to catch them. She had a ridiculous vision of the time she had serviced the shop owner downstairs lying between two trays of jellied eels.

Then something solid struck her on the side of the head and she fell heavily onto the floor.

As the man leaned over her she tried to scream but the blood running into her throat was choking. She saw him raise his hand again and she caught a glimpse of his eyes. They seemed black and empty almost like the snakes she'd seen when the circus had come to Hampstead Heath. She was still staring at his eyes when he reached into her chest and ripped out her heart.

5

Whitechapel, London, September 1st 1888

Jacques pulled the sheet up closer round him. There was an unfamiliar taste in his mouth and he swallowed trying to produce some saliva to moisten his throat. His head was pounding and his arms and legs ached inexplicably.

He remembered his walk from the night before; the public house and the woman. A smile played on his lips; she was probably waking up this morning with a worse headache than his.

Another stab of pain made his brow crease and he decided he might be better off out of bed. He clambered out from under the thin sheet.

As he tidied the sheet on the bed, he noticed a brown flakiness on his hand and on the mattress. He'd forgotten about cutting his thumb on the scalpel.

He examined the cut closely. It wasn't very deep; he guessed it would only need two or three stitches.

He walked over to the porcelain bowl that sat on a table over by the window and   poured some water into it from the jug that stood beside it.

Cupping his hands he threw water onto his face hoping it might help to clear his head.

The water was cold and refreshing and he breathed in sharply as it ran down his neck and onto his chest.

A sudden shout from outside drew his attention to the

window and he looked down onto the street.

There was a crowd of people gathered round a newspaper seller and there seemed to be some excitement. Several of the crowd appeared to be remonstrating with a policeman who was trying to calm them down.

Jacques threw on a shirt and skipped quickly down the stairs and onto the street.

The newspaper seller took the penny and handed Jacques a paper. The headline read:

'MANIAC LOOSE IN WHITECHAPEL'

Jacques skimmed the cover story quickly.

As he read, vivid images flashed into his mind; the ginnel; the steps up to the room; the woman from the tavern lying on the floor, her body open and bloody. He squeezed the paper in his fist and looked round.

"Took her 'ead clean off, I heard," said one.

"It says 'ere they found bits of 'er all over the place," said another.

Jacques turned and ran back up to his room. He flung open his door and rushed over to the drawer of his desk.

Frantically, he pulled out his medical case. He opened it expecting to see a bloody scalpel and remnants of human flesh soiling the green satin but it was lying snugly in its place as clean as usual.

He put his hands to his head. *'What was happening to him? Maybe the fever he'd contracted on the expedition was somehow making him hallucinate, perhaps he'd never even been into a tavern. Last night he could remember feeling unwell. Was it possible that he'd just fallen asleep and his mind was fabricating images based on what he had just read in the paper?*

Feeling decidedly unnerved, he decided to finish dressing and pay a visit to the professor.

The cab ride over to St. John's Wood had taken only a few minutes, but in that time Jacques had begun to feel significantly better. The headache had subsided and he had managed to convince himself of the ridiculousness of what he had been suggesting.

He had now decided against telling the professor about the strange 'flashbacks'; he was sure they were probably just another symptom of the intermittent fevers he had been experiencing since returning from South America. Maybe a brisk walk every day was all he needed to get himself back to normal.

He was now comfortably ensconced on a large Chesterfield settee in the professor's drawing room.

"Glad to see you're feeling better, Jacques. Jonathan and I were getting quite worried about you," said Mrs. Arnold, offering Jacques a scone to go with his tea. Jacques smiled brightly and took the scone.

"Now that you are back on your feet again, perhaps you could assist me in theatre this week," suggested the professor hopefully.

"I would be honoured, sir," said Jacques, feeling that things were finally getting back on track after the expedition.

"How are you finding your lodgings?" asked Arnold," I believe there was some kind of trouble not far from you last night, something to do with a prostitute."

Jacques, taken by surprise, choked on the scone and began coughing uncontrollably.

Mrs. Arnold rang a bell and a butler appeared. She told him to fetch a glass of water.

Jacques was still coughing when the butler returned a few minutes later.

"Please forgive me," said Jacques. "I must have, how do you say? …swallowed something the wrong way."

Arnold smiled at the Frenchman's attempts at

colloquialism.

"I believe there *was* an incident," said Jacques trying to sound as vague as possible. "The body of a woman was discovered late last night. Apparently the police think she may have been murdered."

"How utterly dreadful," offered the professor's wife, lifting her handkerchief to her mouth for maximum effect.

(In truth she abhorred those types of women and what they represented. One fewer might not be a bad thing.)

Jacques continued coughing, his eyes were watery and his face was turning puce. The professor stood up and patted his back.

"I think perhaps you need to get a little more rest to ensure you are fully recovered from your fever, young man."

He lifted Jacques by the elbow indicating that the afternoon tea was over. Jacques followed suit nodding his agreement.

As if by telepathy the butler appeared at the door holding Jacques' overcoat and hat.

"I will expect you Wednesday at the hospital then, three o clock. Until then, get plenty of rest and keep yourself warm."

They shook hands and Mrs. Arnold walked with Jacques to the door.

"I do hope this terrible business with the murder hasn't given you a dreadful opinion of we English, dear. Take care now," she said in maternal tones.

Jacques gave what he hoped was his most charming smile.

"Of course not Mirand; for the tea I must say thank you. It was most delightful. Au revoir."

He turned and walked onto the street in search of a carriage.

"What a refreshingly polite young man," thought Mrs.

Arnold as she closed the door. *"My husband is such a fine judge of character."*

6

Ashworth Maximum Security Mental Hospital, England
1997

The huge steel door creaked painfully open and Donovan
stepped through. He waited while the guard pulled it shut
behind them and carefully reset the combination locks.
Although the corridor was windowless and gloomy, the air
inside was fresh and smelled of disinfectant.

Donovan felt uneasy; it was only his second meeting
with Brady and the first hadn't exactly been what you'd call
a success. Brady had been wary of him and very guarded.
No doubt he'd had his fill of gutter press reporters offering
him thousands for his story; why would this one be any
different?

The guard led him through two more doors before the
corridor gave way to a more open, hospital style set of
doors and rooms. The total silence added to Donovan's
unease and he licked his lips nervously. His palms were
cold and sweaty.

They turned left and came to a small glass kiosk in
which a solitary guard sat surrounded by television
monitors. Donovan scanned the screens and recognised the
solitary figure of Brady in one of the rooms. The two
guards greeted each other and swapped formalities as
Donovan studied Brady on the screen.

"This way, Mr. Donovan." The second guard stood in

the doorway, small, almost insignificant. Donovan thought he looked more like a bank clerk than a prison officer. He pointed to a door twenty metres along the corridor. "You have fifteen minutes."

Brady was tapping away at his typewriter in the Common Room by a barred window that overlooked a small garden.

"Good morning, Mr. Brady," said Donovan. Brady didn't acknowledge the reporter but continued typing.

Donovan took off his coat and pulled a chair across and sat down.

Brady looked even older than he had last time Donovan visited, if that were possible. If he *were* ever released no one would recognise him. Everyone remembered the face of Brady from the sixties; the slicked back hair, the down turned mouth, and the arrogant poise. Now his almost-white hair was confined to a small area above his ears and his heavily sunken eyes were yellow and lifeless.

Donovan took out some cigarettes, drew one out of the packet, and put it in his mouth.

Without turning his gaze away from the typewriter Brady announced tersely, "I would prefer it if you refrained from smoking. According to the Surgeon General, it can be severely damaging to one's health."

The irony of the statement was not lost on Donovan especially as he knew Brady had always had a particular penchant for strong French cigarettes.

He put the cigarette back in the packet. It was not the way he had wanted the meeting to start. He tried a different tack.

"I thought you might like these," he said, lifting some books from the plastic carrier bag at his side.

He knew Brady had a fascination with the Nazis and the Holocaust. He'd called into a bookshop in Covent Garden that morning and bought all they had on the subject.

Brady barely moved his eyes, just enough to acknowledge the gifts.

Donovan placed the books on the desk and sat back down desperately trying to think of another way of getting Brady's attention.

Suddenly Brady stopped typing, picked up one of the books and stared intensely at the cover. The picture on the front of the book was Hitler during one of his famous speeches at the *Berlin Sportspalast,* his fist crashing down dramatically on the lectern. Brady seemed transfixed.

'Touché' thought Donovan sensing a breakthrough.

"I have a proposition for you, Mr. Brady," he said eventually.

Brady, still clutching the book was now looking out of the window.

"In exchange for a small item that you have in your possession, I am willing to write an article in my newspaper which chronicles your full return to health and sanity. I already have the written opinions of several of the doctors and psychiatrists here who have indicated that you are a model citizen and no longer represent a threat to society."

He waited for a response. There was none so he continued.

"I have spoken to Longford this morning and he feels that the social climate is right at the moment to petition the Home Secretary for your immediate release. My article would go a long way in support of that petition."

Donovan knew that he was talking bollocks and that even if he wrote the article, his editor would never agree to it being published. Still he'd give the man a blow job if it meant him parting with the key. The money was just too good to fail.

Brady turned fully round for the first time since he'd arrived and, for a millisecond, Donovan caught what he thought was a glimpse of the evil behind Brady's eyes. Then it was gone. Donovan turned cold.

Brady leaned forward and it reminded the reporter of the scene from *'The Silence of the Lambs'* when Hannibal Lecter says: *"and then I ate her liver with a nice Chianti."* He expected Brady to say something equally as appalling before telling him to fuck off.

To his utter surprise, Brady smiled and reached into a cotton bag on the floor. He took out the key. It was wrapped in a grubby, white handkerchief.

As he handed it to Donovan, he put his other hand on his shoulder, the pressure slightly uncomfortable.

"Everything comes to he who waits," he whispered.

The mouth smiled; the rest of his face didn't. Donovan assumed he was referring to his impending release and smiled back like a benevolent uncle who's just bailed his nephew out of the shit.

The thought had already crossed his mind though that it had been incredibly easy, too easy almost.

What hadn't occurred to him, however, was that he hadn't actually mentioned to Brady what the item was that he had wanted. Donovan clutched the key and stood up.

"I'd better go and get the ball rolling then."

He wiped his sweaty hand on the side of his trouser leg before offering it to Brady, but by this time he'd returned to his typewriter and begun tapping away again.

Donovan left the room without further comment as the guard signalled that time was up.

Brady finished the line of typing and pulled the sheet of paper out of the typewriter. He held it up and smiled. He added it to a growing pile of other pieces of paper on the floor under the table, all of which had the same message typed on them: *'The time has come, my Lord'*

7

Whitechapel, London September 8th 1888

"Right, that's me done for tonight, Annie. You comin' ?"

The two prostitutes were standing under a street lamp at the entrance to a derelict warehouse. The sign which hung above the boarded up doors read, rather appropriately: *'Hanbury Street Meat Market'.*

"Nah, I'll try me luck fer another half hour or so, pubs'll be shutting soon.

"I'll see yer then. I'll leave the door off the latch, and do me a favour will yer: Don't wake me up when yer get 'ome".

Annie nodded, "And thanks again Rosie fer letting me stop. I'll see yer right, I promise."

The older of the two women turned and walked away. The younger one hitched up her stockings and rearranged her dress. She could hear voices approaching and could just make out two figures walking her way. The fog wasn't as bad tonight as it had been.

As they got closer, she stuck her chest out and lifted one side of her dress up slightly.

"Evenin' gentlemen," she called out chirpily. "Looking for a bit of entertainment tonight? I can do two fer the price o' one while it's gettin' late." She hoped the light from the lamp would play generously on her breasts.

The two men looked to be gentry. They were heading

36

towards Bishopsgate. They chose to ignore her and strutted on, placing their canes even more firmly to the ground as they walked as if to emphasise their contempt for her.

"*Toffee nosed tossers,*" she thought.

If either of them had been walking home alone they'd have taken her up like a flash. She'd had more clients from that neck o' the woods than anywhere else in the East End. She usually charged double as well.

The rebuke made her wish that she'd gone with her room-mate earlier when she'd had the chance. She was cold and tired and the small bottle of gin that she dug out from beneath the hem of her dress provided little comfort. Noisily, she drained the dregs of clear liquid from the bottle before throwing it into the nearest alleyway. She hitched up her skirt and set off miserably down the dark, deserted street.

Although it was quicker to cut through the park, she didn't like walking that way on her own. She decided to stick to the streets. (She had also heard about the murder a few days before; she wasn't taking any chances tonight.)

She glanced over her shoulder and peered into the darkness behind her. The dim street lamps were just visible, struggling to penetrate the thickening blanket of fog.

She quickened her pace, keeping close to the fence that ran round the edge of the park; Somehow, it made her feel more secure.

She hoped that Rosie was still awake when she got home and hadn't sprawled herself across the entire bed. It was bad enough having to share a bed without having to heave *her* out of the way as well. Still, she should count her blessings that she had somewhere to doss. (If she hadn't spent her rent money on gin, she'd be tucked up in bed alone in the lodging house in Dorset Street. She'd see that bastard landlord right for turning her down a night's credit.)

This thought reminded her that she still had only a half

penny in her pocket; she'd have to have a better night tomorrow than she had tonight. Maybe she'd go down the docks and try her luck with the sailors; if a boat had just come in she could earn her rent and even have some left over for a drink or two.

'*What a bloody way to make a living,*' she thought to herself.

She turned to cross the street and stepped off the pavement. As her foot hit the cobbles, she felt a sharp tug at her skirt as if someone had grabbed her from behind. She shrieked and turned to face her attacker but there was no one there, just the empty street and the fog.

She breathed a sigh of relief as she realised that the hem of her dress had caught in the heel of her boot when she had stepped onto the road. She bent down to free it.

Her heart was still pounding but she managed to smile to herself as she pulled the torn material from her heel.

She stood up and turned round to continue her journey home.

The steel blade caught her a glancing blow across the bridge of her nose. Blood spurted into her eyes and she suddenly felt herself being lifted swiftly upwards.

A hard punch to the middle of her back knocked the breath from her and she tried to scream but couldn't. She thought she'd been dropped to the ground for a second but she felt strange, as if she were floating almost.

The pain in her back was incredible and she was gasping for breath. It was only as the blood cleared from her eyes and she looked up at the black-coated figure that she realised she was impaled on the railings which skirted the park.

The dark figure stepped closer and she saw the eyes; they were black, bottomless, and filled with evil and even though most of his face was covered by a scarf she knew that there was a smile on his lips.

She knew the pleasure he was experiencing because in her line of work she had seen that look of pleasure more times than she cared to remember.

She felt the cool steel of the blade as it slit her throat and then again as it cut her torso wide open. She could see the steam rising up from her intestines and she felt something tugging at her insides. Then she heard a squelch and something spattered her face.

As she looked at her heart squarely sitting on the spike of the next railing her final sane thought came into her head again: *"What a bloody way to make a living."*

8

The Victoria and Albert Museum, London, 1997

She was clutching at the air as it rushed past her. She was falling faster and faster, further and further, into the black abyss. The scream was lodged in her throat and even if she could scream, who would hear her, a thousand miles from anywhere? Why had she come to the site alone? More so, why had she tried to climb down into the cave without help or even a rope? Did she think she was Harrison Ford, for fucks sake!

There was a pinprick of light below. It was getting bigger and bigger as she fell rapidly towards it. Her heart was pounding in her ears and her eyes were filling with tears. She prepared herself for impact and instant death. Still, the scream wouldn't come. Suddenly the light exploded filling the cave and a voice said:

"Excuse me."

Startled, she jumped up and let the man by. Looking round, she could see the hall emptying.

Dr. Schwarz was still at the podium answering questions about his presentation; the presentation she'd been looking forward to all year and now she'd missed because she'd fallen asleep.

She cursed herself inwardly and grabbed her backpack from the floor. She stomped down the aisle dragging her pack across the tops of the chairs in anger and frustration.

The contents of Dr. Schwarz's seminar was going to provide her with further ammunition to take to the British Archaeological Foundation where she would apply for funding for her expedition.

(She was planning to go to the Sudan in search of what she believed would be the oldest civilisation ever discovered.) She'd even forgotten to turn on her mini recorder at the start of the presentation so she didn't even have that!

It seemed to be the story of her life. In fact, the epitaph on her gravestone would read something like:

'Here lies Katherine Stone. If ever there was an opportunity to be missed, she was the girl to miss it'

For once in her life she just wished everything would go according to plan.

She decided to try and cheer herself up and see if her friends were still in the Student Union bar. That's where they usually hung out after a hard day's sitting about doing very little but listening to stereotypical Open University type lecturers wearing tweed suits and white checked shirts.

As she rode on the top deck of the bus on the short trip across the city she marvelled at the way in which people organised themselves in order to make sense of life. The bus passed under a flyover and she saw several winos sitting on an old settee with no cushions. Beside the settee were two battered supermarket trolleys: one containing masses of stamped-upon steel and aluminium cans and the other with what looked like cardboard boxes.

The winos were sharing a one pound-fifty bottle of sherry and smoking reconstituted cigarettes made from stumps they'd retrieved from bins and the roadside gutters where inconsiderate car owners had emptied them from the ashtrays inside their automotive wombs.

The winos had virtually nothing yet somehow they managed to organise themselves each day in a way that gave life a meaning; they were surviving. Every day they *had* to wake so they could gather the 'fodder' that kept them alive.

They would sell the cans to the recycling companies for a few pounds, not much, but enough to keep them going. The boxes were probably their equivalent of a one bedroom flat.

Below her sitting in the next lane to the bus, revving the engine impatiently, she observed the other end of the social spectrum: a product of Thatcher's Britain.

The man could have been no more than twenty-four or five. As he waited for the lights to change he was shouting agitatedly into a car phone. He was clearly late for an appointment because he kept checking his gold Rolex.

He thumped the steering wheel of his BMW as the lights changed back to red with no apparent movement of traffic in front of him and she could lip read the string of expletives that he was trying to force through his windscreen using a sort of verbal osmosis to the cars ahead. His filofax lay open on the seat beside him. It may as well have been a ball and chain.

'At least the winos were laughing,' she thought.

The bus was crossing Westminster Bridge now and she could see the lights from the Houses of Parliament casting a reflection on the inky black surface of the Thames.

'And that's where the future is decided,' she thought philosophically, *'the future of millions, decided by the thinking of a few hundred.'*

It wasn't that she was against the idea. In fact, she

always described herself to anyone who asked as politically illiterate (which was funny, really, because her father always said that was the first pre-requisite for becoming an MP!).

She just found it fascinating that such a complex system could evolve from the kinds of early civilisations she had spent the last four years studying; civilisations that were based on making human sacrifices to gods that dictated every aspect of life. A wry smile crossed her face as she considered.

'Nothing much has changed really; it's just that the rich people are now the gods.'

She jumped up and took the steps two at a time just in time to hop off the platform as it passed the Student Union building in St. John's Square.

She could hear the sounds of music and laughter filtering down the spiral stairwell as she pushed the heavy double doors open. She nearly fell flat on her face as someone simultaneously pulled the doors from the other side.

Both Kate and the man said *'Sorry'* at the same time in that peculiar way that only the British do when something happens that isn't their fault.

As Kate looked up, she saw the dark mop of jet-black hair and piercing blue eyes of Michael Donovan smiling down at her.

"Well, well if it ain't me old mate, Katy Brick," he laughed, in a mock Cockney accent.

No one had called her that for ten years, not since she'd left Little Stanton, the tiny village in Suffolk where she was born.

She looked more closely at the features, and then it was her turn to smile.

"My God," she said putting her hands on her hips, "Scoop Donovan!"

She leaned forward grabbing the straps of his camera.

"Still looking for the big story, I see."

They both stepped forward and hugged each other affectionately.

"So, what have you been doing with yourself?" Donovan asked.

"Oh, this and that. You know the usual stuff; been to college, got my degree, bummed round for a year ...and now I'm doing a masters at St. Martin's...and you?"

"Er, me..." Donovan suddenly realised he'd been staring at Kate's chest which was covered, just about, by a very clingy Lycra body top, "I finally made it to the 'Big Time' ... I worked as Sub Editor on The *Billingsgate Fishmonger's Monthly* for a year before deciding that a career move was in order and I decided to take the job as Senior Current Affairs Correspondent for *The Times*."

"The Times!" gasped Kate, moving to one side to allow a dreadlocked Rastafarian carrying an enormous art portfolio under one arm and an even bigger ghetto blaster under the other to pass.

"Yeah, *The Lambeth Times*, bloody hard work though."

As she looked up, she saw the familiar twinkle in Donovan's eyes and realised he hadn't lost his sense of humour. It was that that had attracted her to him seven years ago when they had both lived in the same village. (Their relationship had only lasted a month or so before he'd gone to live in London. They'd promised to keep in touch but after the first few letters, things had fizzled out.)

She laughed to indicate that she realised he was joking as two more students pushed past them to get into the Student Union.

"Listen, do you fancy going for a drink somewhere?" Donovan asked. "Perhaps somewhere a little less hectic than a corridor; there's a pub just over the road. We can catch up on old times."

"Sounds great," said Kate, aware of a fluttering sensation in her stomach that she'd not felt for a while. This might even make up for missing Dr. Schwarz's lecture.

It was after eleven when Kate and Donovan finally left the 'Frog and Firkin'.

They had filled each other in on what had been happening in their lives for the last seven years and Kate reflected as she sat in the back of a black cab on her way home. It had felt like they'd never been apart.

It was strange how things worked out; she'd only decided to go to the Union bar to console herself after missing the lecture. If she hadn't she'd never have bumped into Michael.

She fumbled in her pocket for the beer mat on which he'd written his number. Pulling it out, she giggled to herself. Things were looking up. This was one opportunity, she decided, she was not going to let pass her by.

9

St John's Wood, London, September 10th, 1888

"It's the most preposterous thing I've heard in my entire life."

Professor Arnold was rubbing his furrowed temple as if he were trying to physically force the information he had just received into his brain.

"Let us endeavour to take stock of the circumstances. You are telling me that on two separate occasions you ventured out onto the streets of London after dark and sought out prostitutes for no other reason than to butcher them in cold blood. You then woke up, at home in bed, with no blood on your clothes, or any other outward sign that you ever left your room, let alone committed these savage acts of murder?"

Professor Arnold sat down and began unravelling the translucent, brown paper from a large cigar; they were one of his few vices.

"I know how it sounds but I can see pictures in my mind. I know how the women were murdered without having to be told. On waking this morning I had no recollection of the night before, only the feeling that there was something that I had done. When I finally read the newspaper, it said only that another prostitute had been murdered yet I saw her lying draped over the railings. I knew then that it was I who had..."

Jacques began to sob.

"You will forgive me for saying so, dear boy, that unless you have a family history of dementia, which I am sure you do not, then I can only conclude that you must be suffering from some kind of Delayed Trauma Syndrome. You say all this started a few days after returning from the expedition?"

Jacques was pacing the room in front of the fireplace where a log fire roared in the hearth. He looked far removed from the immaculately dressed, well-groomed young man with whom Arnold was familiar. His hair was unkempt and matted, his eyes were sunken and his stubbled cheeks drawn. His eyes were wide and despairing. He was displaying all the symptoms of a nervous breakdown.

He stopped pacing and looked at Arnold.

"Yes, the day after we arrived back in London, I began to feel unwell. I attributed it partly to the change in climate and also to the fact that I had not slept well since the incident at the camp."

Jacques sat down and rubbed his forehead, trying to remember anything else of significance. He did not wish to tell the professor of the strange nightmares he had been having every night since he had fallen down the ravine. He was unsure why he didn't want to tell him, it was almost as if there was a voice inside him telling him not to. He stood up and began pacing the room again.

Arnold rose from the leather armchair and guided Jacques toward the sofa and sat him down. He crouched down in front of him and placed both hands on his shoulders. He spoke gently.

"I have only ever come across one such case before where a trauma manifested itself as hallucinations a number of weeks after an accident. I once treated a woman who had been knocked down by a hansom cab in Aldgate High Street. She suffered several broken bones and lacerations to her face and body but she made a swift recovery and was walking about, albeit with a cane, several months later. One night there was a knock at my door; it was her husband. His face was bleeding profusely and he told me that his wife had hit him with a poker. He explained that for a number of weeks she had been exhibiting increasingly strange behaviour towards him and accusing him of being the son of the Devil. She had attacked him on several occasions and on this particular evening, as he entered the house, she was hiding behind the door with a poker in her hand. He wanted me to certify her insane and have her committed to the asylum."

Jacques was looking up now; the despair in his eyes contained a flicker of hope.

"What became of her?" he asked, eager to know the outcome.

"After sedating her, I admitted her to the hospital where I observed her behaviour for several days. During this time, she continued to have delusions and at one point she had to be physically restrained when she tried to kill one of the nurses who were attending to her.

Apparently, she thought the nurse was in league with her husband and they were conspiring to sacrifice her to the Devil. Unfortunately, I had no option but to ..."

He looked at Jacques to gauge his response that looked at his feet again and put his head in his hands.

The professor was physically pained seeing Jacques so desperate; he had grown very fond of him over the last seven months or so. He was almost like the son he'd never had. (He'd been far too busy concentrating on studying and furthering his ambitions in medicine to start a family.)

It seemed he was powerless to help, but then a thought occurred to him. The Police Surgeon, Dr. Frederick Gordon Brown, was an associate of his. Surely *he* would have examined the bodies of the victims.

Maybe he would be in possession of facts that would prove that Jacques could not have been responsible for the deaths. It was worth a try.

Not wishing to raise Jacques' hopes unnecessarily, he rang for his butler and asked him to prepare a room for his colleague who would be staying for a few days.

The professor told Jacques that he had to go to the college and advised him to get some rest until he returned.

10

London, 1997

Donovan whistled loudly and a black cab performed a swift U- turn from the other side of the road and swung to a halt in front of them.

He held open the door for Kate and followed her into the back.

The driver looked in his mirror waiting for directions. Kate looked at Donovan. She had enjoyed the evening and was reluctant to let it end just yet.

"Coffee?" she asked, hoping the question came out as if it were a courtesy and nothing more. She was very attracted to him but she was unsure if she read the signals she was receiving from him correctly.

"Why not!" he said, smiling brightly. "After all, it might be another ten years before I see you again."

Kate gave the driver her address and they settled down for the ten- minute drive across town.

The streetlights shone in through the cab windows and Donovan found himself staring at Kate's profile. She had matured a lot since their 'fling' back in Little Stanton. All the qualities that had drawn him to her when they were younger were still there but now she had something more. Back in Little Stanton she'd been good- looking (Not a stunner; she was still carrying a few pounds of puppy fat and she wore a brace on her slightly crooked teeth.) but now she was like the butterfly that had emerged after a week inside its cocoon, her legs were crossed and protruded through the slit in the emerald green skirt that she was wearing. Donovan felt himself stirring and the beat of his heart became a touch more rapid.

Kate turned her gaze from the street lights and smiled. Donovan had to stop himself from kissing her (perhaps she just saw him as an old friend.)

He smiled back, "Listen, are you sure it's not too late? Maybe I should just see you home. You've probably got a busy day tomorrow...."

Kate's heart sank. "No. No, honestly, I'm meeting a friend of mine for a late breakfast," she lied. "So I don't need to be up till at least nine."

"Well if you're sure...."

Donovan was interrupted as the cab slowed down and came to a halt outside Kate's flat.

Back in Donovan's apartment, the key, which was still in his bag from when he'd visited Brady at Ashworth, was beginning to glow faintly. Small changes were taking place. The eyes on the figure were beginning to open slightly and the wound on the torso bled a tiny drop of blood onto the cotton handkerchief that covered it. Something was stirring...

Kate paid the driver, despite Donovan's protests. He had paid for dinner and she wanted him to know that she was a modern woman who believed in paying her way. Not that she was a raving feminist; she just liked things to be on an even keel.

She led the way up the few steps outside her flat and put the key in the lock. She could feel Donovan close behind her and the smell of his aftershave was beginning to turn her on. It had been a long time since she'd broken up with her long term boyfriend, two years in fact, and apart from the odd drunken one night stand, her sex life had been confined to watching slightly pornographic, subtitled French films on Channel Four and early morning rendezvous with her vibrator.

Entering the flat, she threw her backpack onto the sofa. She shrugged off her coat and as it dropped round her shoulders she felt strong arms encircle her. She reached behind as he kissed her neck and pulled him more tightly towards her. He spun her around and their mouths met fiercely. Their hands began tugging at each other's clothes. His fingers were frantically trying to unbutton her shirt and hers were struggling to unbuckle his belt.

They were both breathing heavily now and Kate could feel herself becoming moist as she pulled at his jeans and began to slide them down. She traced the length of his erection through his boxer shorts and then slipped her hand inside.

His hands were inside her blouse and he deftly flipped the clasp on her bra with one hand whilst the other searched for her breast. They were both completely lost in each other now.

They fell to the floor and he lifted his weight slightly while she reached up, slid her panties down and kicked them onto the rug.

His tongue explored her mouth and she sucked and bit it gently. She gasped slightly as he entered her and she raised her legs a little so she could push against the floor as he pushed deeper inside her.

Donovan moved in and out slowly at first and then his rhythm became faster as he felt Kate push up as he thrust down. They could both sense the urgency that the other felt and their movements became almost desperate.

Kate rolled him over and sat astride him. She arched her back and pushed herself down onto him. Her movements became frenzied as she felt her climax building. Suddenly she exploded inside and her nails dug into his chest as she finally lost control. Donovan was oblivious to any pain as he thrust himself finally to a shuddering release.

Kate's orgasm seemed to last forever and she squeezed her thighs together, the exquisite pleasure making her writhe.

When she looked down, Donovan's eyes were still closed; there was huge smile on his face. She collapsed forward onto his chest and they both burst out laughing.

Later as they lay in her bed, holding each other as only new lovers do when sleeping, Donovan's mind was filled with strange, disturbing images. He was re-living the evening, but it was as if he were being controlled in some way by an outside force. He couldn't explain it but it was almost as if a voice were telling him exactly what to do and say.

As he watched himself following Kate up the steps to her flat he could see, a few steps behind him, a shadow. It was almost imperceptible, like the shimmer of heat that rises off a road on a hot day. It was whispering to him *"Get her inside. Wait until she gets inside."*

Kate was giggling and telling him not to expect too much, her flat was only small.

As they both stepped inside, he saw himself suddenly lunge forward. It was like watching a movie except he knew this was for real. Up until now it had been a little like watching a scene from a play but now it changed. His hands were round Kate's throat. He was looking directly into her terror filled eyes. They were pleading: *'Why?'*

He lifted her up by her neck and threw her sideways against a full-length mirror on the wall. She fell heavily onto the floor and her head lolled back, blood trickling onto the carpet from her mouth. His camera swung from his neck and he casually lifted it to his eye and snapped off a few frames, the auto-wind filling the eerie silence and the flash lighting up Kate's battered body. Then he heard the voice again:

"Finish her, disciple! I command it!"

The view changed then and he was hovering above the scene again. He watched as he lifted the camera strap over his head and flicked the film out of the back. Then to his horror he saw himself raise the camera high above his head and...

"Michael, what is it?"

Donovan's eyes opened and he saw Kate's worried expression; she looked like a frightened child. He pulled her close to him and held her tightly.

"Michael, what is it?" she repeated. "You're drenched in sweat. Are you okay?"

Donovan still held her close to him.

"I'm fine," he said, kissing the top of her head. "Just a bad dream, that's all."

Kate sighed and kissed his chest. She could still feel him trembling and she held him more tightly.

Donovan was relieved it had just been a dream; he had had vivid dreams before but never anything quite as terrifying as that.

He closed his eyes and tried to let his tiredness overcome the uneasiness that now engulfed him but no matter how hard he tried, he couldn't banish the image of Kate's battered body from his mind.

By the time the first rays of sunlight filtered into the bedroom, the left side of the bed where Donovan had been was long since cold. In his place was a crumpled Fuji film box opened out into a flat sheet with the message written in pencil: *'Call me - 0717 230041',*

11

St John's Wood, London ,1888

The huge oak door flew open and Arnold literally ran into the house.

"Jacques, where are you? Come into the library at once!" he shouted excitedly up the stairway.

He didn't bother to remove his hat or coat despite the fact that he was soaking wet and water was dripping onto the wooden floor. It was just as well Mrs. Arnold was attending a meeting of the Women's Guild, otherwise he would have received a severe reprimand for such inconsiderate behaviour. Good staff was hard to find these days without giving them justification for asking for salary rises due to extra cleaning duties.

The Professor was agitated in the extreme.

"Jacques, for goodness sake, get down here. I have some excellent news."

Arnold began removing his coat now and at the same time instructed his butler who had come to see what on earth all the excitement was about, to fetch some glasses and a bottle of claret; there was some celebrating to be done.

Jacques appeared at the doorway, rubbing his red-rimmed eyes. He had managed to fall asleep for an hour in spite of the constant whispering of voices that seemed to infiltrate his every thought.

Arnold rushed over and placed his arm round his shoulders.

"Sit down, Jacques. I have some crucial information that proves beyond doubt that you could not possibly be the perpetrator of the terrible crimes which have taken place recently."

Professor Arnold explained how he had been to see his friend Dr. Brown.

The police, it seemed, were investigating a number of murders in the East End, all of which they were fairly certain were committed by the same individual.

The victims were all dispatched in a very similar manner and in a very violent fashion. Dr. Brown had provided the professor with detailed information about the deaths and the way in which their bodies had been mutilated. Indeed, at times, he struggled to hold back the bile, which rose in his throat as the grisly details were recounted. But the most important piece of information came toward the end of the meeting.

Dr. Brown had been explaining that, in his opinion, the killer must have some kind of medical background in order to locate so precisely the organs and remove them without causing too much trauma to the surrounding tissues, (a fact which did not in fact serve to help eliminate Jacques from suspicion) when he happened to mention that the murder of the first victim, Martha Tabram, took place on the 7th August.

The professor had asked Dr. Brown to confirm the date and on doing so was amazed when Arnold suddenly stood up and began pumping his hand vigorously, conveying inordinate amounts of gratitude. In fact, he had rushed from the office leaving behind a very perplexed police surgeon.

"But why is this so important, Professor?" asked Jacques. "The Doctor has merely confirmed my fears; the killer most definitely has surgical knowledge. You see the pieces of the mosaic come together...."

Jacques' face once again betrayed his inner torment.

Professor Arnold pulled open the top drawer of the bureau in the corner of the room and triumphantly drew out his journal. He flicked through the book, searching for a particular date. Then he handed it to Jacques.

"Look closely, my dear boy. Observe the date. You could not possibly have killed Martha Tabram on the 7th of August because you were approximately seven thousand miles away in South America."

Jacques read the entry in the journal. It read:

'August 5th 1888 -The expedition has been extremely fruitful. I have little doubt that the specimens we will take back with us will advance our medical knowledge a great deal. Tomorrow we leave for Arequipa.'

12

Whitechapel, 29th September 1888

It had been over two weeks since Professor Arnold had put Jacques' mind at rest about the killings, and he was beginning to feel relatively back to normal again. The letter, which had been sent to Scotland Yard via a newspaper a few days earlier, from a man claiming to be 'The Ripper' and boasting that he had killed the prostitutes, had also gone a long way to helping him believe the professor's prognosis of Delayed Trauma Syndrome.

It had all seemed so real though. In some ways he supposed he had been fortunate; delayed trauma was often permanent according to the professor. He had seen some patients who had developed complete and overwhelming dementia.

The only other positive thing was that, from a professional perspective, his experience had given him an insight into sickness of the mind. He could now truly empathise with some of the unfortunates he had seen in the asylum.

On the page of the textbook he had been reading, *'Gray's Anatomy'*, the diagram of a heart was caged behind a mass of lines and Latin labels. The picture suddenly looked unfocused and began to swim on the page. He removed his spectacles and rubbed his tired eyes.

He looked down again at the page and closed the book.

The clock on the mantelshelf told him he'd been studying for over four hours. It was no wonder he was beginning to see double. He stood up to stretch his legs and walked over to the window. It was a cool evening and the setting sun painted the sky above London purple and red.

He decided to walk down to the stationers and pick up some writing paper before it closed; he hadn't written to his mother for over three weeks.

He pulled on his overcoat, picked up his hat, then turned to check the time again. Something on the shelf seemed different. He couldn't fathom what it was at first but then it struck him; the key he had brought back from Peru, which had been sitting there almost forgotten since his return, had changed. He rubbed his eyes again thinking the double vision he'd experienced a few minutes ago was returning. *No, he was sure, the figure on the side had definitely had its eyes closed when he had first discovered it but now they were half open, giving the figure a kind of sleepy appearance.*

He picked it up to look more closely and immediately felt an intense pain shoot through his upper body. He almost fell to the floor. It was as if he had been struck a violent blow to the chest. A surge of *something* had run through him the second he had picked up the key.

He was now on one knee, the key still clutched tightly in his left hand. His head was spinning and he felt faint and nauseous. Then he reeled back in amazement as a figure stepped out in front of him. It had appeared from nowhere.

Jacques thought that the man looked familiar even though he could only see his back. He walked across the room to the desk and opened the drawer where Jacques kept his medical kit.

Jacques tried to push himself up and open his mouth to complain about the man's audacity at coming uninvited into his house but nothing came out and instead of rising to his feet, he felt himself falling backwards to the floor. Just as his head touched the ground, the intruder turned round and Jacques stared in horror as he realised that the man he was staring at was... himself.

As the door closed behind him, Jacques blacked out into unconsciousness.

"Jacques, Jacques!"

Jacques was standing at the top of the Eiffel Tower in Paris with his father. They were laughing happily and marvelling at the view over the city. His father lifted him up in a mock gesture of throwing him over the ledge and he squealed with delight. Suddenly his father climbed up onto the ledge himself and began to 'tightrope walk' along it.

Jacques was imploring him to come down; the joke wasn't funny anymore. His father was still laughing, although he was swaying from side to side trying to maintain his precarious balance. Jacques tugged at the leg of his trousers and screamed at him to come down.

"Papa, please get down, I don't like this game, please."

Still his father took a pace forward apparently unaware of the danger. Then he turned and looked round at the small crowd of people now focusing on his death defying antics.

The crowd slowly, one at a time, began to applaud until, eventually, a crescendo of applause filled Jacques' ears. His father bowed as naturally as a performer on the theatre stage. Jacques breathed a sigh of relief now as he realised the performance was over.

His father bowed again and tried to resume his standing position on the ledge but as he straightened up he began flailing his arms wildly, desperately trying to maintain his balance. The look of blind terror on his face transferred to the faces of the crowd as they realised he was going to fall.

"Jacques, Jacques!" he screamed, as he clawed frantically at the air.

Jacques reached out to his father, his fingers inches away and he watched as his father disappeared over the parapet.

Jacques leapt onto the ledge; he could still hear his father's fading voice as it called out to him.

"Jacques, Jacques!"

Tears filled his eyes, blinding him, as the words grew fainter...

Suddenly, he was looking into a pair of bewildered eyes and his hands were tightly gripping what he thought were his father's shoulders.

"Jacques, wake up, it's me!"

Professor Arnold not only looked bewildered but frightened as well.

The professor helped Jacques up from the floor and sat him on the edge of the bed.

"Jacques, you are still weak. You need to rest more."

Jacques looked confused, "I was studying, I..."

"You must have stood too quickly, how long were you sitting?"

"A few hours; I can't remember..."

"The door was ajar when I arrived and you were lying on the floor. I thought at first an intruder had caught you unaware but there are no marks on your head or face and everything in the room looks normal."

The image of a figure leaving the room jumped into Jacques' mind.... then it was gone. He looked up at the clock, it couldn't be possible; it was nine thirty and judging by the daylight entering through the window he'd been unconscious for over twelve hours!

The professor handed him a glass of water and for the

first time, Jacques noticed that he was holding something else: a newspaper. Their eyes met and Jacques knew instinctively that this was more than just a social call.

Professor Arnold handed him the newspaper.

"There have been two more," he whispered solemnly.

The Headline said it all:

"THE RIPPER STRIKES AGAIN"

Jacques read the article explaining how a man had been disturbed in a dark court off Berner Street as he was disembowelling a woman known to locals as Elizabeth Stride. He hadn't managed to complete the job so he had lurked around until after one in the morning looking for another victim.

The police knew it was approximately that time because his second victim, Catherine Eddowes, had been detained at Leman Police station until well past midnight for being drunk and disorderly earlier in the evening.

The article also mentioned that the second victim's face had been mutilated beyond recognition. The police had to use her clothes and jewellery to ascertain her identity.

Professor Arnold asked the question Jacques had been waiting for.

"Jacques, where were you last night?"

13

Ministers' Chambers, House of Commons, London 1997

Donovan absent-mindedly fingered the groove in the dark wood panelling on the wall. Henderson was unravelling the stained cotton handkerchief from around the key.

Donovan couldn't understand why he referred to it as a key; to him it looked more like a bottle, albeit a very strange one.

He couldn't help but notice the look of awe on Henderson's face as he finally opened the handkerchief and revealed the key. He seemed entranced and Donovan got the impression that Henderson had forgotten that *he* was still there.

He coughed falsely.

"I take it that it is what you were looking for."

It was rather an obvious statement but it did the trick. Henderson turned to a drawer in the large mahogany desk that dominated the room.

There was a laptop computer on the desk; Henderson had been working at it when he first entered the room. The power-saver screen was the Commons crest on a black background. He noticed that the computer was sitting in a red leather case and then he realised that it was the new Minister's Box that he'd read about recently.

Apparently, all ministers had been issued with one to replace the mountains of paperwork that they inevitably amassed during the parliamentary term. The computers could only be accessed using a special ring dedicated to each minister and the ring was worn at all times in order to maintain security. Some newspapers had reported the idea as ludicrous and a National Security risk, particularly with reference to the ones used by the Ministry of Defence.

Donovan scanned the desk for anything of interest and he was surprised when he saw what appeared to be an ordinary signet ring lying by the side of a notepad.

Henderson reached into a drawer and lifted out a plain brown envelope.

"Michael, you've done well," he said. "It's all there including the bonus."

He handed the envelope across keeping hold of it as Donovan tried to take it. Donovan looked at his fingers. There was no ring, but on the third finger he noticed a circle of red, angry spots. The skin was broken where Henderson had been scratching the rash. Obviously his ring didn't agree with him.

"Michael, remember... this never happened, you understand?"

The look that Henderson gave him had concrete slippers and motorway flyovers written all over it. Donovan got the message. To be honest, he was relieved to finally get rid of the key. Since the incident at Kate's flat, he had felt uneasy being in possession of it. Although there was no direct connection between the dream and the key, he couldn't help feeling that it had some significance.

He slipped the envelope inside his trench coat and pulled an imaginary zipper across his lips. Henderson smiled and walked to the door.

"I'll be in touch when I need you again," he said as he held the door open for Donovan.

The heavy oak door shut behind him and he breathed a sigh of relief.

"Fucking weirdo," Donovan whispered silently to himself as he patted his inside pocket and bounced down the stairs two at a time.

Inside the chamber, Henderson was pouring himself a large scotch. He looked out of his window at the city and raised his glass.

"Not long now," he sighed, before emptying the glass with one swallow.

Donovan was in a cab heading toward Fleet Street when his mobile rang. It was Kate.

"Michael, it's me," she said uncertainly. (She had been worried about calling in case he didn't want to see her again and their 'reunion' the other night had just been a one night stand for old times' sake.)

"Kate, it's brilliant to hear from you. Where are you?"

The smile that he'd had on his face since he'd left Henderson became even wider. Could his day get any better?

She explained that she was at college, studying in the library but she would be finishing soon and going home.

"Listen Kate," said Donovan. "I've just had a stroke of luck and I'm going out later to celebrate...."

Kate thought he was trying to rush her off the line and anticipated the next line: 'I'll be in touch' or 'I'll see you around' Instead he said "I've just got one small problem."

"What's that?" she asked, now trying to sound cool and detached; Ms. Independent.

"All my friends have died and my parents are on a two year cruise in the Caribbean," he laughed, "which means I'm looking for someone to go out with."

Kate resisted the urge to jump up and down and scream out loud; she decided the library wasn't the best place in the world to receive good news on a mobile.

"Erm, I'll just check my diary."

She placed the phone next to the journal she had been

studying. She flicked a few pages over next to the ear-piece then picked up the phone.

"You're in luck," she said. "I'm in between orgies and dinner parties tonight. Where do you want to meet?"

"I'll pick you up at eight," said Donovan.

"Great, see you then."

She was too excited to study now and besides she only had an hour to buy something to wear for tonight. Hurriedly, she checked out the books she wanted and headed out of the library.

14

St. Johns Wood, London, 1888

The professor had not reacted in quite the way Jacques had expected. He thought he would try and persuade him to commit himself to the asylum. After all, he had just described in minute detail the way in which both new victims had been killed.

Arnold had called Doctor Brown immediately upon reading about the murders and acquired details of the deaths that obviously Jacques could not possibly know unless he was the killer. The other disturbing fact that Brown divulged was that the modus operandi of the killer seemed to be different from when Martha Tabram had been killed and that the police were now exploring the possibility that she was in fact the victim of a different killer altogether. He had then gone to see Jacques to confirm his whereabouts at the time of the murders. Jacques had recounted the story of the 'intruder' the night before and had gone on to describe how the second victim had been gutted like a fish and had her entrails thrown over her shoulder.

It had taken nearly half an hour for Jacques to explain about the strange key that he had found in Peru and the strange dreams about the creature with eyes 'like the pits of hell itself.¢

"Jacques, tell me about the actual killings. Are you

aware at the time what you are doing or are you in a state of trance?"

Jacques stared into space, focusing on nothing as if trying to recall a distant memory.

"I'm not sure.... it is difficult to know what is a dream and what is not. Last night, I remember the vision of myself leaving the house.... then nothing. Yet when you began to tell me about the murders it was like *déjà vu*.... how do you say? .... watching myself.... *au théatre*... at the theatre. It is like a scene from a play in which I have acted."

Professor Arnold looked fascinated; his eyes glistened with what Jacques took to be excitement.

"But Professor, I don't understand. If I am the killer then you need to contact the police."

Professor Arnold walked to the dressing table and picked up the figurine.

"You said you felt something strange happen last night when you touched this?" he asked.

Jacques stood up and walked over to him.

"Yes, almost as if something had passed into me for a second and then, as I explained, I must have fallen because I was looking up at... myself."

"There's something about the figure that ties in with the last victim. Look at the eyes; the way they are closed like slits, and the ears...."

Jacques noticed for the first time that the girl had none.

"Catherine Eddowes' eyelids had been slit and both her ears were missing from her head," said the professor. "And this," he pointed to the mark above the heart. "In each of the victims, the heart had been removed."

Jacques' eyes met Arnold's.

"I remember something else from last night," he said. "The eyes were different. That's what made me pick it up in the first place. Last night the eyes were open slightly."

Arnold paced up and down the room.

"What I don't understand is why the key seems to have played no part in the previous murders. You have no recollection of handling it before?"

Jacques shook his head. Arnold replaced the key on the shelf.

He stood in front of Jacques and asked him to sit down.

"You realise..." he continued, "...that if you are in fact the killer, then someone else must have killed the Tabram woman, which means there is another murderer running loose round London as we speak. So even if we go to the police and confess, it may not necessarily mean the end of the blood-shed."

From the expression on Jacques' face, it was clear that this had not occurred to him.

"Jacques, I think at this moment we should not involve the police..."

"But I am...." Jacques began incredulously

"Let me finish, please," begged the professor. "I believe we have a unique opportunity to observe something that has never been witnessed before in the realms of medical science. You are convinced that this artefact is somehow transferring some kind of power to you that is making you commit horrendous acts of savagery. It is my belief that when you fell down the ravine in Peru and banged your head you somehow damaged the part of your brain that controls emotional thinking. If I can observe you closely in a controlled situation, maybe I can draw some conclusions about your condition which will help cure you and others who are at this moment committed to the asylum for the rest of their lives."

Jacques could see the logic in what the professor was saying but the overwhelming sensation of being out of control was terrifying.

"But Professor, what if I kill again? Haven't I murdered enough innocent people already?"

Arnold sat opposite Jacques and spoke softly.

"Jacques, you would not put a man in gaol because he had a fever or because he had been injured in the factory. What you have is a medical condition. That does not mean you are a criminal. Besides, if keeping you under observation will lead to a breakthrough in scientific understanding, isn't it worth doing?"

The professor explained to Jacques that he would prepare a room at home. It would contain a bed with restraining straps so that at night there would be no possibility of him wandering onto the streets. There would be medication on hand to sedate him should the delusions become of a violent nature. During the day he would lead a normal life and continue with his studies.

Jacques pondered on what the Professor was saying. Wouldn't it be better to use the situation to advance medical knowledge rather than hanging at the end of a rope?

After a few minutes, he nodded. The Professor was sitting beside him now and had his arm round his shoulders.

"There is just one thing," Jacques whispered. "We must construct a box with a lining made of lead. The key must be stored inside, out of sight."

The professor squeezed Jacques' shoulders. "I will contact a carpenter immediately."

15

Café Bergère, Oxford Street, London, April 1997

"Would Madame care for coffee?"

Kate looked across the candlelit table at Donovan. He answered for her.

"I think we'll leave coffee for half an hour or so. Could you bring us another bottle of..." He lifted the empty bottle of champagne from the silver, ice-filled cooler at the side of the table. "...this please."

The waiter nodded and smiled genuinely; he was even more hopeful of a generous tip now. He scurried away quickly.

"So, Kate," said Michael. "What exactly are the plans for this expedition that you're so excited about?"

She had in fact only mentioned the trip once in passing. If the truth were known at this moment, the last thing on her mind was archaeology.

"Actually, I'm in the middle of two projects at the moment. In two weeks I'm due to fly out to Australia to do some research on the aboriginal tribes that live in the Northern Territory."

"I should have been an archaeologist, you never see one working anywhere that the sun doesn't shine," teased Donovan. Kate gave him a glare of mock disdain then continued.

" ...The aborigines' culture has provided us with lots of

information about ancient civilisations and we want to see if we can link any of the cave art which displays their religious ideas with similar paintings in North Africa."

The new bottle of Möet Chandon arrived and the waiter filled both their glasses.

"Here's to a successful trip then," said Donovan raising his glass. He took a long draft then said. "So what else have you got in mind?"

"Well I'm also trying to get the funds together for the second part of the expedition to The Sudan next year. I believe that there is a civilisation that once existed there to rival the complexity of the Ancient Egyptians. If I manage it, the follow up work will provide me with material for my doctorate."

"Dr Katherine Stone, eh?"

Donovan leaned across the table and kissed her gently on the mouth. "It all sounds very intriguing. I have some very interesting artefacts back at my apartment. Maybe you can find time to examine them later and tell me what your conclusions are."

The alcohol was going to Kate's head now and she had that delicious light-headed feeling that only drinking champagne brought.

"I think I can fit that into my itinerary," she tried to say, but it came out 'itrinery' and she giggled.

The next morning Donovan woke up to the smell of bacon cooking. He rubbed his eyes and looked at the *'Star Wars'* alarm clock at the side of his bed, it was in the shape of *'R2D2.'* The liquid crystal display added to the futuristic reality of the android, at least it had done twenty years ago when he had first bought it.

The alarm call was actually the John Williams soundtrack from the film.

He sat up as Kate emerged from the kitchen carrying a glass of orange juice and a bacon sandwich.

"Morning, Obi Wan Kenobi," she said handing him the sandwich and taking the clock from his hand.

"A present from my mother," he lied, biting into the sandwich.

There was a muffled thump at the door and Kate looked at Donovan questioningly.

"Paperboy," he explained.

Kate opened the door to the apartment and picked up the bundle of newspapers and smirked. There was a copy of every major National and two or three of the local rags.

"A bit of light reading?"

"Got to keep up with what the opposition are doing," said Donovan.

Kate put them on the table.

"Mind if I use your shower?" she asked.

"Only if you let me share it with you," he said grinning. "There is a water shortage you know, we all have to do our bit."

Kate let the sheet she was wearing fall to the floor and put her hands on her hips.

"Well, don't be too long, we've only got ten minutes for you to 'do your bit'. I've got a lecture at ten."

Donovan threw a pillow at her as she dashed into the bathroom and it hit the door as it closed.

He climbed out of bed and realised he had an erection already. For some reason, despite the fact they had spent all last night making love, it didn't seem right to walk into the bathroom with a hard-on.

He heard the shower click on and the water begin to flow. He grabbed a tea towel off the table and tried to wrap it round himself unsuccessfully, it looked like a tent.

Just then the alarm on the clock chose to go off and he stifled a laugh and looked down.

"Fuckin' light sabre.... Let the force be with you, my son," he said in his best Alec Guinness voice and pushed open the bathroom door.

Donovan whistled tunelessly, a cup of coffee in one hand and the pile of papers under his arm. Kate had left ten minutes ago and he'd decided to read the papers before getting ready to go out. On a Friday, he was officially off work in lieu of the fact that he worked every weekend and Bank holiday. In reality, he never stopped working; the world didn't stop just because it was his day off. He was usually so paranoid about missing *'The big story '* on his day off that he spent more time on the streets than on any other day.

Today, though, he was feeling a little more relaxed than usual so he settled back into the soft cushions of the big sofa and began to read.

Most of the front pages concentrated on the recent visit of Sinn Fein leaders Martin McGuiness and Gerry Adams to the Houses of Parliament and their subsequent refusal to take the Oath, swearing allegiance to the Queen. The tabloids, as usual, dealt with the situation in their usual manner, one of them even comparing Gerry Adams to Guy Fawkes.

At the bottom of page ten of the *Daily Mail* there was an article which wouldn't normally have caught Donovan's eye but because of the conversation he'd had with Kate last night about her trip to Australia, he read it. The headline read:

'Another Brit backpacker missing Down Under '

The story told of how a twenty three year old male travelling around Australia on a working holiday had left Tennant Creek in the Northern Territory to travel down the Stuart highway to Alice Springs.

There were several sightings of him during the next few days mainly from people with whom he'd hitched rides.

He'd told them that he planned to stay in Alice for a day or two where he was meeting up with a friend travelling north from Port Augusta. Then they were hitching out to Ayers Rock.

Unfortunately, he had never made the rendezvous. His backpack had been discovered hidden behind some rocks by day-trippers at a beauty spot called Bond Creek, just north of Alice Springs.

The backpack was untouched, it seemed, and still contained valuables such as a portable CD player and about six hundred Australian dollars. This fact, said police, appeared to rule out a mugging and left them with very few leads to follow.

The article concluded by saying that the disappearance now meant that twelve backpackers, all Europeans, had disappeared in mysterious circumstances over the past eighteen months. There was also some advice for would-be travellers not to hitch rides alone.

Donovan thought about Kate and her visit but his concern, he decided, was unfounded. She wasn't exactly a backpacker although she could pass for one easily. Neither would she be on her own. Still, he'd tell her to be careful before she left.

He drained his coffee mug and went to get dressed.

16

St John's Wood , London 8th November 1888

Jacques looked round the room. It had taken a week to set up the room as Professor Arnold had required.

The bed had been requisitioned from the asylum where the professor had explained that he was doing a study on the effects of hypnosis on patients with personality disorders. As these people would be regressed to incidents they had experienced earlier in their lives, their behaviour would be unpredictable, hence the need for the bed. The asylum had conveniently arranged a cart for its transfer.

The bed had iron legs and a padded headboard. At each corner there were leather straps attached to large steel bolts underneath.

At the side of the bed was a silver tray upon which was arranged several glass vials and a large hypodermic syringe. There was also a writing table at the foot of the bed on top of which stood an oil lamp and a leather-bound journal. None of the pages had yet been written upon. The heavy bedroom door had been fitted with several steel plates and the padlocks hung from them ominously.

The 'key' was not yet in the room; it had been locked inside the specially constructed box, downstairs in the library, since the previous week.

As Jacques took it all in, he was thinking that what he saw in front of him was probably the permanent alternative to the experiment, had the professor gone to the police.

He wasn't sure what would come of this but he consoled himself with the thought that although he would now probably never fulfil his dream of becoming a surgeon of world renown and helping people in need, he would at least be helping to advance the scientific understanding of the mysteries of the mind.

His thoughts were interrupted as the door swung open and the professor entered.

"Ah, Jacques, there you are, I have just returned from seeing off Miranda. She is now on the way down to Richmond to visit her mother for a few days which means tonight it will be possible to begin the observations."

Jacques recognised the look of excitement in the professor's eyes; it was the same look all learned people get when they feel they are on the verge of a new discovery.

Jacques was tempted to ask the professor simply to throw the key into the Thames, since there had been only one dream and no incidents since it had been placed in the safe.

He knew he was clutching at straws though and that the murders had nothing to do with the key. He had just used it as an excuse because he was terrified of admitting that his brain really was damaged, probably beyond repair.

"We will begin after dinner this evening," announced the professor with a little too much relish for Jacques' liking. "I have given Charles the night off so we shall not be disturbed."

Jacques nodded without a smile. He felt how he imagined a man might feel being served his last meal before his execution.

It was just after seven thirty when the butler came into the drawing room and asked them if there was anything else he could do. The professor told him there wasn't and bade him goodnight.

Jacques couldn't help but notice the slight impatience with which Arnold watched him depart down the steps and onto the street.

The minute he had disappeared from view, the front door was bolted.

On his return to the room, Arnold poured them both another brandy and then sat down opposite Jacques on the other side of the fire.

They both said very little as they finished their drinks and eventually it was Jacques who stood first.

"We may as well begin," he said, almost as if they were contemplating playing a rubber of bridge or a game of charades.

The professor led the way up the stairs.

The air in the room was cold despite the fact that a fire had been lit in there an hour or so earlier. Jacques removed his house jacket and shoes and lay on the bed. The professor tied the straps round his wrists and ankles.

"It is more comfortable than the one at my house," he joked. "Maybe life in the asylum would not be as bad as I feared."

The professor was too engrossed in preparing the sedative to acknowledge Jacques' attempt at lifting the gravity of the circumstances.

"I am sure this will not be necessary but I think it is a prudent measure, just in case the situation gets out of control," he said, as he pulled the plunger on the syringe upwards.

Jacques made himself as comfortable as one could possibly be having been strapped to a bed; whilst Arnold went down to retrieve the key from the safe.

Jacques felt extremely vulnerable and almost laughed at the irony of a psychopathic killer feeling vulnerable. The very thought of himself leaving the room and killing someone now seemed absurd and he began to wonder if he *were* actually asleep and enduring some terrible nightmare.

He heard footsteps coming back up the stairs and the professor entered the room holding out the key at arms length as if it were about to explode.

He placed the key on the table at the side of the bed with the engraved figure facing Jacques. The eyes were shut, Jacques noted.

He then removed a ring of keys from his waistcoat pocket and walked back to the door where he proceeded to lock the padlocks. There were four in all.

Jacques turned and looked at the tall double-sashed window which looked out onto the road and wondered if even a deranged, possessed, motiveless killer would be prepared to jump three storeys to escape.

The professor then sat down at the table, checked his pocket watch and spoke out loud as he wrote the first entry in the journal: *The experiment commenced at eight twenty seven precisely.*

Jacques closed his eyes and decided the best approach was to try and get some sleep.

It was the slightest of noises that woke Jacques. At first he wasn't sure where he was but then he remembered. Across the room he could see the professor at the door. He appeared to be unlocking it. Jacques was unsure as to why he would need to leave the room; he had been meticulous in his preparations to ensure that they could both remain in the room all night.

Jacques called out but the professor continued as if he had not heard him so he tried again, this time more forcefully.

"Professor, what is it, did you forget something? ... Professor please, answer me."

Jacques was beginning to worry now. Instinctively, he tried to move but the restraining straps had been tied well. They bit painfully into his wrists.

It was then that he noticed the hypodermic needle on the floor at the side of the professor.

'What was he doing? Maybe he had fallen asleep and was sleepwalking.'

Jacques turned to look at the strap on his wrist to see if there was any way of release, then he noticed the key.

The eyes on the figure were wide open. They were also glowing, The final thing he noted was the faint trickle of blood running down the torso of the figure.

The sound of the door opening made him turn his attention back to the professor.

He stood in the doorway with his back to Jacques. Then he slowly bent down to pick up the needle. As he did, Jacques caught a glimpse of his face. It was not what he expected. The face was the professor's but younger...much younger. The cheekbones were more thickset and the nose more aquiline. The mouth was wide and thin and the chin was longer than the professor's own. But it was the eyes that held Jacques' gaze. They were black and malevolent. The pupils were thin and vertical like those of a lizard or snake.

A flash of recognition filled Jacques' mind as he realised where he had seen them before...It was in the jungle, at the bottom of the ravine when he had first discovered the key.

'Arnold' left the house via the back entry. He wore a long, black overcoat and a deerstalker hat. He also carried his black medical bag.

He moved quickly and with purpose along the pavement, heading towards Whitechapel.

Late night revellers bade him 'Goodnight' as they passed but none saw his face. The night was dark, misty, and cold and his collar was pulled up tightly round his neck.

It was fifteen minutes before he reached the narrow

streets of the East End.

There were few people about when he approached the lady sitting on a low wall opposite 'The Crown Vaults' tavern just off Miller's Court. She appeared to be having some difficulty standing and didn't react until he was virtually at her side.

From the way she was dressed, she was obviously a prostitute. She looked up at 'Arnold'.

"Sorry, luv, I'm not working tonight. I'm not feeling too good. Try me tomorrer."

Her eyes were red-ringed and watery.

"Tell yer what, though, I'd appreciate it if yer could give me a hand gettin' 'ome. I only live 'cross the road there...up the duff yer see, can't catch me breath," she said wearily.

The collar of Arnold's coat still shadowed his face and she took his lack of reaction to mean he needed more persuasion.

"Awright then, help me get 'ome an I'll give yer a taste of what yer after."

She tried to stand but she lost her balance and staggered forward. He managed to catch her before she fell and he carried her across the road. There was still no one about.

They approached a narrow, arched opening at the end of a cobbled ginnel, the wall of which bore a ragged poster offering a reward of a hundred pounds put up by a Mr. S. Montagu for 'Information leading to the arrest of the Whitechapel murderer.'

"It's just 'ere," she mumbled. "Number thirteen."

There was a window next to the door with a piece of muslin drawn across. Two panes of glass were smashed and some cotton sacking had been shoved into the gaps in an attempt to keep out the draughts.

As he put her down she reached inside the top of her boot and pulled out a small brass key. She opened the door and went in. 'Arnold' followed shutting the door quietly behind him.

Mary Kelly threw her shawl onto the bed.

"Now about that..." she began and turned around.

The syringe hit her directly in the left eye and she staggered back screaming. Bewildered, her hands clutched frantically at her eyes and they closed round the hypodermic needle protruding from her face. Then she felt cold, leather-gloved hands enclose her own and she was spun round and thrown across the room.

She screamed out in pain as her head caught the edge of the dressing table and she fell to the floor. She peered up into the gloom, now almost oblivious to the syringe protruding from one of her eyes. She saw the dark shadow loom over her and tried to drag herself physically into a corner that didn't exist.

It was a small mercy that she could not make out that he now had a scalpel in one hand and a bone-saw in the other.

'Professor Arnold' felt both terror and excitement as he carefully made the first incision. It was as if all his senses were heightened. He was now experiencing the pleasure he normally felt during an operation when he could locate an organ and almost instinctively know what to do to repair it. The difference now was that the feeling was far more intense, almost sexual in nature. At the same time, somewhere deeper inside, there was a feeling of revulsion and nausea.

The wide, arcing incision he made across the prostitute's abdomen seeped blood, mirroring the grin on the professor's face.

For over an hour he worked at the body, removing all the major organs including the uterus and the newly formed foetus, placing them carefully on the table at the side of the bed. Each was laid out with meticulous care.

The heart was the final organ to be removed and as he

carried it over to the table, he lifted it above his mouth and let the still warm blood drip into his mouth. With each drop he felt more powerful and the urge to go out into the streets and seek another victim was almost overwhelming. Deep inside his head he heard a voice whispering: *"Quickly, Get it done, I need it now."*

When the body cavity was completely, empty he lifted the body onto the bed and arranged it so that the arms crossed the chest and the legs were together. Then he removed the syringe from the eye and cut off her eyelids so she appeared to be gazing up toward the sky. He then placed the heart inside her mouth and took a step back to survey the 'altar'.

He knelt down at the bottom of the bed, closed his eyes and breathed in deeply. Suddenly the room filled with light and he squinted even though his eyes were closed. A blast of air rushed past him threatening to knock him over and he braced himself against it.

The smell that accompanied the blast was foul and foetid and he fought the need to vomit. Then, just as suddenly, it was dark again.

He opened his eyes. The body was still in the same position, the eyes still gazed upward but the mouth was empty.

17

Arnhem Land, Northern Territory, Australia May 1997

Kate stepped out of the small twin-engine Cessna and onto the dry rocky ground. The searing heat hit her in the face and she pulled the wide brimmed hat down to shield her eyes from the brilliant glare of the sun. Pippa, an undergraduate from the faculty of anthropology at the university, stepped out behind her. The two women had known each other for two years now and they got on incredibly well.

"Jesus, I knew it was going to be hot but this is ridiculous, I'm sweating like a racehorse," said Pippa, wiping her forehead with her bandana.

About two hundred yards away there was a small shack, which judging by the rusty corrugated roof and rotting wooden boards that made up its frame, was no longer in use.

Beyond that there was a huge expanse of bush and scrub giving way in the distance to the magnificent sandstone escarpment, which they had flown over on their three-hour flight from Darwin.

Suddenly, the door on the shack flew open and a figure jumped down the steps of the veranda and began walking towards the plane. As he got closer it became obvious the man was an aboriginal. Finally, he stood in front of them.

"G'Day and welcome to Gumbalanya, I'm Peter," he

declared.

Kate was a little disappointed. She had somehow expected the aborigines to be naked except for a lizard skin thong and covered from head to waist with white and ochre mud paint.

Peter was wearing 501s, a *'Rolling Stones'* tour t-shirt, and a pair of *Adidas* trainers.

"Hi, I'm Kate Stone and this is my colleague Pippa Johnson. We're delighted to be here. Thank you so much for issuing the permit."

Pippa leaned forward and shook Peter's hand.

"Pleased to meet you Peter," she said.

Kate watched Peter's face as he saw for the first time Pippa's incredibly alluring smile that all the men she met found so attractive. It always had the same effect.

Peter was no different; Kate could see he was smitten already.

"Right, let's get yer gear and we'll go and have a chat in the station," said Peter suddenly returning to the land of the living. "Reg won't be here for another hour yet. He radioed in a bit back, the jeep had a blow out in a dry creek bed."

Peter picked up most of the baggage whilst Kate and Pippa carried the archaeological gear.

The 'station' turned out to be the shack.

Inside, the shack was actually quite welcoming with two electrical fans managing to make the atmosphere only marginally uncomfortable. There was an old chest freezer in the corner of the room from which Peter produced three cold beers. He handed them one each and offered them a seat.

After quenching their thirst Kate explained over the noise of the generator, which whined away at the back of the shack, what she intended to look at during their three-week stay.

Peter explained in return that he couldn't guarantee that

she would be able to see all the sites that contained rock art, as there were a number of different tribes living in Arnhem Land, some of whom led traditional lifestyles. These people were wary of letting white people onto their land. Also a lot of the sites had great spiritual significance and were not to be disturbed.

Suddenly there was a hiss of static on the radio.

"...Calling Gumbalanya, Peter do you read me? Over."

Peter picked up the handset.

"Reg, this is Peter. Where are yer, mate? Over."

"I've managed to change the wheel and I'm just passin' Kubarra Creek I should be there in ten minutes. Any sign of the two Pom sheilas yet? Over."

Kate and Pippa looked at each other and giggled.

"Affirmative, mate. They arrived about half an hour ago. Over."

Peter turned and winked at Kate.

"Righto mate, pour me a cold one. See you in ten. Over."

Peter replaced the handset and sat back down on the wooden chair opposite the girls.

"That was Reg," he explained sheepishly. "My boss."

"So how did you come to be involved in the administration of the reserve?" asked Kate.

"My dad was the chief elder of our tribe when they decided to lobby the government for the return of the lands to us back in sixty three. A kind of tribal council was set up and each tribe sent a representative to be a part of it. The cooperative was established so that the land and its riches could be managed effectively.

For example, the mining rights for uranium deposits alone are worth a fortune. The deposits actually belong to the government but they need our permission to mine them. For us, it is more important that the land be preserved in the state it was in when it was given to us by the *Spirits of the*

Dreamtime. Without the Council there wouldn't have been a way of sorting it out. I was round at the time and just sort of helped out whenever I could. I've been doing it ever since."

Peter went on to explain that both he and Reg were originally from a village on the tip of the Gove Peninsula called Nhulunbuy on the north east coast of Arnhem Land. He was interrupted by the sound of a vehicle coming to a halt outside and they all got up and walked out onto the veranda.

Reg jumped down from the jeep. His jet-black hair and brown leathery skin was covered in red dust.

" G'day. Sorry I'm a bit late, bloody tyre gave out an' I couldn't get the bloody jack to stand up straight. Anyway, better late than never, eh?"

His whiter than white teeth shone out from a smile that went from ear to ear. Kate smiled, she knew she was going to like Reg. Peter handed him a cold beer.

"Cheers mate, give me five minutes to hose meself down an' we'll get a move on."

He swallowed the beer in one swig, crushed the can and threw it into an oil drum that sat on the veranda. Then he went inside to grab a quick shower.

Pippa and Kate loaded their gear into the jeep whilst Peter attached the trailer that contained all the camping gear onto the back of the jeep. The temperature was still rising and by the time they had finished they were dusty, hot, and thirsty. They were sitting on the steps of the veranda when Reg emerged from the shack looking cool and fresh from his shower.

"Righto, let's hit the road, can't sit relaxing all bloody day yer know."

Peter glanced at Pippa and Kate who couldn't help but grin.

Fifteen minutes later they were heading down a rocky

track, being thrown from side to side.

Peter looked over his shoulder.

"Don't worry it gets a bit flatter about thirty kilometres further on," he said with a wry grin.

The girls hung on to the undersides of their seats and tried to smile.

"So when's the other bloke meetin' up with yer?" Reg asked.

Pippa explained that Steve Johnson, another anthropologist and the expedition photographer, had stayed behind in Darwin to pick up the mobile camper van that was going to be their home and base for three weeks. They had flown in ahead of him to get things up and running. It would take him two or three days to drive to Maningrida and meet up with them. He was bringing the rest of the archaeological equipment as well as a laptop computer that he was testing for the Technology Department. It was supposed to have some kind of satellite link so information about the expedition could be sent back daily to St. Martins.

Kate was looking out of the window. Despite the fact that the terrain had looked exactly the same for the past twenty minutes and showed no signs of changing, she was fascinated by it. She was thinking how amazing it was that the aborigines had managed to survive so successfully for forty thousand years in such a harsh environment.

Ahead of the jeep the heat haze made everything shimmer, behind it the clouds of dust billowed away into the distance.

Inside the jeep everything had a coating of red dust and when Pippa lifted her hat off to wipe her head with a dampened bandana, Kate laughed. There was a line across her forehead white above, red below. Unfortunately, it was Hobson's choice: either live with the dust and a 'cool ' breeze with the windows open or bake with them shut.

They had been travelling for about three hours when Kate was awakened from a light sleep by the sound of the jeep slowing down. It was early evening by now and the sun was low in the sky. Even so, the temperature was still in the nineties. Kate straightened up to see why they were slowing down. Ahead of them, just off the road were two aborigines.

Peter said something to Reg in the dialect of the Yirrkalla tribe then turned to the girls.

"They're *Gurindji*," said Peter. "They're one of the traditional peoples we told you about earlier."

As the jeep came to a stop the two men approached. They seemed friendly enough and smiled when they spoke.

Unlike Reg and Peter, they were for the best part naked. They looked as Kate had imagined aborigines to look. They both carried spears with three vicious looking prongs that splayed out at the end. The slightly younger of the two had a leather strap round his waist from which hung three very large but very dead lizards.

Kate and Pippa watched as Reg and the two men spoke. Every now and again the men would point toward the escarpment and make animated gestures.

At one point they became very excited and the older man drew a pattern in the dirt with his spear. Both Reg and Peter seemed to scrutinise the pattern and ask questions to which the men responded with more pointing and more drawings.

After several minutes of talking Reg went round to the back of the jeep and brought out a bottle of cold water from the cooler box. He gave it to the men who drank thirstily and with obvious relish.

When they had finished they shook hands with Reg and Peter, nodded and smiled at the girls, then turned and walked back into the bush.

Back in the jeep, Kate could hardly wait to find out

what the conversation had been about.

Peter explained that Reg had asked them if they knew of any ancient sites where there were cave paintings. They had said that there were many and that they had spent last night in such a cave.

The drawing in the dust was a map illustrating how to find that particular cave. As it was not considered sacred, it would be okay to visit and take pictures as long as nothing was removed.

He had also mentioned that some of the other caves in that particular area contained paintings of Namarrgon; *the Lightning Man* but those caves were strictly out of bounds to anyone other than the *Gurindji.*

"Is it possible to see it now?" asked Pippa eagerly.

" 'Fraid not," said Reg. "It's a bit too far, about thirty kilometres, I reckon. It'll be dark before we got half way there. In fact, we'd better get a move on and set up camp for tonight. If yer like, we can take a look first thing tomorrow."

Kate felt a mixture of excitement and disappointment. She felt the buzz that she always got at the start of a new expedition but she felt frustration at not being able to go and explore immediately.

Reg started up the engine and pulled back onto the track. The sun was just disappearing over the escarpment.

Andy Jefferson sat down heavily on his backpack and a cloud of dust billowed up round him. He heaved a sigh of frustration and swore under his breath as he watched the mobile camper that had just passed him without stopping, disappear into the distance.

He knew he was being unfair; the van was obviously bursting at the seams with whatever it was carrying and the driver *had* held up his hands in that '*Sorry I would if I could* ' type gesture.

Still, he was entitled to be a little bit pissed off; he'd

been trying to hitch a ride for four hours now. In that time only three vehicles had passed. None had so much as slowed down.

He dragged a map from the backpack and studied it carefully.

"Bastard, bastard, bastard," he swore out loud. He was at least fifty kilometres short of the nearest campsite and probably sixty from his intended destination: Jabiru.

He looked up as the sun finally disappeared behind the escarpment and the twilight turned everything sepia-coloured. The temperature dropped immediately and he shuddered involuntarily. He contemplated his options.

He had another litre of water and enough food to see him through the night. He'd have to find a rock or a bush to sleep by for tonight (that wouldn't pose a problem at least!) then start hitching first thing tomorrow.

He put his map back in the pack, lugged it wearily onto his shoulders and stepped off the track to search for a suitable spot. He had only walked about fifty yards or so when he heard the distant but unmistakable sound of a car engine.

He looked back up the track. In the distance he could just make out a small black speck followed by a trailing cloud of dust.

Andy's heart lifted and he ran back toward the road, his head suddenly full of cool showers and warm food.

He waved as the pick up got closer and assumed his *friendly hitchhiker pose,* all smiles.

The truck began to slow down as it approached and there appeared to be two people inside.

It finally pulled up a few yards in front of Andy and he walked forward quickly hoping it didn't contain a couple of teenagers who were going to roar off, showering him in kicked up rocks and dust the second he got alongside.

The truck had an American-style elongated front seat

with enough room for three people. The driver and his passenger were both aborigines.

Andy felt a little uncomfortable; up until now he had not hitched a ride with anyone other than white Australians or other travellers who had hired cars.

The passenger stuck his head out of the window.

"We're going as far as Jabiru, mate, if that's any good to yer."

He was about thirty, Andy guessed, and he looked friendly enough. The driver was perhaps a little older.

Andy looked back at the inhospitable scrubland round him, and then turned back to the truck. He'd be drinking a cold beer in half an hour.

He threw his backpack into the back of the truck and slid into the space beside the passenger.

18

St. John's Wood, London. 11th November 1888

Jacques had waited, helplessly strapped to the bed and unable to do anything for over four hours.

Finally, he had heard the professor return to the house but no amount of shouting had succeeded in summoning him to the room. In the end, Jacques had fallen asleep from sheer fatigue.

It was daylight the next morning when Jacques was awakened by the tugging of the straps at his wrists; they were raw and sore due to the hours of struggling the night before. When he opened his eyes and looked into the professor's, he instinctively knew what had happened.

Unlike Jacques' encounters the professor had been able to recall the events from the second he had awakened. The professor and Jacques had discussed the situation until they could discuss no more and eventually a decision had been made.

It was decided that the key, now back in the lead lined safe in the library, be kept there where it appeared unable to exert any influence.

At first, they considered throwing it into the murky waters of the Thames as Jacques had almost suggested before the experiment but both agreed that the possibility of it being washed up and found by someone else was too high. If that happened then neither of them was in any doubt that the killings would begin again.

They would both carry on with their careers for the time being until a more permanent solution could be found. They would not inform the police and in time the killings would become just another unsolved mystery that most people would either have forgotten about or never heard of. Besides, although they couldn't alter the past they were certainly more use to society as physicians than locked away in prison as convicted murderers.

They agreed never to mention the killings again unless it became absolutely necessary.

19

London 1997

Donovan was missing Kate even though she'd only been gone a few days. He had not heard anything from her since she'd called in the middle of the night to say she'd arrived safely in Australia. The fact was that very little of newsworthy value seemed to be going on and the time was dragging very slowly. He had staked out all his usual haunts in search of a good story but none was forthcoming.

He was presently sipping coffee in a dingy café off the Tottenham Court Road feeling thoroughly depressed. The rain beating against the steamed up windows and the smoky atmosphere inside the cafe were doing nothing to help cheer him up.

The door suddenly opened allowing a blast of cold air to enter the café and Donovan looked up as two women carrying over laden shopping bags and dripping umbrellas entered.

They sat down at the table next to his and ordered a pot of tea for two. Donovan stopped watching them and his thoughts returned to Kate. She would be gone for three weeks at least. He hoped she was missing him as much as he was she.

The two women were now slurping their tea noisily.

"So what's your Jim up to these days, is he still not working?" asked the one wearing a headscarf tied under her chin to disguise the fact that she was actually wearing rollers.

" No, didn't I tell you? He 's got a job as a labourer on that Millennium wotsit across the river. Bloody good money too. In fact, he's put in so much overtime the last few weeks I've hardly seen him."

The mention of the Millennium project made Donovan look up from his coffee cup.

" 'Ere you sure he's doin' overtime? He might 'ave a bit on the side yer know," suggested the friend.

"I never thought o' that," replied the woman now studying the contents of the paper napkin that she'd just used to blow her nose.

"Still might not be a bad thing if he was, it might stop him pestering me for sex, eh?"

Both women guffawed loudly in between loud slurps of tea.

Donovan stood up and left the café. Maybe he'd take a cab across to the site and take a look round. He knew that Simon Henderson had something to do with the project and there was quite a lot of public debate going on about it at the moment.

Maybe he could write a satirical pseudo-political piece about it while he waited for some real news to come along. Of course, he'd have to put it in using a *nom de plume* in case Henderson happened to read it; he didn't want to kill the goose that laid the golden egg.

Twenty minutes later, Donovan jumped out of the cab outside the entrance to the construction site.

Forming a kind of archway entrance onto the site was a huge billboard bearing the names of all the companies that were involved in the funding of the construction.

Donovan scanned down the board and thought that with all the major multinationals and recently privatised utilities present, if they'd put current share prices alongside the company names it would've been just like reading the Financial Times.

Another board giving details of the construction company responsible for building the Dome accompanied the billboard:

'ACADEMY CIVIL ENGINEERING'.

Donovan noticed the company was actually based in Greenwich. At least the work had gone to a British based concern. One of Donovan's major political bugbears was how the government frequently gave huge, financially lucrative contracts to foreign companies when there were plenty of British companies capable of undertaking the work. As far as he could see, not only did it make sense to provide employment for British workers but surely the money they earned would stay in the British economy!

He suddenly realised he was drifting into one of those inner self discussions that he occasionally got into when his inherent, slightly left of centre political conscience had been pricked. He put it down to his Welsh origins. His grandfather had been a miner in a South Wales colliery for fifty years.

Fortunately, the rain had stopped now but it was still very cold and he pulled his raincoat tighter round himself.

The site was surrounded by seven feet high wire mesh fence. At the entrance were a dozen or so portakabins; around which milled workmen in bright orange boiler suits and others in suits and hard hats carrying clipboards and rolled up plans. He was amazed at the scale of the work going on.

The area that had been cleared and levelled was immense.

About three hundred yards away, roughly in the centre of the site, he could see a massive, almost circular, concrete base. There were very few workers actually around the base, just two or three on the far side of the compound who looked like they were carrying out electrical work.

Donovan wondered why so few people were around. He heard laughter coming from one of the portakabins as a worker exited through the door and walked down the steps. Donovan looked at his watch. Twenty five past twelve; of course it was lunchtime.

The worker walked to the next cabin, which looked like a portable toilet facility. He took off his hard-hat and hung it on the banister rail before climbing the steps that led up into the cabin.

Donovan seized the opportunity. He slipped through the steel gates and strolled nonchalantly past the first two cabins. As he passed the toilet block he lifted the hat from the rail, placed it on his head and carried on walking.

His camera was already inside his coat protected from the earlier rain and with his mobile phone in one hand and his notebook in the other, he passed easily as a site official.

As he made his way across the muddy ground a man jumped down from the cab of a JCB and made towards him. As he passed, Donovan smiled and the man greeted him with an "Awright guv." He nodded noncommittally and strode on.

Eventually he reached the large expanse of concrete. There were several more portakabins dotted round its perimeter and there were two compounds on one side.

One appeared to contain construction materials whilst the other was obviously a workers' village containing cabins for eating and resting. The front cabin looked like an office and Donovan could see a few men inside studying plans on the wall.

He ducked behind a cement mixer and was about to take a few snaps to accompany the light hearted article that was forming in his mind when a figure crossed directly in front of him, heading towards the spot where the three men were working.

Donovan instinctively shrunk back further behind the mixer.

The man looked familiar to Donovan as he approached one of the men and they walked away to the materials compound.

They stopped just inside the gates and a conversation ensued. Donovan couldn't quite make out the features of the man but he was sure that he knew him from somewhere. The worker seemed agitated as they talked and continuously looked round like a schoolboy sneaking a smoke behind the bike sheds.

It was only when the man produced a large brown envelope and passed it to the worker who slid it inside his boiler suit with another wary look around that Donovan realised why he looked so familiar.

"Well, well, well," he whispered to himself.

He quickly pulled out his camera, swapped the lens for a zoom, and clicked off half a dozen shots.

Five minutes later, Donovan watched as Henderson walked away towards the site entrance and the worker returned to his colleagues. He saw him gesture to them both that it was time for lunch and they downed their tools and headed for the compound.

Donovan was intrigued now and the adrenaline rush that he felt every time he got the smell of a story ran through him making him shiver.

He waited a few minutes then wandered over to the spot where the men had been working. Everything seemed perfectly normal. They appeared to have been laying electrical cables in a furrow that, as far as Donovan could see, ran all the way round the perimeter of the concrete base. Looking around to ensure he wasn't being observed, he surreptitiously snapped off a few frames of the furrow and the site as a whole. Then he returned the camera to his coat before making his way back to the entrance.

20

Arnhem land, Australia, 1997

The jeep rounded the large outcrop of sandstone slowly. Reg didn't want to lose another tyre like yesterday; he only had one more spare.

They had set off early in the morning to search for the cave that the two *Gurindji* tribesmen had told them about the day before. The last ten kilometres had been off road and were even more uncomfortable than yesterday's drive, if that were possible. Once again the heat was incredible even though it was only eight a.m.

Kate hung out of the window carefully scrutinising the outcrop for any signs of a cave entrance. The outcrop was, Peter estimated, about three kilometres long by about five hundred metres wide so the cave wouldn't be too difficult to find.

The outcrop was almost like a miniature version of Uluru or Ayers rock and was surrounded by nothing but scrubland and the odd pandanus palm. Pippa suddenly screamed out.

"Stop! What's that over there?"

She was pointing to a large boulder that had obviously fallen from the top of the rock sometime in the last thousand years or so. Behind the boulder was a shadow.

Reg pulled the jeep up immediately.

"Could be...." said Peter. " Let's go and take a look."

Kate was first out and quickly she made her way across the uneven scrub toward the rock. Pippa and Peter followed whilst Reg hung behind to get torches in case they were needed.

As they approached the rock, it was obvious that the dark patch behind was not just a shadow.

The opening was dark and only about three feet high. Near the entrance, there were human footprints in the sand leading inside. Peter grabbed Kate by the shoulder to stop her from going any further..

She turned with a puzzled look on her face.

"Dingoes," he whispered quietly, pointing down to paw tracks also in the sand. "They usually steer clear of humans but if you corner them they can get pretty nasty."

He turned and shouted to Reg to bring the torches.

"Chances are they used this place to sleep in last night and have moved on already but yer can't be too sure."

Reg stepped from behind the boulder clutching four torches and a rifle. They each took a torch then Reg lead the way crouching down low to clear the overhang to the cave.

The beams from the torches lit up a narrow passage about twenty feet long then it began to open up; the roof became higher as they moved along.

"Jesus, it's cold," whispered Pippa. "How can it be so cold when it's a hundred outside?"

The vapour from her breath rose in the torch beam. Reg suddenly stopped and knelt down.

"Well looks like the dingoes left already," he said pointing to more tracks.

"How do you know they left?" asked Kate.

Peter answered for Reg. "They're going in the opposite direction."

Reg stood and continued walking into the cave. The roof suddenly rose up abruptly and the passage opened up into a large chamber. They shone their torches up to the roof. It was about thirty feet high.

Lower down on the walls were painted pictures of lizards, kangaroos and men. Kate excitedly ran over towards them. She recognised them instantly as the x-ray type, typical of the Northern Territory. The bodies of the animals depicted were drawn as if the artist could see the internal organs. It was easy to identify the intestines and the kidneys in most of the animals and Kate noticed that the heart in each of the animals was particularly prominent as if it held some kind of special significance.

"God, these are fantastic," she gasped and immediately began to remove her backpack.

Pippa was also beginning to explore. In the back of the cave there were some large flat shaped stones about two feet high. They had score marks running horizontally across the top. They had been shaped and sculpted to form a kind of low table. Scattered round the stones were hundreds of bones of all shapes and sizes.

To one side of the stones was a blackened dip in the floor; the hearth?

Pippa's mind was already analysing the information and putting together an image of what life had been like in the cave thousands of years earlier. The stone table must have served as a butcher's block for cutting the meat before it was roasted on the fire.

The cave suddenly lit up and for a millisecond the entire scene inside the cave could be seen. The flash on Kate's camera took Reg by surprise and he let out an involuntary scream.

Kate laughed. "Sorry Reg, I should've given you a warning."

"It's a pity we can't take some of these bones back to the lab and carbon-date them," said Pippa. "I'd love to know how long this cave has been in use"

Peter's voice echoed from even further into the cave.

"Well, I reckon even if you'll never be able to tell how old *they* are at least I can tell you that someone other than the *Gurindji* has been in here quite recently."

Pippa and Reg made their way over to him. Kate was still busy taking photographs of the paintings.

Peter held up what looked like a piece of paper. It was just as well the darkness hid Pippa's face; she blushed as Peter held up the centrefold of a '*Playboy*' magazine.

He folded it over to the front cover and scanned it with his torch. The date showed it was the previous month's issue.

Reg shone his torch on the floor searching for anything else. There was something half buried in the sand. He bent down to see more closely and brushed away the dirt. Reg picked the object up carefully. It was a watch, but more incredibly it was actually showing the time and date correctly.

Peter examined the strap for damage; maybe it had fallen off the owner's wrist as he slept, maybe a traveller sheltering from a storm. It was very unusual to find things like this in a cave that so few aboriginals even knew about let alone a tourist.

Once again Reg and Peter broke out a conversation in their tribal dialect.

Pippa waited patiently.

Peter stopped in mid sentence and apologised. "Sorry Pippa, sometimes I forget. We were just saying that it is difficult to imagine a *Gurindji* who would have access to such items and it is even more difficult to imagine a traveller finding the cave by chance as it is a very remote site."

"Could it be possible for a *Gurundji* to have brought a traveller out here to see the cave?" asked Pippa.

"It's possible I suppose," said Peter. "But it would be

very unusual. They are a traditional tribe who do not like to share their lives with outsiders. The *Gurundji* we met only gave us the information about this site because we told them you would be supervised and not allowed to remove anything."

Kate had finished taking pictures now and had come over to join them. They explained to her what they had found.

They looked round for a further ten minutes or so but to no avail. Other than the two items, there was nothing else.

It did not go unnoticed by Reg or Peter, though they said nothing to the girls, that the area immediately a round where the objects were found appeared to have been brushed over with something as if someone had tried to cover their tracks. If that were the case it was odd that they had left behind the watch and the magazine. Then again, the magazine had been behind a rock and the watch was mostly buried in the dirt.

Although the two men didn't say as much, it was pretty obvious to Kate that they were both disturbed by what they had found. She preferred to believe that some tourist had paid a 'rogue' tribesman with a few dollars and some personal items to show them the cave. The items had probably been hidden there for him to retrieve at a later date.

Kate hoped this wouldn't affect Reg and Peter's willingness to guide them to other sites.

They made their way back through the low passageway towards the circle of light at the entrance and finally emerged from the cave and out into the daylight and the heat.

Back inside the cave at the deepest point, beyond where they had been standing, was what appeared to be the back of the chamber.

Had they examined the wall closely, they would have

discovered that what looked like a shadow when light was shone onto it was in fact a narrow crack. The crack was just wide enough for a person to squeeze through sideways and then it widened out into a small inner chamber.

The walls of the chamber were covered from top to bottom in paintings.

The ones closer to the bottom were similar to the ones Kate had been photographing in the main chamber but, higher up, the paintings were of a different kind altogether. There were strange winged creatures with snarling jaws and demonic faces.

There was a large rendering of serpent with several heads; it was beckoning below to what looked to be a crowd of people. The crowd was surrounding an obelisk and there appeared to be something emanating from its surface. Although the paintings were in the style of traditional aboriginal art, they were much more complex and intricate.

Covering most of the length of the chamber floor was a flat stone similar to, but much bigger than, the one in the main chamber.

On the stone lay a corpse. His lidless eyes stared upwards towards a painting on the roof of the chamber. His chest was split wide open and the intestines and other organs were strewn about the floor. His mouth was set in a terrified grimace and his lips were caked with dried blood.

In between his teeth were remnants of flesh. To be precise, flesh from his own heart.

The Lightning Man stared back at the corpse from the roof of the cave. His lips were also covered in blood, some of which still dripped onto Andy Jefferson's lifeless body below.

In the jeep, Kate was doing her best to steer the conversation away from the strange discoveries in the cave and onto the arrangements for the rest of the expedition.

She was worried about how quiet Reg and Peter had become since they'd been in the cave.

"So we should arrive in Maningrida by nightfall, giving us most of the morning to set up and establish an itinerary before Steve shows up in the afternoon."

"That's if he's on time," said Pippa. "He does like to settle himself in slowly and get to know a place. Do you remember Egypt last year? He was two days late joining the camp and he only came then because an Egyptian shop owner threatened to cut off his ears because he was trying to chat up his wife in the bazaar."

Kate laughed at the memory. He was certainly a character. In fact, he'd tried it on with both Kate and Pippa on more than one occasion. If Kate hadn't been aware of his reputation she might have even gone out with him. As it was they were all now extremely good friends and apart from being a terrific flirt, he was an excellent photographer.

"I reckon as long as we hit no problems we can be there for about sixish," said Reg.

"Just in time fer some home-cooked tucker!" said Peter. "My sister's a terrific cook."

Kate looked at Pippa and winked. She was relieved they were a little more back to normal now.

21

Waterloo Station, London April 10, 1912

The two men sat, grave- faced, in the carriage of their London & South Western Train. One was in his eighties, his face thin and lined. His hair was almost completely white and although his body looked frail, his eyes still sparkled with life. An observer would have described him, in his tweed suit and brown leather brogues, as distinguished. They would not have been mistaken in their assumption

The younger man was in his late forties. He was square jawed and sported a small moustache, which somehow added an air of illustriousness to his considerable good looks. His skin had that olive appearance, typical of men who originate south of the English Channel and his thick, black, slicked back hair still retained its youthful shine.

The older of the two was reading a newspaper; the younger stared out of the window as the train pulled slowly out of the station and gathered speed.

"We are fortunate that the coal miners have come to their senses at long last," said the professor. "I was beginning to wonder whether we would be able to sail or not. According to my newspaper, supplies are having to be procured from other vessels in order that our ship may sail."

Jacques was only half aware of what the professor was

saying. His thoughts kept returning to the events that had occurred nearly twenty-five years earlier.

Although in some ways the memory was distant, he could remember certain aspects so vividly that it was as if they had happened only yesterday.

Since the night the professor had returned from his fated visit to the East End, the key had been safely stored away. There had never been a recurrence of the 'happenings' and both men had managed to get on with their lives normally.

Neither had ever mentioned the killings or the key to anyone and in fact they had not once in the past twenty-five years spoken to each other about them. Not until about three weeks ago anyway...

The professor had been retired for the last five years. Jacques was the Senior Physician at St. Margaret's hospital. They were still very close and Jacques often visited the professor either on social calls or to ask for his advice about medical matters, as the professor was still highly respected as one of the leading surgical minds in Europe.

Jacques was surprised however when the professor made a personal visit to the hospital and was waiting for him as he came out of the theatre one afternoon. The serious expression on his face told Jacques instinctively what the visit was about.

He had supposed that one day (after the professor's death, most likely) he would have to make a decision about what to do with the key. It was simply too dangerous to be left where it was. But he guessed now, looking at the professor's face, that a decision had possibly already been made. He helped the professor to a chair and sat down beside him.

"It is the key. Is it not?" said Jacques quietly

The professor nodded.

"I have a friend in New York with whom I have

maintained correspondence since he left England to take up a post there fifteen years ago. He wrote to me recently to tell me of an expedition that he is organising to South America. It is an archaeological venture to excavate ruins in Peru. According to the information he has sent me, the area they are bound for is very close to where ... where you discovered the key."

Jacques face was ashen now; it had been so long.

"I think we should take the key back, Jacques. Return it from whence it came. The responsibility is ours as only we know of its potential for evil."

Jacques wiped his brow; he was sweating profusely even though he actually felt cold.

"You are right, of course we cannot take the risk of leaving it where it is."

"I will contact him immediately and request that we join the expedition when it departs New York in a little less than a month's time."

Jacques nodded and placed his hand warmly on the professor's shoulder. At last they would finally be able to forget the past.

So, they had made plans to join the expedition. They would keep the key in a lead-lined wooden case during transit. As far as anyone else on the trip knew, they were going to collect botanical specimens for medical purposes. The expedition would leave New York bound for Lima on Saturday the 20th April.

The sound of a lady's voice from the corridor brought Jacques back to the present. The carriage door was slightly ajar and as she walked past he heard her ask the lady in front of her what time the ship was due to sail. As she passed, she glanced into the carriage and looked briefly at Jacques and the professor.

Jacques was particularly drawn to her eyes. They were emerald green framed by ebony lashes.

Jacques guessed she was in her early twenties. She was slightly embarrassed at having been caught looking at him and her face reddened. She nodded her head slightly and carried on up the train.

Jacques looked up and found the professor smiling at him.

"What is it?" he asked sheepishly.

"A very handsome young lady, Jacques, and travelling on our ship I suspect."

He continued smiling as he returned to reading his paper.

It was 9.30 am when they arrived at Southampton. They disembarked and made their way down to the dock along with what the professor estimated to be about two hundred other passengers.

As they rounded the corner and stepped onto the dockside they stopped in their tracks. They knew from the brochures that they had received with their tickets that the ship would be something special but they were not prepared for the sight, which lay before them.

The ship was enormous. It was like the sleeping Gulliver in a book that Jacques had read recently surrounded by hundreds of tiny people rushing round. There was a buzz of anticipation now and everyone round them was chatting excitedly.

As they approached the boat there were signs directing First Class passengers one way and Second Class passengers another.

There were a number of black-coated men verbally directing a large number of people along the dockside to waiting queues. The queuing people appeared to be waiting for examination by men sitting at tables. They were being given pieces of paper which certified them 'fit to travel' before being allowed to walk up the gangway and onto the ship.

"Steerage passengers this way please!" shouted one of the men again, as Jacques and the professor walked in the direction of the second-class gangway.

Opposite Jacques on the first class gangway about thirty yards further towards the bow of the ship he noticed the girl he had seen on the train. She was quite obviously a woman of some means judging by her dress and the small entourage accompanying her.

When they reached the top of the gangway they were welcomed aboard by two stewards who checked their tickets and confirmed that they were on the correct part of the ship.

Jacques noticed a sign that read 'Promenade Deck B'. The length of the ship was now even more readily apparent. It was truly magnificent. Hundreds of people were leaning on the rails; many others were strolling along the deck marvelling at the splendour of the vessel.

The professor turned to Jacques. "I have some business to attend to before we sail. I will meet you here in..."

He took his pocket watch from his waistcoat, "...twenty minutes."

Jacques wandered along the promenade, thinking that the last time he had been aboard a boat had been when he returned from Peru carrying the key in his pocket. If he could turn back time he would never have picked up the cursed thing.

Still, on the voyage back home in a month or so he would celebrate with a bottle of vintage champagne and finally put it all behind him.

At twelve noon precisely, there was a triple blast of the ship's horn heralding her departure and the professor appeared at Jacques' side. They leaned on the deck rail and waved along with everyone else to the friends, relatives, and sightseers on the dockside.

"Looks like *they* missed the boat." said Jacques

pointing to five or six men who were desperately waving and running along the dock at the stern of the boat.

Jacques felt a sudden overwhelming sense of relief as the ship was towed forward by the tugs and away from the dockside. It was as if a huge weight had been removed from his shoulders. After twenty-five years he would finally be free from the nagging ache that the key had inflicted upon him.

Although he had never spoken about it, a day had barely passed when some memory or other hadn't haunted him. At last, he could be totally free again. Three weeks from now it would be back from where it came.

He wondered why the idea to return it had never occurred to them before. Maybe the power of the key, although diminished by being kept in the safe had still been strong enough to influence them so that they *couldn't* think of returning it. If that were the case, why now all of a sudden?

Further up the dock two boats were moored side by side. They were dwarfed by the ship slowly making its way toward them. The swell from the ship made them bob in the water.

Jacques felt a tap on his elbow. When he looked round, the professor was pointing to the nearer of the two boats. Its stern was moving out into the channel towards their ship. Other people had noticed it too and there were concerned conversations as the stern rope attaching it to the dock sprung free and its drift became more pronounced. The excitement of the departure was now turning to bewilderment as the two ships looked set to collide. The professor could imagine the headlines:

'The 'Unsinkable' Sinks at Southampton Dock.'

Just then, a tug appeared at the stern of the ship and one of the crew threw a line aboard the drifting boat. Fortunately, the throw was accurate and the line was quickly secured. The tug pulled the boat towards the dock as the gigantic ship slipped past not ten feet away. The relief amongst the passengers was almost tangible. People began laughing and giggling nervously.

Jacques overheard someone confide to his wife "Now that *would* have been a disaster."

The professor and Jacques looked at each other and both knew what the other was thinking.

"Relax," said the professor. "The key is secure in its case in the ship's safe. I deposited it with the Purser the minute we boarded. "

Slowly the ship's engines roared into life and the lines to the tugs were released. They were on their way.

22

Mid Atlantic April 14th 1912

Jacques was leaning over the rail of the ship. At his side was Eleanor Harvey. They were admiring the setting sun. They had been at sea now for four days after picking up more passengers at Cherbourg in France and Queenstown on the southern coast of Ireland.

It had only taken twenty-four hours for Jacques to contrive a meeting with the 'handsome lady from the train' as the professor referred to her.

He had simply waited for her to take an after lunch stroll on the promenade and when she stopped for a rest on one of the many benches dotted along the deck, he approached.

"Please forgive me, Mademoiselle, but my curiosity will not allow me to pass you by without asking you if we have met before at some point. I feel sure that I know you and although I am usually very good at recalling names, I cannot for the life of me remember yours. Maybe you could save me from further embarrassment..." He trailed off, hoping she would take the bait.

She didn't disappoint him.

"Why, I do believe we shared the same Boat Train from London. I seem to recall you were with an older gentleman. Your father, perhaps?"

Jacques feigned sudden recall.

"Of course," he said smiling. "The train."

He offered her his hand and she reciprocated. He kissed it and introduced himself.

It transpired that she was the daughter of a Mr. John Harvey, a very wealthy businessman who had made his fortune in mining and prospecting. They were on their way to New York to visit friends. It was her first visit to the States.

Jacques had explained that he and the professor were going to Peru to do botanical research, a fact that excited her enormously as she had a great interest in horticulture. She told him that she would much prefer to be going with him than visiting some 'stuffy old relatives' in New York.

They had talked for over an hour before Eleanor's mother and aunt had arrived on the deck and whisked her away to afternoon tea in the Palm Court. By that time he realised that he was hopelessly infatuated.

Since that first meeting they had become virtually inseparable and each was growing fonder of the other by the day. The professor had assumed that infuriating smile when Jacques first announced that he had met her but later when he had been introduced to her, he was almost as smitten as Jacques.

"If I were fifty years younger..." he'd said patting Jacques firmly on the shoulder later.

Jacques placed a shawl around Eleanor's shoulders; it had become increasingly colder every day.

"So when will you be returning to England?" asked Jacques.

"We will stay in New York for a week before travelling up to Maine for a further week. My father has some business there to attend to and then we shall return to Southampton on the twenty second."

Jacques' heart lurched. The thought of leaving her in a few days time was almost unbearable.

"I have an idea," he said. "When you return why don't you come down to London for a few days and I can show you the sights?"

Eleanor turned to face him. "Jacques, that would be wonderful. You realise, of course, that Mother would insist on chaperoning me."

"Of course. I'm sure your mother would enjoy visiting London. It is a very big city. We would need to be very careful that we did not become separated from her whilst visiting the sights. It might lead to us being on our own for a few hours at the very least."

"Jacques, you are terrible," she declared smiling. "If Mother knew what a scoundrel you were she would not let me near you let alone allow me to visit."

Jacques bent his head down and kissed her gently on the mouth. Her lips parted and he felt the tip of her tongue touch his. They held each other tightly as the kiss became more intense and Jacques could feel himself becoming aroused.

Their lips parted momentarily, "Not here, Jacques," Eleanor whispered breathlessly. Jacques looked deeply into her eyes, they told him what he wanted to know. He grabbed her hand and led her back along the Promenade deck.

Instead of taking the double doors that led into the First Class Lounge, he led her through a door with a sign that said 'crew only'.

They skipped down the stairs and found themselves in a narrow passageway on the lower deck. There were a number of doors leading off to their left. Jacques was still holding Eleanor's hand and he could feel her trembling now that he had stopped and was deciding where to go.

About halfway down the passage one of the doors had no number on it. Jacques tried the handle. It creaked as it opened. He felt for a light switch inside the door and the room suddenly lit up, revealing it to be a storeroom.

There were several mattresses thrown up against one wall and a pile of spare life vests against another. The room would no doubt in time become dank and dusty but as the ship was brand new it was clean and pleasant.

Eleanor squeezed Jacques' hand and he stepped behind her to close the door. When he turned round Eleanor had slid one of the mattresses down onto the floor and had laid her coat on top. Jacques stepped forward and once again they kissed passionately. This time they did not part and Jacques lifted her gently and laid her down on the mattress. As he laid her down their eyes opened.

Eleanor's were misty with tears. "I love you, Jacques," she whispered.

Jacques pulled her to him and laughed.

"Then marry me," he said.

Their lips met again and they lay back embracing each other tightly.

The ship sailed on through flat, glassy waters.

In the First Class restaurants the ladies were drinking spritzers and commenting on how fantastically comfortable the ship was whilst the men retired to the smoking room and discussed the Stock Market over brandy.

On the lower decks, the steerage passengers had for the most part retired to their bunks. There were one or two card games still going on and the odd drunk still saying goodnight to his bottle of liquor but by and large it was very quiet.

In the ship's safe in the Purser's office on 'C' Deck the key was beginning to glow. The eyes on the engraved figure were open wide and staring intently.

Professor Arnold stretched up from his bunk to turn out the light. He was very tired for the port and brandy at dinner had been particularly good tonight.

23

Maningrida, Arnhem Land Australia, 1997

Pippa and Kate were studying the map closely. It was a mass of crosses, pencilled in over the last half hour or so as Peter and his sister, Noola, pointed out sites with which they were familiar and which might be of interest to the expedition.

Reg was snoring loudly from a hammock behind them that was slung between two rafters on the veranda.

"Right all we need to do now is decide which ones to look at and we're away," said Kate throwing the pencil onto the table and stretching back on the wicker chair she was sitting in.

Peter leaned forward and drew a ring round two of the crosses.

"We can do these in one day. The nearest one is only fifty kilometres away. If Steve shows up this arvo we can probably get out there tonight and be ready to look at them tomorrow."

"If he shows up at all," said Pippa.

Kate was studying the map again.

"Peter, the *pukimani* burial poles, they are at which site?"

Peter pointed to one of the sites he had circled.

"And you say that there are some human bones actually at the surface?"

"Yes, it is very unusual to find the poles on the mainland; they are usually made by the *Tiwi* people whose homelands are Bathurst and Melville Islands off the north coast. There are also many paintings at that site. We must be very careful whilst we are there; it is a very sacred site. Many aborigines visit each year to pay their respects to their ancestors and the Spirits of the Dreaming."

Peter was speaking in a hushed manner now in deference to the religious significance of what he was talking about.

Suddenly, Reg turned over on his hammock, raised his buttocks and produced a huge fart.

They all fell about laughing.

"Now *that's* aboriginal dreaming for yer," said Peter shaking his head laughing.

It was just after two o clock when the camper van rolled up in front of the house.

Steve jumped down from the cab as Pippa and Kate, closely followed by Peter and Noola, scrambled outside to greet him.

"Steve, what the hell's going on?" asked Kate.

Steve gave her a puzzled look.

Kate tapped her watch with her finger.

"You're actually on time for once. What was the problem, nothing in a skirt between here and Darwin?"

He grabbed her and gave her a bear hug.

"That's what I've missed these last few days; companionship, wit.... sarcasm!"

Pippa came over and reached over Kate's shoulders to put her arms round his neck. She gave him a peck on the cheek then spat out in mock disgust.

"Different continent; same cheap aftershave," she laughed.

Peter coughed into his hand behind them and they all

turned round

"Oh, Steve, this is Peter and his sister Noola. Peter works for the Aboriginal Federation. He'll be showing us a round."

The two men shook hands.

"Pleased to meet you Peter," He turned his attention to Noola. "And Noola," he said, taking her hand in his and lifting it so that he could kiss it in the style of a nineteenth century gent. "No one told me there were going to be any beautiful women on this expedition."

Noola blushed.

"Don't you ever stop!" said Kate. "Come on. Let's get some lunch then we can make a start. Reg says we can make it to the first sites this evening."

It was early evening and Kate and Steve were taking a walk by the Glyde River. They'd arrived and made camp about an hour earlier. The campervan was quite spacious now that a lot of the equipment had been shifted outside. The evening was clear and warm. The sound of bush crickets filled the air.

Kate had suggested they take a walk so that she could fill him in on what happened at the cave the day before. She'd deliberately waited for Pippa to begin writing her journal in the hope that she would decline the invitation. That way she could talk to Steve about her plan. Reg and Peter were mulling over the engine of the four-wheel drive.

They stopped and sat down on a low sandstone ledge overlooking the river. It was moving quite slowly but its banks were full. The 'dry' season was still a few months off and Reg had warned them to beware of crocodiles. Apparently during the dry season they tended to migrate into concentrated populations in areas of low ground where surface water remained. At the moment, he'd said, they would still be present in most streams and billabongs.

"So you reckon someone, a non aboriginal, had been

into the cave for some reason a few days before you?" asked Steve.

"Well, what do you make of it? Someone had to have been in there in the last few weeks according to the magazine we found. The watch still held the correct time... and there was this..."

She pulled something from her pocket and handed it to him. It looked like a piece of coloured cloth.

She had found it in the cave also half buried in the sand as the others walked ahead of her. She was going to tell them about it when they got outside but by then she'd noticed the change in Reg and Peter and decided to keep it to herself.

When he opened it out to its full size his reaction surprised Kate.

"Jesus, I've seen this before!" he said, his voice full of surprise.

"I passed a bloke... a backpacker. He was wearing this just the day before yesterday, I swear. I remember thinking that if the van wasn't so full with all the equipment, I'd have stopped and given him a ride; could've done with the company myself. I knew he was a Brit, you see, because of the flag."

The 'cloth' was actually an old baseball cap. It had at some point had a small union jack flag sewn onto the back to act as a sun guard for the neck of whoever was wearing it.

Steve turned the cap inside out and pointed to the black stitching holding the flag on. It was very crude.

"See. He must have made it himself. What are the chances of there being two of these knocking round? "

"When did you see him?" Kate asked.

"Day before yesterday, six o clockish, about thirty miles short of Jabiru. I know because I remember thinking that he'd be lucky to get there before it got dark."

"Well, if it is his, then he must have managed to get a ride pretty quickly. We got to the cave at about ten yesterday morning, which means if he *was* in the cave it had to be on the night you actually passed him."

"That's quite a way, Kate. He would have had to travel most of the night to be there then. There must be another explanation. Anyway, according to your description the cave was so off the beaten track it's unlikely that he could've found it himself, having been dropped off by whoever gave him a lift."

"Unless of course his ride took him there," said Kate, "Steve, I want to go back to the cave and have another look around. At first I thought maybe some other student or anthropologist or whatever had been nosing round knowing something about the site we don't. But now I'm intrigued. Maybe we can go on the way back to Darwin when we've completed the tour of the sites. Peter and Reg will be stopping on in Maningrida when we've finished."

Steve nodded. He was as curious as Kate. It also appealed to his natural sense of adventure.

"Look, let's keep it to ourselves for now. There's no way we can go back until we've completed the study."

"Shouldn't we tell Reg?" suggested Steve.

"I saw the look on Peter and Reg's faces when we were in the cave. It was almost as if they knew something but weren't letting on. I've got a feeling that if we tell them they'll get spooked again and have us out of here before we had a chance to go back."

"What about Pippa?"

"Come off it, Steve. You know Pippa can't keep secrets. Remember the surprise birthday party for your sister? Or 'not surprise' birthday party as it turned out."

Steve nodded, remembering how Pippa had inadvertently spilled the beans to Gemma. *"So where's Steve and Mike, Pippa?" "Oh they're back at your house getting it ready for the part... oops. "*

Kate was right, it was better that just the two of them knew for now.

They stood up and strolled back to the camp. Kate glanced at Steve. He was kicking loose rocks and dust into the river as he walked. In some ways he reminded her of Michael.

She could still see why she had found him so attractive when he'd made a pass at her twelve months ago. She wondered what Michael was up to in London and smiled to herself at the memory of their last night together before she'd left.

Michael had bought her what he called an *'Outback Survival kit'*

It consisted of a baseball cap that he'd sewn corks onto all along the peak, a packet of Earl Grey teabags (her favourite), a toilet roll; three ply (*"toilets are few and far between in the outback"*) and finally a Saint Christopher on a chain.

She twisted it between her thumb and index finger as she walked. He'd told her it would keep her safe until they were together again. He'd bought it because of an article he'd read about hikers disappearing Down Under and he was going on to her about being careful. Maybe he did love her after all.

Suddenly, she realised the significance of her thoughts.

"My God, Steve...."

"What? Kate, are you okay?"

Kate had stopped in her tracks. Her face had paled.

"I've just had a thought. Something a friend said to me before I left."

Her eyes were focused in the distance now as if she were trying to remember the details of the conversation

"He'd read in the papers that quite recently something like... twenty backpackers had disappeared into thin air whilst travelling round Australia. You don't think..." she trailed off again.

Steve was staring into the distance now as well.

"Naah...just a coincidence. Bound to be. When we get back to the cave we'll probably find a gang of New Age hippies have moved in or something."

Kate looked at him. She could tell he was trying to convince himself.

She slapped her thigh to tell herself to pull herself together. She was behaving like a bloody idiot. She'd watched too many *'Hercule Poirot'* movies.

"Come on, let's get back. They'll think a croc's got us," she said as a shiver ran down her spine.

24

The North Atlantic, April 14th 1912

The engraved figure on the key glowed brightly inside the safe. The eyes were wide open and liquid oozed from the mark on the chest. Had Mr. McElroy, the ship's purser, not been busy conversing with passengers he may have noticed a slight knocking sound as the heavy, wooden case containing the key began to tremble against the walls.

On the bridge, the Quartermaster had said good night to the Captain and was holding a steady course. He was looking through the bridge window at the slick, black, ocean ahead when he felt a slight tug to starboard on the helm. He looked immediately at the ship's compass and waited, realising that it would take a minute or two for any deviation from the course to register. Suddenly, he felt it again, almost imperceptible, again the pull was to starboard. A conversation he'd had in Southampton with Tom Andrews, the ship's designer, sprang into his mind:

"We could run over most other ships in this thing and not even realise it, let alone worry about the consequences"

No, surely it would have to be a very small boat if the lookouts couldn't see it in time. He laughed at the ridiculousness of his thought processes. Obviously, Andrews had been exaggerating. It was probably just his imagination. After all, he'd had a long day and was very tired.

He looked down again at the compass and was surprised to find that the ship's course had actually altered by a degree to the north, so there had been a pull to starboard, albeit only a small one. Perhaps they had hit a whale. This stretch of ocean was apparently renowned for whales heading north to their feeding grounds in the Arctic.

He gently drew the wheel slightly to his right; he would have it corrected in a minute or two, nothing to worry about. He glanced over to where the First Officer, Murdoch, was busily chatting to Moody, the other officer on duty, on the bridge. They were laughing about something (everyone was always a little more relaxed when the Captain had retired for the night).

The helmsman decided not to mention the incident. It was probably nothing and they might both think he was foolish for bringing something that minor to their attention. He looked at the compass and saw that the ship had come back to port.

Inside the safe, the key suddenly stopped trembling. The engraved figure seemed to be almost smiling now as if it was contented; the eyes were closed once more.

Up in the crow's nest, the watch was just changing over. The two men handing over were bitterly cold and they stamped their feet as they made way for the new watch.

"Righto lads that's us done," smiled one of the men, obviously relieved that the shift was over.

"I hope you've brought yer long johns it's bloody perishin' tonight," joked the other.

One of the new men produced a half bottle of gin from his pocket.

"We'll not be needing any long johns. Don't worry about that!" He smiled and offered them the bottle.

"No thanks," said the first. "I'm getting off to my bunk. It'll take the rest o' the trip to thaw my feet out."

He brushed past and began making his way down the ladder. The second took the bottle and pulled on it thirstily. He wiped his chin and handed it back.

"Cheers, mate." He turned to leave then turned back again. "Oh, nearly forgot, keep yer eyes peeled fer small bergs and growlers; the Captain had a couple of ice warnings on the wireless earlier. G' night."

He made his way down the ladder whistling tunelessly to himself, presumably to keep his mouth from icing up.

The two men stood side by side looking ahead as the mighty ship sped on.

There was no moon but the sky was clear and dotted with a thousand stars. One of the men leaned forward as if he was trying to see something in the distance.

"See something, Tom?" asked the other.

"I don't know. Pass me the glasses, Les."

"You'll be lucky, they've not been seen since Southampton. What is it?"

"It's nothing," he said, resuming his normal position. "Just my eyes freezing over, I expect."

"Here, this'll sort 'em out," said Les. He passed Tom the gin bottle.

The professor awoke with a start. He sat up straight in his bunk and fumbled for the light switch. He was sweating profusely and his heart was thumping against his chest. He felt very uneasy.

He tried to recall what he had been dreaming about but it eluded him. Suddenly, the image of the key jumped into his mind. He closed his eyes in an attempt to see the image more clearly.

There was a flash of something else... people screaming and shouting hysterically.

He opened his eyes again and rubbed them with the back of his hands and beads of sweat rolled down his face.

He swung his frail legs slowly off the bed. His head

was swimming a little and he thought back to earlier in the night trying to remember exactly how much he had had to drink.

He instinctively closed his eyes as he cast his mind back and immediately the images came again. This time they were clearer. There were people running up and down the decks of the boat, women crying, children screaming. It was almost as if he were hallucinating, the images were so vivid.

He noted that the deck of the ship was at a strange angle and some people had fallen and were beginning to slide inexorably down the wooden deck in slow motion, desperately flailing their arms in an attempt to grab something that would halt their fall. He forced his eyes open. He was trembling now.

"Oh no! Dear God, no," he mouthed.

He realized what was happening...the key. He must retrieve it from the safe before it was too late, if it wasn't too late already.

He stood up as quickly as he could manage. His arthritic joints were painful and restrictive at the best of times but having just gotten out of bed it was agony. He struggled to pull on his trousers.

Tom took another slug from the gin bottle.

"Jesus, it's cold," he said. "Why couldn't we have signed on for a bloody cruise that went somewhere hot?"

Les laughed, the gin was starting to take effect.

"Knowing our luck we'd have been suffering from bloody sunstroke now if we had. I had this uncle who joined the Foreign Legion. He was stationed out in the desert an ..." He stopped mid sentence.

"So.... go on," encouraged Tom.

Les was staring straight ahead. His mouth dropped open.

"Lord, help us!" he whispered.

Tom turned to see what Les was staring at and immediately grabbed for the bell rope and began swinging it frantically. Les was still staring, his expression frozen.

"Les, get on the bleedin' blower, tell the Bridge!"

Les didn't move.

Tom pushed him roughly out of the way and grabbed the brass pinna of the voice pipe. He twirled the ringer handle frantically, and then he heard the voice of the Sixth Officer at the other end.

"Bridge. Moody here."

Tom swallowed, trying to summon up some spit so that he could get the words out. Finally they came.

"Iceberg! Right ahead!"

Jacques' eyes opened and he looked up into the darkness. Something had jarred him from his sleep. It had felt like a bump. Maybe he had been dreaming. He turned and looked at the sleeping figure of Eleanor beside him. She looked like an angel. His eyes misted over. His love for her was overwhelming and he wished again he didn't need to leave her in New York.

The room was quite cold now and he pulled his coat over her to keep her from chilling. He couldn't be sure of the time, as they'd fallen asleep, although he was sure she would get into trouble when she got back. No doubt her mother would have been looking for her. His eyes slowly adjusted to the dark and he could make out his clothes. He stood quietly and began dressing.

The professor opened the door and began making his way slowly along the Second Class corridor. One or two passengers were conducting conversations at their cabin doors. They were wearing dressing gowns and pyjamas. They'd obviously felt the vibration that had resonated through the ship about five minutes ago.

He was trying to hold back panic now and as he walked his breath escaped in spurts from his lungs. He *had* to get to the Purser's office.

A steward appeared from round a corner and smiled pleasantly.

"Are you feeling alright, sir?" he asked the professor. "You look a little pale."

"No, no I'm fine. Thank you. Just getting a little exercise before retiring, as is my routine."

The professor smiled back weakly.

"By the way, what was that slight bump I felt just now?"

The steward's expression was that of an adult trying to reassure a frightened child.

"Oh, that was nothing sir, probably thrown a propeller blade I expect, same thing happened to *The Olympic* last month. It'll slow us down a bit but not much. After all *The Titanic* has triple screws. Nothing to worry about at all. We'll still get to New York on time."

The professor nodded and the steward padded away happily to complete his rounds. The professor quickened his pace; he was not reassured in the slightest.

Jacques eased the door slowly shut behind him, not wanting to wake Eleanor. He would reconnoitre the First Class decks to ensure that Mrs. Harvey had retired before returning to inform her that it was safe to go to her cabin. They would at least have time to think of a plausible explanation as to their whereabouts for the latter part of this evening.

He couldn't stop smiling to himself as he leapt two at a time up the steps toward the Promenade Deck, and he couldn't recall a time when he had felt happier.

He pushed open the door that led onto the deck slowly for he didn't want to have to explain to anyone why he was coming out of a door marked 'crew only'.

As he stepped out, he looked up and down the deck. At the very end of the promenade there were two men leaning over the rail peering downwards. One was a crew member; the other appeared to be a passenger.

Jacques was too immersed in thinking about Mrs. Harvey to consider what they were doing and tiptoed quickly up the deck in the opposite direction. It was only as he was stepping off the deck and into the First Class Lounge that something caught his eye.

About thirty yards aft of the doorway, lying on the wooden deck floor, was a dark shape about the size of a man. Jacques thought at first it was maybe a passenger who had fallen and was lying prostrate on the floor. Quickly, he made his way toward it. He got within five feet of it before he recognised it as the biggest chunk of ice he had ever seen.

The professor hurried across the landing. The purser was locking the door of the office and had his back to him. There was no one else around.

"Forgive me," said the professor.

The purser jumped, the sound of the professor's voice taking him by surprise.

"Good heavens!" he said turning round, hand on his heart. "Sorry, sir. You took me quite by surprise."

"I'm dreadfully sorry. I didn't mean to startle you, it's just that I was hoping to catch you still open. I need to withdraw something from the safe."

The purser removed his pocket watch from his jacket. "Well, strictly speaking sir..."

"It is very important," interrupted the professor, "It is my condition, you see." He coughed at this point for effect.

"My medication is in the safe. I miscalculated my dosage for tonight and now ..." He coughed again. "I am in need of more."

"I see, sir," said the purser lifting his keys back out of his pocket. He placed the key carefully inside the lock and turned it. There was a click and he pushed open the door.

The professor followed him into the office.

Inside, the purser opened the safe.

The professor was sweating. The heightening tension he had been feeling since he had awoken increased now that he was in such close proximity to the key again.

"A wooden box you said, sir?" asked the purser, his head inside the safe.

"Yes indeed, not very large...."

"Ah, here we are," said the purser leaning forward. "Cor blimey what you got in there? It weighs a bit, don't it!"

The professor took the box from him, ignoring the question.

"Thank you very much. I appreciate your co-operation," he said, handing him a farthing.

The Purser smiled at the unexpected tip. "Thank you very much, sir. Pleased to be of service." He touched the peak of his hat and bade the professor goodnight.

The professor turned and walked from the room. He thought the box felt warm. Or was he just imagining it?

The other curious thing was that although he only had hold of the box for a minute or so, his whole body suddenly felt different. His joints felt less stiff, his breath came without effort, and most amazingly, he actually felt stronger.

A worrying thought occurred to him and he cast his mind back to the night of the *experiment*.

'*I must find Jacques* ' he thought urgently.

25

Darwin, Australia, 1997

The drops of condensation on the outside of the glasses glistened in the afternoon sun.

"Cheers," said Steve as he raised the beer glass.

There was silence as the three of them relished the luxury of the cold amber liquid. It had been a long two and a half weeks.

Pippa put her drink down first and started laughing. The other two looked at her and then at each other shrugging shoulders indicating that neither of them knew what had amused her.

"I'm sorry," said Pippa. "I'm just thinking of you two and that cave. Did you honestly expect to find a decomposing corpse?"

Kate punched her playfully on the arm.

"Alright, alright so I have a vivid imagination," she said. "It's still a mystery how the things got there though, isn't it."

"Like I said," offered Steve. "Likely as not some pervo on a day out decided he needed a bit of female company of the paper variety and slipped inside the cave for a swift 'five knuckle shuffle'. His watch came off while he was in there and he accidentally dropped the magazine as he left."

"Is that the kind of thing blokes do when they're in the outback?" laughed Pippa.

Kate resigned herself to the fact that she was in for a lot of ribbing for a while to come and took another swig of her beer. Still, she couldn't help thinking about the baseball cap.

They had arrived at the cave the day after saying fond goodbyes to Reg and Pete in Maningrida. The expedition had been a great success and Kate had plenty of material to take back to St. Martin's.

Steve had tried to persuade Kate to confide in the aborigines about their plans to revisit the cave but she was adamant that it would only cause problems.

At first they had told Pippa that they wanted to take a few more photographs but she eventually dragged out of them the real reason why they wanted to go back. Though she wouldn't admit to it now, at the time she had listened in awe to what Steve and Kate said and had thoroughly expected to find something odd at the cave.

As it transpired, despite spending a good hour inside digging round in the sand searching for further objects, they had found nothing.

Pippa stood up, empty glass in hand. "Well, Holmes and Watson, fancy another?"

She turned, giggled, and headed for the bar without waiting for a reply.

Kate wished their flight home was today instead of the day after tomorrow; she was missing Michael.

She looked at her watch and did a quick mental calculation about the time difference. It would be about eight thirty in the morning in London. She'd give it an hour then call. Meanwhile, she needed to use the toilet.

She excused herself and made her way across to the foyer of the motel.

The toilets were hidden away down a short passageway across from the reception area. She made a mental note that the telephone was also along the passageway and glanced over at the kiosk to check that it was coin operated and not one of the newer card-operated ones. She hated the cards as they always ran out at the most inconvenient times or you finished the call with so little credit left that it wasn't worth using it for another.

The kiosk was framed by a large cork notice board full of the usual pinned messages left by backpackers trying to keep in contact with other travellers. She read a few of them out of curiosity.

Peanuts, See you in Alice, Monday 10^{tth.} Jake

Jane, can't make Jim meet you in Katherine at Globetrotters, Stefan

Looking for a ride to Adelaide? Room for one more in VW combi leaving Tues 15th. Petrol & food share. Call Andy on 56478054

Kate was caught between trying to form a mental picture of what someone called Peanuts might look like and wondering why all the messages sounded like they were written in code, when something caught her eye at the bottom of the board. It was no different to any of the other messages; it was the name of the place that caught her attention.

Dave, Missed you in Jabiru. (What happened?!!!)
If you're still up north give me a call at Frog's Hollow.
Ellen

Kate was sure that Jabiru was the place that Steve had mentioned when he had told her about the hitchhiker *'Stop it!'* she scolded herself. *'Why can't you let it go? It's not your problem!'*

A few minutes later, Kate walked past the notice board

in the opposite direction. She didn't know why but she looked at the message again and noted the name of what she presumed was a hostel.

When she arrived back at the table she noticed Pippa was now sitting where she had been earlier, on the chair closest to Steve. They were both giggling uncontrollably.

"Not still laughing about the bloody cave?" enquired Kate feeling more than a little annoyed that Steve now seemed to think it was all a big joke as well

"Oh, come on, Kate," said Pippa. "You've got to admit it's funny."

Kate noticed that Pippa's hand was now resting on Steve's thigh. She was surprised by the sudden surge of jealousy she felt and pretended to look at her watch in case her face betrayed her thoughts.

"Listen, I'm going to grab a quick shower before we go for something to eat. I'll see you down here at eight." She turned and left them looking bemused.

As she passed into the foyer she heard them burst into laughter again. It was all the encouragement she needed. Instead of going to her room, she approached the man at the reception desk and asked him how to get to Frog's Hollow.

Half an hour later, Kate was standing outside a white-bricked hostel on Lindsay Street. There was a picture of a large green frog sitting astride a kangaroo above the doorway welcoming guests.

Kate stepped inside. The air conditioning hit her as she entered and sent an involuntary shiver through her body.

There were several people lounging about the entrance area cum common room. They were chatting and eating traditional backpackers fare: pot noodle, toast and the like.

Kate looked round for a likely looking Ellen even though she had no idea what she looked like. A voice from behind her made her jump.

"G'Day. Can I help you?"

A blonde haired, tanned-faced girl of about twenty stood behind the reception desk smiling broadly.

"Ermm yes, I hope so..." faltered Kate. She hadn't actually given any thought as to what she was going to say. "...'I'm looking for a friend ...I think she may be staying here."

The girl turned her attention to a VDU and her fingers hovered above the keyboard as she waited for the name. Kate realised what she was waiting for.

"It's Ellen."

The girl waited for the surname.

"I'm afraid that's all I know," said Kate apologetically.

The girl looked up; there was no trace of irritation on her face.

"Mmm let's see..."

Her finger pressed the down arrow and the list of guests scrolled down on the screen.

"Here we are. Ellen Montgomery. Bunk four, room seven."

Kate smiled. "Thanks very much. I appreciate it."

The girl directed Kate through some patio doors and out onto a large pool area. She stepped into the sunshine.

The pool was surrounded by double storey bunkrooms and there were sun loungers nestled in amongst shady palms.

Kate was astounded. It was a far cry from the youth hostels that she'd encountered back in Britain when she had spent a couple of summers bumming round.

She made her way past the pool to room seven. There was a girl relaxing on a lounger directly outside.

"Excuse me," said Kate

The girl raised her head and lifted her hand to her brow to shield her eyes from the sun.

"I'm sorry to bother you, I'm looking for Ellen Montgomery and was wondering if..."

"That's me." interrupted the girl, sitting up a little further trying to recognise Kate's face.

"I read your note on the board at Larrhakeay Lodge; the one to Dave."

"Do you know him?" asked Ellen hopefully.

Kate felt a little stupid now. Where did she go from here?

It took her fifteen minutes to explain that she'd seen a young man heading for Jabiru a few weeks back but couldn't offer him a lift because of all the equipment in the van. (She decided, at this point, not to tell Ellen everything. She didn't want to cause unnecessary worry, especially if it was unwarranted). During this time, Ellen confirmed that Dave Ellis, a young man she had met on the aeroplane on her way to Australia, had arranged to meet up with her in Jabiru so they could do some bush walking in Kakadu National Park. He hadn't shown up.

Ellen was keen to get back in touch even though she hardly knew him because she figured it would be safer to hitch with a man rather than on her own.

"Can you describe him?" Kate asked.

"Erm... dark hair, tanned, about six feet..." she searched for something that would make him stand out from any other backpacker.

"... His backpack was quite unusual, it was one of those army type camouflaged ones. You know the sort."

"Did he ever wear a hat of any kind?" Kate asked, optimistically.

"Now that you mention it, yeah. In fact I was there when he made it. He wore a baseball cap but his neck kept burning so he sewed a handkerchief onto the back to protect it. He looked like one of those foreign legion blokes when he wore it ...except for the Union Jack of course."

Kate was getting more and more agitated the more she heard. She felt that she had to tell Ellen the rest of what she knew.

She apologised for being economical with the truth and then began to tell her everything.

It was seven thirty-five by the time she got back to the motel, having called into the local police station after seeing Ellen.

She'd asked to see the missing persons register, if they had one, on the pretence that she thought she had seen a woman who she thought may have been on a missing persons poster she'd seen a week or so before.

She had been amazed when the officer handed over a huge brown ring file. Inside were posters for over three hundred people, and that was just for the Northern Territory. The officer led her into an interview room then left her alone, apologising but saying that he had paperwork to catch up on.

It took her a good ten minutes to flick through the posters and note down how many were actually backpackers. She also wrote down the location at which they were last seen or their supposed destination.

A plan was forming in her mind.

She informed the officer that she must have been mistaken and realising how late it was, set off to jog back to the motel.

At dinner later that evening, Pippa and Steve were both flabbergasted when Kate informed them that she wasn't going home the next day as planned but was stopping in Australia for an extra week.

After an hour trying to persuade her that she was once again being ridiculous, they realised just how serious she was.

Finally, Steve agreed to postpone his return too, but for a week at the most.

Pippa had stopped giggling by now and in fact looked decidedly put out. She had to get back to London for her brother's wedding in four days time.

Kate, still feeling a little wary about her decision, smiled nervously and ordered three extra large Kahlua and Cokes whilst Steve tried to contact the airline to change the tickets.

26

North Atlantic, April 14th, 1912

Jacques leaned over the rail of the deck and peered down. The ship had come to a halt.

He looked towards the stern of the ship. The two men he had seen a few moments ago were no longer there but in the distance about five hundred yards behind the ship he could just make out what he thought they had been looking at.

The iceberg was enormous, towering even at this range above the height of the boat deck. His thoughts turned to Eleanor still asleep in the storeroom. His immediate thought was to return to her but then he could see no signs of panic on decks. There were no crewmen rushing about or alarm bells ringing. He decided to find a steward and enquire what had happened; the damage couldn't be too great and after all the ship *was* unsinkable.

He made his way up the promenade deck, into the lounge, and up the staircase to the next deck. There were not many passengers about but those that were remained calm, sitting and chatting, apparently unaware of the collision.

As he came to the top of the stairway he almost bumped into two men coming down. He recognised them as the two men he had seen looking over the rail earlier. One of them, the one dressed in civilian clothes, was carrying what appeared to be a rolled up document, and he looked pale and worried.

Jacques suddenly realised who the man was. They had been introduced at dinner on the second night; his name was Andrews. He was one of the designers of the ship itself.

Jacques grabbed his elbow as he passed. Andrews turned and looked at him. His eyes betrayed his inner desperation.

"I am sorry to bother you," said Jacques. "But I am aware that we have struck an iceberg. Could you possibly reassure me that everything is alright?"

Andrews licked his dry lips nervously.

"Unfortunately, sir, I am unable to provide you with the reassurances that you request." He looked round quickly. "My advice is to locate your loved ones, ensure they have a life vest and make haste to the nearest lifeboat. The ship has less than two hours."

Jacques suddenly felt numb; an image of the key flashed into his mind. He cursed inwardly as panic began to take hold. His mind was whirling: Eleanor, the professor... the key.

The professor banged on the door again. "Jacques open up! This is of the utmost urgency."

There was still no answer.

He looked down at the box in his hands; the box that twenty minutes ago he had struggled to carry. He was confused. The urge to open the box was almost overwhelming and even though he was well aware of the evil that lay within he couldn't help but marvel at the well being he felt. There was no pain when he walked, his joints were free, and his breath came easily instead of in wheezes.

A smile played on his lips, and then he shook his head as if dazed. "Jacques, my boy, where are you?" he thought.

He turned back down the corridor and set off at a pace.

He'd give it another ten minutes; then, if he still hadn't found Jacques, he would hurl the cursed thing overboard. He turned the corner and almost ran up the stairwell.

There were now quite a number of passengers who had obviously become aware that something was wrong and were wandering round the boat trying to find out what had happened.

The professor suddenly realised that the ship's engines had stopped. He halted for a second and strained to listen. The low hum of the gigantic engines was no longer there.

The doors in front of him swung open and a crewman ran past him banging on cabin doors as he went.

The professor stepped through the door and out onto the deck. When he had left the Purser's office there had been hardly a soul about and all was calm; now there was a distinct feeling of suppressed panic. There were people milling round one of the ship's officers who appeared to be handing out life vests. Further down the deck, another officer was directing two crewmen to lift the covers off a lifeboat.

The professor scanned the faces round him hoping Jacques was amongst them. His head was beginning to swim and the energy force building up inside him was incredible. He knew now what was happening; he had felt this way once before and he knew he was succumbing to the power inside the box. He made a decision; he couldn't afford to wait for Jacques any longer.

He made his way towards the quieter stern end of the deck and peered over the rail. He lifted the box above his head. The inky, black water ninety feet below was like glass and a thousand tiny pinpricks of light reflected up at him. He imagined the box sinking slowly down to the bottom of the sea, safe out of harm's way forever.

His arms began to tremble and a terrified voice inside his head screamed at him *'Throw it, do it now, no time to lose, Do it!!'*

He fought to summon the will power to throw it but it felt like he was pushing against an invisible force. Despite his new found strength, his muscles burned and perspiration rolled down his face.

He screamed out in a last ditch attempt to release it and a sharp pain exploded above his eyes. His legs buckled and he fell to the floor. His eyes were squeezed tightly shut in pain and the image of a dark, sinister figure filled his mind.

A demon stared down at him, its yellow teeth set in a snarl, screaming something at him; something that, although hard to make out, seemed to make sense.

He knelt forward and placed the box on the deck. He flicked the two brass clasps upwards and there was an almost inaudible hiss as the seal was broken. He slowly raised the lid and became transfixed. His eyes glistened with excitement and he breathed in deeply as if relishing the moment.

The figure on the key stared out at him, its eyes glowing a deep red. He knew exactly what he had to do.

He lifted the key from the box and tucked it into his pocket. He stood, threw the box over the rail, and walked quickly to the rear of the ship.

There were three lifeboats to which none of the crew or passengers had yet turned their attention . Looking around to ensure no one was watching, he jumped up onto the davit from which one of the boats hung and swung himself out of sight.

There was a large steel winch handle stored at the base of the davit which when locked into position was used to swing the boat out over the rail before lowering. He pulled the winch easily from its housing despite the fact that it normally took two men to lift it into position.

Instead of attaching it to the winch, he lifted it high into the air and brought it squarely down onto the gears of the winch. It took three more blows before some of the teeth sheared off and he knew it would be inoperable.

For good measure, he swung the handle against the gunwale of the boat, the timber splintering with each blow. Eventually there was a gaping hole, two feet wide in the side of the boat.

He smiled, turned, and still holding the handle, headed toward the next lifeboat.

Jacques swung open the storeroom door. Eleanor had gone but the sweet smell of her perfume still hung in the air. His mind was whirling and there was a knot in the pit of his stomach. Andrews had said the ship had less than two hours and it had been at least forty minutes since the collision. He had no time to lose. By now Eleanor would no doubt be making her way up onto the boat deck with the other passengers and getting ready to board the lifeboats. As a woman, her safety was assured.

He decided to look for the professor first. Surely a sick old man would warrant a place in the lifeboats alongside women and children. He suddenly thought about the key in the safe. At least if the ship did sink the key would go with it to the bottom of the ocean.

At that moment, two crewmen came running down the corridor. They stopped in front of Jacques and one of them stepped into the storeroom oblivious to the fact that the door was already open.

"Ere matey give us a hand will yer. Grab as many life vests as yer can and take 'em up to the boat deck. There are first class passengers up there climbing into lifeboats without 'em."

Jacques stepped in and began bundling up the vests.

"An' mind yer don't get conned into givin' 'em to any steerage passengers, we ain't got enough for them."

Jacques looked incredulously at the man but his mind was still in too much of a spin to contemplate the full implications of what he'd just been told.

Ten minutes later and he was up on the deck. There were people running about everywhere. Some of the lifeboats were being launched and women were weeping as they left their husbands behind. Some clutched babies whilst others held onto personal possessions. All were in shock at the realisation of what was happening.

Jacques spotted a family peering over the rail of the boat, none of whom had life vests. He ran over and insisted they put them on.

The man looked pale and panic stricken despite the fact that he was trying to maintain a brave countenance for the sake of his children. His wife had tears rolling down her cheeks as she helped the children on with their vests. Jacques smiled at her hoping it might provide some comfort and then he turned to begin the search for the professor.

He realised that with nearly fifteen hundred passengers on board he had little chance of success but still...

The ship had a definite list now and all manner of objects were beginning to slide along the deck. The passengers, who up until now had been relatively calm, were beginning to panic and Jacques was struggling to fight his way through the tide of people heading for the front section of the deck towards the lifeboats currently being filled.

There was a stairwell down to the lower decks a little further down the boat. Maybe the professor was still in his cabin, asleep and unaware of what was going on. He sometimes took something to help him sleep, especially if his joints were causing him discomfort.

Jacques was sweating now despite the intense cold. He was nearly at the stairwell. As he clambered across some chairs that had fallen onto the deck, he heard a shout to his right and a loud clang as metal struck metal. He peered along the deck and saw a large black object fall onto the deck from one of the spaces in between the aft lifeboats. As it hit the deck the object let out a moan and Jacques realised it was a man.

Another figure appeared immediately after the first and straddled the crumpled body on the deck. The figure held something above its head.

Jacques instinctively screamed out and the figure looked up.

Jacques was mesmerised. The professor stared at him for a moment but there was no recognition.

Jacques realised immediately what had happened; he remembered the night of the experiment and how the professor had left him strapped to the bed. He'd had that look then.

Jacques launched himself along the deck and hurled his full weight at the professor. They both hit the floor together and Jacques felt the breath knocked from him.

The professor was underneath him but was already beginning to push him off. Jacques tried to use his superior weight but the professor's strength was immense. Jacques heard a low growl then felt himself being lifted. Suddenly he was thrown backwards against the steel frame of the deck rail and there was a sickening thud as his head hit metal.

He looked up through a haze of pain and stars. The professor was standing over him holding something in his hands. His red, lizard eyes met Jacques' and for a moment he thought there was a tiny flicker of recognition. Then the professor's lips were pulled upwards-revealing yellow dripping fangs beneath. The object was raised a touch higher and Jacques closed his eyes in anticipation of the blow.

Instead, there was a loud crack and Jacques looked up to see the professor keel over sideways almost in slow motion.

Standing behind where the professor had been was an officer holding the remnants of an oar. The splintered end dripped with blood.

The officer's mouth dropped open and he tried to speak. Nothing came out.

Jacques groggily began to get to his feet. His head was still spinning and he fell down onto his knees.

He crawled toward the crumpled body of the professor.

One side of his head was completely open, grey matter glistening and steaming through the shattered skull. The eyes were open and staring and Jacques knew they *were* the professor's eyes now and not those of the terrible demon he had battled with a few minutes earlier.

He leaned his face close to the professor's mouth but felt no breath. A tear rolled down his cheek and fell onto the professor's face.

He bent down to kiss the cheek of his friend and gently pressed the eyelids closed. The officer's voice behind him filtered through into his thoughts.

"Jesus, I've killed him. I didn't mean to kill him but I thought he was going to... He was sabotaging the boats, the bastard was trying to wreck the boats..."

Jacques looked at the professor again and once again cursed the night he had left the tent in Peru.

He noticed the slight bulge in the professor's topcoat and drew his breath swiftly in. He could hardly bear to look. Gently, he grasped the lapel and turned it over. The top of the key protruded from the pocket. Jacques' sorrow turned to anger and he ripped the key from the coat. In one massive release of energy he jumped up and hurled it over the side of the ship.

It arced out into the blackness and disappeared.

Jacques fell onto the deck rail and began to sob.

27

Ministers' Chambers, House of Common, London 1997

Donovan opened his filofax and pretended to study the pages. He lifted his head and smiled as a man, dressed in the apparently parliamentary requisite navy pinstriped suit, walked past him.

He waited until the man had turned the corner then scurried across the corridor to Henderson's chamber door.

He had waited outside for Henderson to leave the building five minutes earlier. He knew Henderson had a twelve o clock appointment at the BBC. He was taking part in a Sunday lunchtime questions and answers programme dedicated solely to the Millennium Project.

The pass that Henderson had provided for him on his previous visit hadn't been difficult to doctor and the security guard hadn't given it a second look.

He stole another glance a round then inserted the narrow steel 'key' into the lock. After several twists, there was a satisfying click and he pushed the door quickly open. Once inside, he stood still with his back against the door. He held his breath and waited for the bang at the door signalling that he'd been seen. It didn't come.

He breathed a sigh of relief, lifted the 'key' to his lips and kissed it. It had been a present from a private investigator friend whom he'd helped out with pictures from time to time.

The air inside the room smelt dank, the faint aroma of pipe tobacco and aftershave, not Henderson's he noted, were legacy of an earlier tête-à-tête.

He scanned the room making a mental note of the position of everything so that he could leave it exactly as he had found it. His eyes fell on the Minister's red box still on the desk. Unfortunately, the computer was off and the signet ring was no longer on the table beside it.

He walked over and tried the first of two drawers in the desk. A pile of documents stared up at him. The top one was a feasibility study for the conversion of a well-known government research plant into a 'Secure Dumping Site' for nuclear waste. He smiled as he thought of the implications if *Greenpeace* got wind of it.

The other documents were less interesting and he tried the second drawer.

There was only one item in the drawer; a book entitled *'The Search for the Stone.'*

It was the last thing he expected to find. He flicked through it and discovered it was actually a biography of an early twentieth century archaeologist called Julian C. Tello. Donovan memorized the name; Kate would no doubt be familiar with him. He'd ask her if she ever decided to return from Australia. He replaced the book and closed the drawer.

Apart from establishing that Henderson had an interest in archaeology, the clandestine visit was proving to be very unfruitful.

He froze as voices outside the chamber became louder. A man and a woman were having a heated discussion, something about the European Monetary Union as far as he could make out. They had stopped directly outside.

The woman's tone became disdainful. "I'm sorry, but I disagree completely. The Germans have every reason to be enthusiastic..."

Donovan stopped listening and looked round the room for a means of escape even though he knew it was irrational and they couldn't possibly get into the chamber.

As his eyes flicked round, something caught his eye. He wasn't sure what, and looked round again more slowly this time. The ring!

It was sitting on top of the bookshelf half hidden behind a picture of Winston Churchill.

The voices outside began to fade as the couple outside moved along. He picked up the ring and pulled the red, leather-backed chair from beneath the desk. At the base of the computer was a terminal. The shape and size were identical to the ring.

He placed the ring carefully onto the terminal and pressed gently. It slid home snugly.

He pressed the reset button and a green light on the processing unit came on accompanied by a whirring sound. The screen lit up and hundreds of digits flicked across the screen before scrolling down to make way for more.

After twenty seconds or so a window appeared asking for the *User Code*.

"Shit!" cursed Donovan. "Just like James fucking Bond...now...let's see..."

Ten minutes later, to Donovan's extreme irritation, the window still flashed *'invalid code'*.

He'd tried the name of Henderson's constituency, his middle name (Montague), his mother's name (Laura), his father's name (Edward), the date that he had become an MP, the date of the last victorious General election, and at least twenty other names or dates he thought might be significant to the minister. All were in vain.

He looked at his watch, and drummed his fingers on the desk. He stood up and walked to the window searching for inspiration.

The brown murky waters of the Thames slipped by

outside. He stared out desperately trying to come up with something.

His thoughts drifted to Kate. He had been so disappointed when she'd called the day before, explaining that she was staying on in Australia for a little while longer. He missed her terribly. He imagined her freckled face, tanned and healthy. He had missed her infectious giggle and her naive, philosophical outlook on life. If she knew what he was doing at the moment, or worse, some of the things he'd done in the past...

He promised himself fervently that once he'd satisfied his curiosity on this one, there'd be no more underhanded deals with dodgy politicians like Henderson. He'd do things strictly by the book.

Once again, he was surprised by the strength of the feelings that Kate evoked in him.

A bright-red double-decker bus crossing Westminster Bridge sounded its horn in frustration at a cyclist who was weaving in and out of the traffic and Donovan looked up. The sign on the side of the bus was advertising the Millennium Experience. It read:

'*The Dome: Gateway to the Millennium '*

He pondered for a few seconds

"... Mmm..... you never know," he said out loud, and then cringed as he remembered where he was.

He turned and leaned over the keyboard once more and typed in: *'Millennium Dome'.*

The *'Invalid code'* window still mocked his incompetence and he thought to himself that if he were a computer programmer, he would have programmed it to say something like *' No way Jose'* or 'Try *again dick head'*

He typed in *' Dome'* and then, *'Millennium Project' but* still there was no response.

Finally, out of sheer desperation, and the fact that it was the only word of the sign he hadn't tried, he typed in:

'Gateway'

The screen suddenly changed and a desktop appeared in place of the window. Donovan jumped up and down on the chair and had to resist the urge to scream out.

He looked down at his watch. He'd risk five more minutes.

28

North Atlantic, 1912

Eleanor watched solemnly as the stern of the giant ship slipped silently beneath the ocean. There was a faint sucking sound, but that was all.

They had managed to row about five hundred yards from the stricken ship. The crewman in charge of the boat had told them that they had to get as far away as possible otherwise there was a possibility of the boat being dragged down when the ship sank.

Apart from himself there was only one other man on board. He had only been allowed on because he had claimed to be a doctor and could be of help with any survivors. Eleanor doubted if he were really a doctor though. He had made no efforts to even comfort any of the sobbing passengers let alone treat cuts and bruises.

The rest were women and children, thirty-four in all. It was a miracle they had managed to row as far as they had.

The scene that lay before them was almost incomprehensible. The water was still and glassy and the stars in the clear, black sky cast an eerie glow on the devastation below.

There were hundreds of bodies floating in the water but none moved other than to bob in the swell created by the ship as she sank. There was flotsam everywhere and only the odd shout pierced the still, night air. From where the shouts came was difficult to tell.

Eleanor was shivering uncontrollably, a combination of shock and the freezing temperature. Her mind was numb. She had been literally thrown into a lifeboat the second she had stepped onto the deck. She'd had no time to find Jacques or her mother after leaving the storeroom. Everything had happened so quickly.

The boat she was in was the first to be launched and at the time there didn't seem to be any real panic. She couldn't understand why the officers were insisting so strongly she put on a life vest and get in the boat. They had said it was just a precaution and they'd probably be winched back up as soon as it was safe. It had been like a nightmare.

The only sound now was the gentle swish of the solitary oar pushing them back towards the floating dead. She gazed across the water at them, searching for any signs of life.

Suddenly, a shout broke the eerie silence and a beam of light appeared about two hundred yards to starboard.

"Ahoy there."

It was another lifeboat and like theirs, it was only half full. Slowly, they drifted towards each other.

As they got closer, Eleanor could make out the pale, frightened faces of the women in the other boat. She felt as though she were staring at her own reflection in a mirror.

Apart from the two White Star men at the front of each boat no one made any attempt to speak.

The crewman on the other boat could have been no more than twenty and looked as shocked as the women. The older man to his credit tried to instil some order into the dreadful situation.

"Come about, we'll raft up. It'll be safer until help arrives."

"They're bound to have...have sent out a distress call

before she sank. I'll bet there are ships on the way already..."

The boy's words sounded as if they were based more on wishful thinking than a genuine knowledge of ships' procedure. "... Somebody said *'The California'* was within a few miles of us earlier. She can't be more than a couple of hours away at most."

The older officer nodded noncommittally then turned to the passengers in his boat. He explained how he wanted them to hold onto the oars of the other boat so that they didn't drift apart again. Some of the women were too shocked or cold to respond; others made weak attempts to follow the instructions.

Eleanor suddenly felt the bile rise in her throat and she instinctively turned her head over the gunwale of the boat. Her body was wracked with spasms as the shock finally took hold and she retched violently into the water.

When the sickness had finally stopped, she opened her eyes slowly and drew a hand across her mouth. She was still looking down into the water when she thought she heard a faint 'plop'. Something had splashed in the water.

Her first thought was that it was a survivor. She straightened up and peered round, scanning the surface for more movement. A glint of light caught her eye to her left and she squinted, trying to focus.

A small object floated into view and drifted slowly toward the boat. As it got close enough she leaned down and scooped it up.

The figure that was engraved on the strange key-like object smiled up at her. Its eyes were closed in an expression of apparent contentment.

Jacques was dying. He clung to a piece of wood, too cold to kick or to shout.

In the distance, he could make out the beam from a torch and heard muffled voices. He could no longer feel with his hands the wood that kept him afloat; there was just the sensation of being weightless.

He had searched in vain for Eleanor right up until the ship began to tilt and it was all he could do to cling on.

He had prayed that she had made it onto a lifeboat and then he had prayed for himself as the stern of the ship was lifted hundreds of feet into the air and the bubbling cauldron of water below began to suck them down.

His eyes closed against the memory and in the dense blackness of his mind a pinprick of light appeared and began to get bigger as if it were moving towards him. As it got closer, it became apparent that there was a figure standing in front of the light.

He suddenly recognised the figure as his father. He was beckoning to him. Then his mother appeared beside him, smiling and saying something that Jacques couldn't quite make out.

The last time he had seen his father, he had been confined to a bed, coughing up blood and wheezing. Now he looked strong and healthy. The bright light behind them both seemed to emanate warmth, and the urge to reach out and embrace them was overwhelming.

Jacques tried to pull his frozen fingers from the driftwood so that he could swim to them but his fingers felt as if they were made of stone and he thought they would break if he forced them any more. He concentrated solely on prising open the fingers one at a time, feeling the skin tear as he pulled each one free. The pain was horrendous but the image of his parents before him, so serene and happy, spurred him on.

At last he felt the last finger break free of the wood and he began to reach forward in the water toward them.

He took one last look at the flotsam that had saved his life and turned back to his parents. As he did so, he saw the light behind them diminish as if someone had stepped in front of it. The expression on their faces changed and they both turned to look at something hidden in the darkness.

The pleasant warmth was replaced by an icy blast of air and a foetid smell filled Jacques' nostrils.

The demon he had seen in the eyes of the professor back on the ship loomed large above them, placing his taloned fingers round their necks.

Jacques clawed at the water in front of him, trying desperately to get to them.

The thing closed its scaly fingers tighter and droplets of blood began to spring forth from the veins in their necks. Their faces turned blue and their eyes bulged from their sockets.

"Noooooooooooo!"

Jacques screamed and flailed his arms but still he only drifted.

The demon raised its yellow, lizardy eyes to the sky, a guttural low growling noise emanating from its throat. Jacques' mother and father were now suspended two feet from the floor.

From behind the demon, more figures began to appear from the shadows to welcome Jacques as he was dragged into purgatory to join them. Figures, he realised suddenly, that were familiar; Mary Ann Nicholls, still holding her intestines that dangled from the slit in her stomach.

"Cat got yer tongue, Frenchie?" she asked mockingly, her over made-up face grinning like a ventriloquist's dummy.

Annie Chapman stepped out from behind her, then another one of his victims; Catherine Eddowes.

The group grew as new faces appeared, smiling, one after the other.

The family he had helped with the life vests were there, no longer looking lost and forlorn, as well as the ship's officer who had killed the professor, still holding the splintered, blood stained oar.

Finally, the professor himself appeared. He looked strong and healthy; apart from the side of his head that was no longer there. He too smiled and raised a welcoming arm.

Jacques could not tear his eyes away from the grotesque tableau before him and as he opened his mouth to scream, he knew for certain that he was finally dead.

29

The Stuart Highway, Australia 500 kilometres north of Alice Springs, 1997

The road disappeared into the shimmering haze ahead of him.

Steve turned to look at the sleeping form of Kate beside him. Her bare feet were resting on the dashboard and her head was resting on a scrunched-up jacket. There were small beads of perspiration resting on the freckles on her nose.

He felt a stirring in his groin. Even in a pair of old jeans and a vest, she managed to emanate sensuality.

He watched her breasts gently rise and fall as she breathed.

"Stop it you randy bastard."

He turned his attention back to the road. He'd always had a soft spot for Kate even though he knew he hadn't the slightest hope of ever becoming anything more than just a good friend; she knew him too well. He smiled to himself and wondered if she had any inkling that he and Pippa had spent her last night in Australia together. Not that it meant anything in terms of a relationship of course; they'd taken advantage of each other on several occasions in the past without it ever developing into anything. They both had needs and both appreciated that it was a convenient arrangement.

He knew Pippa and Kate were good friends but he didn't think Pippa had confided in her about their occasional *'rendezvous'*.

The memory of Pippa sitting naked in his hotel whirlpool was doing nothing to diminish his hard-on and with the prospect of not arriving in Alice until tomorrow becoming more of a certainty he tried to think of something to take his mind off sex.

Kate stirred and she yawned loudly.

"God, I needed that," she said, stretching.

"Feel better?" asked Steve, squirming a little in his seat hoping his semi erection wasn't too obvious through his Levi's.

Kate nodded and smiled.

"How much further, before we get to Bond Creek?" she asked picking up the road atlas.

"About fifty kilometres or so. I reckon another hour maybe."

Kate studied her watch.

"That will mean it'll be about sevenish when we arrive and eight by the time we've found a motel for the night."

She pulled a small notebook and map from the inside pocket of her jacket.

"According to the missing persons register, at least eight people, six men and two women, have disappeared within a two hundred kilometre radius of that spot, the last being..."

She flicked the book open and scanned down the list of names.

"...a Jeremy Harding, twenty three, originally from Bedfordshire, England. The police found some of his possessions including his backpack at Bond Creek."

"Maybe we can ask round, see if anyone saw him in the area prior to his disappearance."

Kate was studying the map now.

"We can give it a try after dinner," she said swallowing, suddenly realising how hungry she was.

She lifted her head and stared out along the highway, deep in thought as if she were searching for a distant memory.

Steve glanced across at her.

"A penny for 'em." he said smiling his best 'big brother' smile.

"Mmm?" Kate's forehead lined in response but her eyes stayed focused on the road ahead.

"I was just wondering what you were thinking of, you seemed to be in a world of your own."

Kate blinked and turned to face him. "Erm... sorry I... something just came to me... then I lost it, you know like when you meet someone you haven't seen for a while and you've forgotten their name. It's on the tip of your tongue but it won't come. Well it's a bit like that only I don't even know what it is that I'm trying to remember."

Steve looked suitably puzzled.

"It's all this driving down bloody dusty roads with nothing for company but me and the kangaroos; it's finally got to you."

"Oh I don't know, I've quite enjoyed being with the kangaroos really," said Kate mischievously.

Steve feigned a hurt expression and Kate snuggled up to him and rested her head on his shoulder.

"You know, I'm only joking Steve. You know how much I love your jokes and stories. And by the way, thanks again for staying on with me. I know you think I'm mad."

Steve felt the stirring in his groin again and decided that the best policy was to concentrate on the driving.

Two and a half hours later they stepped out of the rowdy atmosphere of the only watering hole within a fifty-kilometre radius of nowhere and out onto a wooden, shiplap veranda that overlooked Main Street.

Main Street was *in fact* Bond Creek. Apart from one avenue off it, Main Street consisted of a petrol station, a hardware store, a general store, a bank, a motel, a few dozen houses and a pub.

It seemed like every farm hand north of Alice had chosen to hit Bond Creek for a drinking spree on the same night. Despite having a resident population of about a hundred, the bar was splitting at the seams.

Fortunately, they'd managed to finish their dinner in relative peace before the majority of the revellers had arrived.

There was only one other person on the veranda; a white haired old man, leaning on the rail, smoking an old-fashioned, clay pipe. He had his back to them, the smoke from the pipe drifted over his shoulder toward them.

There was a dusty plastic table and three chairs just beyond where he stood and Kate and Steve had to pass him to sit down.

"Excuse me," said Steve in an exaggeratedly loud voice, "Is anyone using these chairs?"

He knew it was a pointless question but it seemed as good a way as any to break the ice.

The man turned round and mumbled something through his beard and pipe, which Steve took to mean 'no'.

He placed their drinks on the table and Kate smiled brightly at the man before taking a seat. She thought he looked a little incongruous, more like a character from a second rate spaghetti western than a native antipodean.

"A bit of a party going on inside." tried Steve again, "thought it might be a bit quieter out here."

The man took his pipe from his mouth and to their surprise sat down on the spare seat. He thrust a grubby, gnarled hand out towards Steve.

"The name's Piper. Tom Piper."

Steve took his hand and introduced himself and Kate.

Kate just nodded and smiled and was thankful he just smiled back and didn't offer to shake her hand.

"Yer picked the wrong night to come to town if it's quiet yer after, mate. Fridays is payday and since there's nothing to spend yer money on and nowhere else to spend it for bloody miles this is the only place to be if yer in the sheep business."

He sucked on his pipe and blew out a cloud of pungent, brown smoke.

"It'll calm down about fourish," he added in a comforting tone.

Kate was glad the 'motel' they'd booked into was a little further up the street, though judging by the singing and the sound of glass breaking coming from inside, maybe it wasn't going to be far enough.

"Of course it wasn't always like this..." began Tom.

Steve and Kate glanced at each other and smiled. It was as good a place as any to start their enquiries.

Once Tom got into his stride there was no stopping him, he obviously wasn't used to having a captive audience and now that he did he was taking full advantage. He went on to provide them with a potted history of Bond Creek and actually turned out to be very pleasant company. He'd lived there since he was five years old and seemed quite proud of the fact that he'd only ever journeyed out of town on two occasions: once in 1957 when he'd been bitten by a redback and had to be taken to the doctor in Alice and once in 1975 when the whole town had to be evacuated due to a plague of mice that had forced everyone to leave until the exterminators could clear up. He laughed to himself at the memory.

Steve ventured back inside the bar to fetch another round of drinks and Tom reached into his pocket for matches to relight his pipe which had gone out whilst he had been talking. Kate took the opportunity to ask whether

Tom knew anything about the backpacker who had recently gone missing.

"Sure do," he said. "Everyone heard about him. He'd been in town a few days before he disappeared. Most people picked him out on account of his accent. It's not often we get Americans in Bond Creek. In fact, I think he stopped at Dean's place whilst he was here. Same as you."

"Hang on, Tom." Kate leaned forward. "American? Did you say American?"

Tom nodded. "That's right. Erm, let me see...California; I think he said ... that's right it was. I remember him having a conversation with Jonno in the bar and asking him where the best surfin' in Austalia was as he was keen on it back home ... O' course Jonno went on fer half an hour about here an' there even though he's been out of town fewer times than I have. Funny, really, since there's not many places in Australia further from the sea than here!"

Tom chuckled to himself again and puffed once more on his pipe.

"I was under the impression he was from England," said Kate.

Tom wrinkled his brow in puzzlement. Then his eyes widened.

"You're talkin' about the other bloke; the one whose gear they found out by the river. He was a Pom fer sure. That was a couple o' months back now. Real mystery that was, cops reckon it was like he'd been taken by aliens straight up off the ground on account of all his gear still being in his pack."

Steve returned with the drinks and Kate continued to ask Tom about the American.

It was after midnight by the time they got back to the motel and they both went to Kate's room to mull over what they'd been told. Mercifully, the noise from the bar was just a faint hum.

In the room, she added the details Tom had given her to the information she had already in her notepad. Then she located on the map the river where Jeremy Harding's pack had been found and the last known sighting of the American; a crossroads about five miles south of town.

The map now had nine red crosses on, all pinpointing the places where people had disappeared.

Kate studied the map intensely. Something still bothered her each time she studied the map. Suddenly, she threw her hands to her mouth.

"Shit! I think I've got something!"

Steve, who had started to fall asleep behind her on the bed, jumped up.

"What? What? ..."

Kate was now rummaging in her backpack. She lifted out a cardboard tube, in which she kept her archaeological maps. She flicked the plastic top up and withdrew the maps. She sorted through them searching for a particular one.

When she had found the one she wanted, she placed it on the floor. She asked Steve to pass her the map from the bed and she placed it over the other so that it was superimposed on top.

Although it was difficult to see through the top map at the details on the map below, the black crosses on the bottom map denoting the location of aboriginal sites in the immediate area were plainly visible.

Steve and Kate looked at each other incredulously.

The pattern of the crosses almost perfectly matched the crosses on the top map, the locations of the last known sightings of the missing persons!

30

London 1997

Donovan was peeling off his wet coat as he entered his flat. Although he'd only had to run two hundred yards from the Parliament buildings to a taxi rank, the rain was torrential and he was soaked to the skin. As he undressed he made his way into the kitchen and poured himself a hot cup of coffee.

Two minutes later and he was sitting in a pair of joggers at a desk in his 'darkroom' scanning through the pictures that he'd taken at the construction site a few days before.

He'd taken about thirty in all; mostly they revealed nothing out of the ordinary, just the usual type of stuff you'd expect on any large construction site. He flicked through to the couple he'd taken of Henderson with the man. He was certain there was something...

He opened a drawer and rummaged round until he found a magnifying glass. He scrutinised the first picture closely, concentrating not on Henderson nor the package he was handing over, but the workman's jacket. The worker was half turned away from the camera so his face was in shadow. Across the back of the man's fluorescent, waterproof jacket was a company name, only half of which was visible. The long distance lens and the relatively fast film speed had combined to make the image grainy and vague but Donovan could just make out the first three letters: a B, an E and a U.

"Yes!" he exclaimed, jumping up from the desk. He hurried into the sitting room, picked up the phone and excitedly punched in some numbers.

"Charlie, it's Michael. How are you mate? Good, good ...Listen I need a favour. I need you to find out as much as you can about a 'Beaumont Construction."

He paused while Charlie wrote it down.

"That's right, Beaumont... Cheers, mate...Yeah as soon as you can. Give my love to Sarah. Talk to you soon."

Donovan replaced the phone and rubbed his hands together eagerly. He loved the feeling he got when he sensed a good story was in the offing. He reached over to his steaming coat draped over a chair and pulled the notebook from the inside pocket. It was inside a plastic wallet so it was completely dry. Flicking open the pad, he carefully read the notes he'd made at Henderson's office.

He'd found mostly insignificant ministerial documents on the hard drive of the computer but one file in particular had caught his eye because it had the same name as the password that had eventually allowed him access into the computer; *'Gateway'*

Inside the file were hundreds of documents. Some were correspondences to companies considering investing in the Dome, some were speeches that Henderson had obviously delivered in *The House* and some were memos to Party Whips outlining strategy for drumming up party support for the venture.

The document that interested Donovan the most, however, was a financial inventory of payments made to companies during the construction so far.

The inventory was predictably dominated by the name *'Academy Civil Engineers'* but the names of other construction companies cropped up here and there.

Donovan had been staggered by the amounts involved.

One of the company names in particular seemed to register something at the back of his mind: *'Beaumont Construction'*. He was sure he had seen or heard the name before. Now of course he knew where. He had noted down the dates of the payments and the amounts before leaving the chamber, there were seven in all, each for a hundred and fifty thousand pounds.

He smiled to himself at the near miss he'd had earlier. Just as he was leaving the Parliament buildings, Henderson's limousine had pulled up and Donovan had skipped past just as Henderson stepped out.

Had he seen him it wouldn't necessarily have been a disaster; it just meant that he'd managed to avoid any potentially difficult questions about why he was there wearing an expired pass given to him by the minister himself.

Charlie was an old school mate of Donovan's who worked as a planner in the offices of Trade and Industry. He had access to details of virtually every business, large or small, in the country.

He and Charlie were still close friends and met up every few weeks for a curry and a few drinks to chat over old times and bring each other up to date on what was going on in their lives. He had helped Donovan with information on a few occasions but Donovan was careful not to take too much advantage of his friend's position. He knew that divulging information of any kind was a dismissible offence and he didn't like to think he was compromising his friend... not too much anyway.

He made a mental note to make the next curry *his* treat and went off to soak in a hot bath, satisfied with a good day's work.

31

November 23 1922, Valley of the Kings, Egypt

A large bead of sweat rolled onto the sand -stained page of the journal. He brushed his hand across his head and continued writing, desperately trying to complete the morning entry:

Today may be the day we give the world the greatest treasures ever found in this land. Soon I shall...

A loud voice, calling out, made him stop and look up. "It is ready, Mr. Carter, sir. Come, we are ready!"

Carter quickly dispatched a runner to the small camp a few hundred yards away and made his way up the rocky outcrop to the newly excavated tomb entrance. White - cotton- clad Arabs milled round, jabbering away excitedly. The sun hovered on the horizon like a hawk biding its time, waiting to pounce on an unsuspecting rodent.

Carter could hardly believe that after fourteen years he might now be on the verge of fulfilling all his dreams, justifying the faith placed in him by his benefactor, George Edward Stanhope, the Earl of Carnarvon. Another two or three weeks and the funding would have been removed.

Now, as he watched the sickly figure struggle toward him, his walking cane in one hand and the arm of the runner in the other, he felt an overwhelming sense of relief. It had been over two weeks since he had informed him of the discovery, two weeks of incredible self-restraint.

In the last few months he had become increasingly obsessed with finding the tomb. The other strange thing was the regularity with which the dreams had occurred during the weeks running up to the discovery.

The 'night terrors' he had suffered as an infant had returned with a vengeance. Every night, despite the tiredness, he would lie and wait for the terrifying visions to fill his mind, hoping beyond hope that the night would bring nothing but badly needed sleep and rest.

Recently, it seemed as if he were two separate entities; one that lived entirely for the sole purpose of furthering the knowledge of the past and another who felt as if an outside force were taking control and guiding it towards something he knew was devastating and uncontrollable.

The night terrors tore away at his mind and tortured him physically as the pains that accompanied them gripped him more with each successive 'dream'.

He was brought out of his reverie by the weight of a hand on his shoulder and a rasping voice. "Howard, my boy, couldn't you have discovered something in a slightly more hospitable location?"

Carter looked round into the watery eyes of his friend and sponsor.

"Delighted you could make it, Sir. I'm afraid the Egyptians were quite inconsiderate when it came to planning the whereabouts of the graves of their dear departed."

The warm smile that Carter gave his old friend disguised the growing uneasiness inside him.

"The tomb is ready to be opened. The photographer is at the site and I have made arrangements for the appropriate paperwork to be made ready in the event that we find anything of importance," Carter muttered quickly. He was impatient to get up to the site after the almost unbearable wait.

"If, my boy, if!" Carnarvon leaned toward him and whispered conspiratorially. " I tell you; this is going to take the entire archaeological world by storm. They have been waiting for this for twenty five years."

He looked up toward the excavation, "Come, they have waited long enough."

The Egyptian workers who had worked tirelessly with Carter on the site over the last few weeks surrounded the tomb entrance. None of them had really expected to find anything, least of all the water - boy who had absent-mindedly been prodding a stick into the sand when he felt it stop at something solid. He now had pride of place nearest to the entrance as Carnarvon and Carter prepared to open the tomb. The desert was silent and an air of expectation hung over the crowd. Everyone's eyes were trained on the stone slab that separated them from three thousand years worth of Egyptian history.

Carter stepped forward and pushed the tip of his cane into the joint of the doorway. He slid it round the edge, deepening the groove, in readiness for the insertion of wooden pegs. Suddenly there was movement above him and one of the men shouted something in Arabic. Carter turned round and looked down toward the path leading to the camp. A growing cloud of dust signalled the approach of someone running rapidly toward the site.

As the figure got closer it became clear that he was holding a piece of paper in his hand. The workers parted to let him through.

The messenger stopped in front of Carter, bowed his head and held out a small, white envelope. Carter took it and glanced across nervously at Carnarvon. He tore it open and unfolded the contents. It was a telegram.

TOMB MUST NOT BE OPENED STOP MUST WAIT FOR INSPECTOR. STOP ORDER OF PRIME MINISTER PASHA STOP ARRIVE NINE O CLOCK

STOP.

The frustration got the better of Carter and he slammed his cane against the sand. "Damn, damn!"

Carnarvon took the telegram from him and slowly read it. Without further consideration, he gave orders for the tomb entrance to be covered over and guarded until tomorrow. "After all this time, a few more hours won't make much difference," he whispered. "Come on, let's get ourselves cleaned up. I've brought something with me that'll raise your spirits."

Inside the tent, the shadows loomed large. The solitary oil lamp cast a warm glow onto the faces of the two men. The bottle of brandy was two thirds empty and both spoke in hushed, slightly slurred voices.

Carter leaned forward and poured them both another finger of brandy. He swung the glass to his lips and with one swift pull swallowed the drink. He opened his eyes and looked at Carnarvon.

Carnarvon followed suit and emptied his glass. Both men smiled and stood up. They embraced each other, then Carter picked up the lamp and they walked from the tent.

There was a hissing noise as air rushed into the hole made by Carter's cane. He tapped away at the hole with the hammer and chisel and slowly the hole got bigger. There was a vague smell of incense, which somehow seemed to intensify the urgency with which he worked and pretty soon the hole was big enough for him to stick his head through. Carnarvon could hardly bear the suspense; he was literally pulling at Carter's shirt to try and see inside.

As Carter turned from the hole and pulled out the torch, his smile was immense. "You simply won't believe it," he said.

Reluctantly he pulled himself away from the hole and Carnarvon stepped forward, stuck the torch through the hole, and peered inside.

From behind him, Carter noticed that his whole body suddenly went rigid, or was it just his imagination? It was almost as if Carnarvon's body went into spasm. He touched the old man's shoulder. "Are you alright, John?" Carnarvon pulled back. " I'm absolutely fine, in fact I'm bloody marvellous," he replied. His eyes seemed glassy though and had a peculiar, vacant look about them.

Carter put it down to a combination of excitement and the brandy they had consumed earlier.

"Howard, I need to see inside more. Make the hole larger."

Carter must have looked surprised; he knew exactly how awkward the Egyptian authorities could be and who could blame them when you saw some of the damage caused to other tombs by European treasure hunters. Take that lunatic Belzoni, for example. He'd destroyed precious artefacts by blasting his way in, then, not content with just that, went on to deface the stones by carving his name on the tomb!

"John, maybe we'd better wait until morning you know..."

Carnarvon interrupted tersely. "Howard I *need* to see more, I could be dead tomorrow. You know my condition."

The vehemence with which he insisted was not lost on Carter.

"I suppose we can always cover it up again after we've been in," he said, attempting what he hoped Carnarvon would recognise as a smile.

Twenty minutes later, both men clambered through the hole. The torch lit up a small chamber. They could hardly control themselves. The room was filled with treasures. Two life size statues of the boy king guarded a sealed up doorway and there was a golden throne with the painted figures of the king and his queen, Ankesenanum, on the back. Three golden beds moulded in the shape of a lion, a cow and a typhon stood along the length of the wall opposite.

Carter watched as Carnarvon dashed from artefact to artefact. It was almost as if he were entranced. He looked down. At his feet lay a bunch of flowers, dry with age. There was something overwhelmingly saddening about them and he found himself almost wishing he had never discovered the tomb; he felt as if they were desecrating holy ground. The strange feeling of foreboding he had experienced prior to Carnarvon's arrival returned and he suddenly felt very claustrophobic.

He looked up from the flowers to see Carnarvon sitting on the throne, holding a small trinket. His eyes were closed and there was an incredibly serene look on his face. The trinket attracted Carter's attention. For a second, he could have sworn it glowed! The figure that was engraved on it seemed to dance momentarily and he noticed the oversized eyes were closed, giving it the same serene repose that Carnarvon had.

"Must be just the torchlight," he thought.

He walked toward his friend and was about to touch his shoulder when his body went rigid again as it had when they first looked inside the tomb. Panicking, Carter thought he must be having a seizure of some sort and stepped forward to try and help. Suddenly, Carnarvon's eyes opened wide and Carter stared into them.

At once, he became terrified. It was like looking into the portals of hell itself. The night terrors that had haunted him throughout his life came rushing out, threatening to engulf him completely and he sensed something evil wrapping itself round him; something slimy and malevolent. He felt as though his chest was being crushed and he sucked in air desperately as he felt himself beginning to suffocate.

He was still staring into Carnarvon's eyes when he noticed a small tiny pinprick of yellow appearing at their centres. Suddenly, he realised that the points of light had a shape, they looked like a face.

The face was slowly getting bigger. Now it was covering the irises and he realised it was laughing. Carter felt rising panic and would have screamed had there been any air in his lungs. Instead his mouth simply hung open.

As the image grew to fill the inside of the eye, Carter began to black out. Suddenly there was darkness.

32

Northern Territory, Australia. 1997

Steve was sitting under the meagre shade of a solitary pandanus palm, soaking his bandana with water from his bottle. The temperature was in the hundreds and, apart from Kate, the only living things out in the open sun, as far as he could make out, were flies.

She'd hardly slept a wink the night before, having discovered the correlation between the disappearances and the aboriginal sites.

At first light, she'd insisted they check out some of the locations to see if they would reveal anything else. He had to admit that it all had to be too much of a coincidence and he was now convinced that Kate was really onto something. Having said that; wandering round in the bush in this heat was taking things a bit far. He'd suggested earlier that maybe they should take what they had to the police in Alice but Kate had simply laughed. He supposed she was right; in Alice the worst crime ever perpetrated was probably sheep rustling. The police would no doubt think they were a couple of crank Poms taking the piss out of the local constabulary.

Kate was still at the opening to the third 'cave' they'd visited so far, searching in the sand for anything unusual. Steve secretly thought she was being a bit optimistic if she hoped to repeat what had happened up in Arnhem Land.

Still, she was like a dog with a bone when she set her mind to something and he knew it would be pointless to try and suggest they call it a day just yet. He wrapped the wet bandana round his neck, stood up, and made his way over to her.

"Any luck?"

"Not yet," Kate answered, without looking up, and continued shifting sand round with her foot.

"Why don't we try one more site then go and get cleaned up and I'll take you out for lunch? I know this great little place in Bond Creek!"

Kate put both her hands on her hips and looked up.

"Don't tell me...Yabbie's?" she laughed. It was *the* only restaurant in Bond Creek.

"Okay. One more and we'll go eat," she sighed in exasperation. "But I want to do at least a couple more this afternoon."

"You have yourself a deal," said Steve, thrusting out his hand to shake on it.

They collected up their backpacks and walked wearily back to the jeep. As Steve climbed into the driver's seat, something caught his eye. Something had glinted in the distance. He scanned the bush ahead and moved his eye line about to see if he could catch it again but saw nothing.

He decided it must have been the heat haze and started up the engine. The heat inside was incredible and it was a relief when they pulled onto the track and picked up a little speed, the flow of air marginally cooling them down.

They'd driven about five hundred metres when Steve saw the glint of light again. This time he asked Kate if she had seen it.

"Pull over for a second, I'll check it out," she said, pulling out a pair of binoculars from her pack. She climbed out of the jeep and peered out in the direction that Steve thought he'd seen the light .The bush seemed endless, flat, dry and hostile. Then, something came into view. It was difficult to judge the size of it because of the distance, but it appeared to be shaped like a dome. At first Kate thought she was imagining it. There couldn't possibly be a building out here in the middle of nowhere. She passed the binoculars to Steve.

"What do you think?" she asked.

Steve took a few seconds to locate it. "I don't know, but it definitely appears to be a building of some sort."

"But what kind of building would anyone put out here? According to the map, there are no homesteads for fifty kilometres and besides, it doesn't exactly look like a farm, does it."

Steve's curiosity was aroused now.

"There's one way to find out." he smiled and jumped into the Landcruiser. "Come on."

They followed the track until they reckoned they were roughly parallel with the building and were surprised when another track appeared to their left, running at ninety degrees to the main 'road' in the direction of the building.

They gave each other a *'How did that get there?'* look. They had to have passed it on the way out but neither of them had noticed it.

Steve turned onto the track.

Ten minutes later, the scale of the building was becoming apparent; they were probably only a couple of kilometres away now. They both looked at each other, suddenly realising what it was: an observatory!

"We may as well have a look now that we're here," said Steve.

"May as well," Kate agreed, shrugging her shoulders and taking a swig of tepid water from her bottle.

As the Landcruiser pulled to a halt outside the building, Kate read a plaque that was screwed to the wall beside the door.

'*Warranboola Observatory Founded 1992*'

The door was closed. Steve touched Kate's arm and nodded in the direction of a small out building at the side of the main building. The front panel of an open -topped jeep was just visible parked round the side.

"Looks like someone's home."

"Well let's be neighbourly and say Howdy," grinned Kate in her best attempt at a Texan drawl.

Steve turned off the engine and they both jumped out.

Kate tried the handle on the door. It turned freely and she pushed it open.

The doorway led into a small anteroom. There was a door immediately in front of them and a spiral staircase to their left. Astronomical charts adorned the walls from top to bottom.

Kate tried a tentative 'Hello, anyone home?' When she got no reply, she walked over to the stairwell and tried again, louder this time. "Hello, anyone home?"

There was a moment's silence then the sound of footsteps skipping down the stairs.

Kate looked at Steve and smirked; she almost felt like they were intruding and shouldn't really be there. Never mind, in for a penny...

Kate had been expecting some kind of white haired, lab coated, boffin type to step from round the corner, instead a tanned, blonde haired man, wearing faded khaki shorts and a bright-red basketball vest appeared.

"G'day, and welcome to Warranboola. It's not very often we get visitors out here. Bit off the beaten track, you see."

"You can say that again," said Kate, unable to avert her gaze from the sapphire blue eyes that twinkled warmly behind tortoise shell glasses.

"Hi," said Steve, offering his hand. "We were out studying the burial sites when we saw the sun reflecting off the dome. We were curious to find out what it was. In fact we only realised it was an observatory when we got really close to it, by which time we figured we might as well say hello."

"I suppose it *is* a little unusual in the middle of the bush and all. I'm Brian, by the way."

Kate introduced herself and realised she was still staring. He was without doubt the most attractive man she'd ever met.

Brian gave her an enormous white-toothed smile and held out his hand.

"I thought they always built observatories at the tops of mountains," said Kate quickly in an attempt to mask the fact that she had been staring.

"That's usually true," explained Brian. "But the atmosphere here is so clear and unpolluted that the lack of altitude isn't really a problem. We also have the advantage of being a long way from any major built up areas so when the sun goes down out here, it's just about as black as you can get."

Kate nodded her understanding.

"Come on upstairs and I'll show you round."

Steve brought up the rear as Kate followed Brian. In a way, he was glad to be doing something not connected to the disappearances; he felt Kate was becoming a little *too* obsessed by it at the minute.

At the top of the stairs was a landing, which opened out into a gallery running in a circle round the inside of the dome. A metal walkway connected the gallery to a platform in the centre of the dome, upon which, sat the huge 2.6 metre reflecting telescope. Brian explained that he was doing a Masters degree at the University of Sydney and at the moment was spending twelve months living and working at the observatory as part of his research on something called *'globular clusters'*. (Steve whispered a gross comment about the contents of his handkerchief after a heavy cold and Kate gave him a dig in the ribs.)

He led them both across the walkway and onto the platform, closing the safety gate behind them.

Kate was fascinated; the only telescope she'd ever seen was the tiny one her father used to have in the conservatory at home. He spent more time noseying at the neighbours than directing it towards the heavens.

Brian spent an hour demonstrating how the telescope worked and Kate was impressed not only with the telescope but Brian's obvious passion for astronomy. Kate's opinion of him was heightened even further when he explained how the telescope was fitted with instrumentation that permitted low and high resolution spectroscopy, photometry from near ultra violet to infra red wavelengths and faint object imaging! She hadn't a clue what it meant but so what: a man with great looks *and* brains!

Steve looked up at the telescope and gasped, "Wow!"

Kate hoped Brian was too engrossed in his subject to detect the sarcasm and punched Steve on the arm when he wasn't looking.

Later, Brian showed them round the living quarters, which lay through the door they had seen as they first entered the building. Far from being a thrown together jumble of furniture and belongings, a camp bed, and a portable cooler box, they were surprised to find a purpose built two-bedroom apartment with all mod cons.

Brian explained that because of the observatory's remoteness and the fact that it was a new building and not some turn of the century relic, its construction had been well thought out. Apart from the once monthly trip into Bond Creek for supplies, it was to all intents and purposes self-contained.

It was late afternoon when they were both climbing back into the Landcruiser outside, both sad that the visit had come to an end. Although Kate and Steve enjoyed each other's company, it had been refreshing to spend a few hours with someone different. The feeling must have been mutual as Brian agreed to meet them for a drink the following evening in Bond Creek.

Brian waved as they pulled away, " Seven o clock sharp at Yabbies."

Kate looked back as a cloud of dust enveloped the waving figure.

Kate reflected upon the visit on the way back to Bond Creek; Brian had been very interested in their archaeological work. (They hadn't told him about the real reason they were still in Australia. When Brian had asked why they were there, Kate had jumped in quickly before Steve could say anything and told him they were doing archaeological research about ancient aboriginal ceremonial sites).

His knowledge of the local area was surprisingly good, considering he wasn't a native, and he had actually given them some interesting pieces of information about the aboriginal sites, the most important being that he'd noticed a pattern to the comings and goings of visitors to them. He explained that sounds travelled a long way across the bush because of its flatness, particularly at nighttime. Therefore, he tended to be aware of any traffic on the 'road' even though it was a good ten kilometres away. He also took note because working on his own for most of the time, he had become particularly adept at picking up sounds. (The only reason he had not been aware of their approach that afternoon was that he had been on the radio to another observatory and had been wearing headphones until a few seconds before they pulled up outside.)

It was only after a few months that he realised the new

moon (or day one of each lunar cycle) seemed to coincide with a nighttime visit to the site closest to the observatory. Without fail, in the last five months a vehicle of some description had visited the site between nine and midnight.

Brian assumed that the aborigines, like other ancient races, had traditions and religious beliefs closely linked to astrological events and this probably explained the timing of the visits.

Kate remained deep in thought for the entire duration of the journey back and said very little. Steve put it down to fatigue and was therefore surprised when she jumped out of the vehicle like a scalded cat the second they arrived at the motel and bounded across the road to the grocers cum pharmacist cum newsagents store with a swift: "I'll be back in a minute, mine's a lager."

Steve shook his head and smiled; where did she get the energy?

He walked the few hundred metres to the bar where they'd had dinner the night before and pulling up two chairs on the veranda out front, ordered two cold beers.

He'd just taken the head off his drink when Kate came running up, waving what appeared to be a small, black book of some sort.

She looked incredibly agitated and could hardly wait to sit down before she flicked open the pages of what was apparently a pocket diary.

She pointed to a date two months previous.

"What do you think of that?" she said excitedly, throwing the book open in front of him

Steve's expression remained blank.

"What, exactly, do I think of what?"

"That!" said Kate, tapping her finger emphatically to some writing in bold at the top of the page.

21st April New Moon

Steve looked at her again, still plainly oblivious to the significance of the date.

"Steve, the twenty first of April is just two days after Jeremy Harding's belongings were found at the dried up river bed!"

33

Munich, Germany, March 28th 1923

The two elderly men made their way carefully down the steps and onto the street. They pulled their collars up against the heavy drizzle and began to walk the two blocks back to the Karlstrasse Hotel where the older of the two men was staying.

They had enjoyed a good meal and had even managed to talk a little business in between courses.

"So your friend is a happy man at last." said Jacob "Do you think there is still more treasure to be discovered?"

Carnarvon let out an involuntary laugh. "Think! I know there is more; this is just the beginning! I estimate that what we have found so far is a small fraction of what remains in the Valley."

Jacob patted his friend warmly on the back. "Well, all I can say is that if the next discovery has as big an effect on you as this one then your investment has been a good one. It has taken twenty years off you. I never saw you look as healthy. You make me feel old, my friend."

Carnarvon winked and smiled as a young woman skipped through the puddles in her stiletto heels on the pavement opposite. Both men laughed heartily and continued on.

Carnarvon had to admit, since he and Carter had entered the tomb in Egypt, his health had undertaken a remarkable turnaround. The physicians in London who had only weeks previously warned him that another British winter might be his last, were astounded by his miraculous improvement.

He put his hand up to his chest to check that the artefact was still there and the reassuring lump in his inside pocket brought a smile to his lips again. He had never spoken of the key to anyone or its apparent effects on his well being, not even to his daughter Evelyn, or his good friend Howard Carter.

He guessed that Carter suspected something odd had occurred after their clandestine visit to the tomb, but neither of them had spoken of what had actually happened that night other than to marvel at the wonders they had found. It had taken on a kind of surrealness that neither of them could explain.

Anyway, all that Carnarvon knew was that, for whatever reason, the key had given him a new lease of life, with the only apparent side effect being the occasional vivid nightmare.

The trip to Munich had been Evelyn's idea; she had noticed the improvement in her father's health and figured that the chances were that it was only a temporary condition perhaps brought on by the excitement of the discovery. She had told him to visit his good friend Jacob as she imagined it would probably be their last chance to see each other before her father finally succumbed to illness.

The two men walked side by side in a contented silence and crossed the road to turn into the long street that would take them to the hotel.

On the corner of the street was a beer hall, outside of which, several men were smoking and talking excitedly. There were billboards pasted upon the building with posters advertising an event, but not having a fluent grasp of

German, the only bit that Carnarvon could understand was the date. Judging by the applause and chanting coming from inside there was some sort of public gathering going on. Jacob noticed his friend looking.

"The new way forward for the Fatherland," explained Jacob. He was smiling yet Carnarvon detected that for some reason, the smile was an uneasy one.

"The latest new Nationalist Socialist Party trying to drum up support. They are unhappy with the Republic's acceptance of the French still occupying The Rhineland."

Carnarvon nodded his understanding. He was aware of the growing feeling in Germany that the time was ripe for them to throw off the political constraints forced upon them after the war by the Treaty of Versailles and start rebuilding some national pride. He looked across the road again as people suddenly began pouring from the hall and in a few seconds there was a tide of people flowing down The Karlstrasse.

Jacob and Carnarvon stopped and waited in a shop doorway to let the crowd pass.

Carnarvon couldn't help but notice how excited and animated they were as they passed. The meeting must have been successful.

After about ten minutes, the street returned to its former state with just a few stragglers hurrying home in the drizzle. The two friends continued their walk back to the hotel.

Carnarvon was contemplating the journey back to Cairo the following day and wondering what new treasures had been uncovered in his absence when a figure stepped out in front of them from an alleyway to their right. He said something to them in German. Carnarvon looked to his friend for assistance. Jacob, he noticed, looked startled. He too had obviously been in deep thought.

The man repeated whatever it was he had said initially.

Then Carnarvon noticed the unlit cigarette in the man's hand and he breathed a sigh of relief as Jacob began rummaging in his pockets for his lighter.

Carnarvon took stock of the man. He was dressed in a strange fashion, especially considering the weather. He wore black trousers tucked into black leather boots and a brown shirt. There was a badge on the pocket of the shirt and an armband round his right arm, which sported a motif of some sort. He wore a black ski hat but no overcoat, which Carnarvon thought strange, especially as he didn't appear to be feeling the cold. (Maybe he had just come from the meeting at the hall.)

Carnarvon's heart was beating quickly, he didn't know why he felt so threatened by this person, and after all, he *was* only asking for a light. Still he took reassurance from the glow of the hotel entrance a hundred or so yards beyond the man who blocked their path.

Jacob said something to the man as he leaned forward to light the cigarette held between his lips. He drew in the smoke deeply and exhaled a thick cloud into the cold night air.

The man laughed in response to whatever Jacob had said. Then, unexpectedly, two more men stepped from the shadow of the alley. They too were dressed in the curious uniform.

Both Jacob and Carnarvon now realised that the encounter was something more sinister than an innocent passer-by asking for a light.

One of the men walked forward and replaced the first man standing directly in front of Jacob; he was holding what appeared to be a horsewhip. Although he was smiling, the man's demeanour was unmistakably threatening. His eyes had the look of a madman.

"Sind sie ein Jude?"

He spat out the last two words as if to emphasise his

contempt for them and stared at Jacob, with just a trace of a smile on his face.

Carnarvon saw Jacob's face drain of colour as the man asked the question again, more forcefully this time.

Despite his lack of German, Carnarvon knew what the man was asking; he just didn't understand why a complete stranger would be asking a question about his friend's religious beliefs.

The third man had walked round to stand behind Jacob now and Carnarvon anxiously scanned the street beyond, hoping that someone would come out from the hotel so he could shout for help. But the street was completely empty except for them and these men.

The three men held a short conversation. Then, suddenly, Jacob's arms were grabbed from behind and the man in front smiled slowly at Jacob's pathetic attempts to resist. He was no match for the brutish man who restrained him.

He placed the horsewhip so it rested on Jacob's cheek then used his free hand to unbutton his overcoat. He reached inside and pulled out Jacob's wallet.

"So that's what it's all about, they simply want to rob us," thought Carnarvon. He quickly reached inside his own coat to pull out his own wallet

"Here, I have money, lots of it. Take it all, but please leave my friend alone. He isn't well."

As he pulled out the wallet, the 'key' came out too and fell to the floor. He instinctively leaned forward to try and catch it but he was too slow and it landed with a dull thud onto the German's patent leather boot. As Carnarvon leant forward to pick the key up, he felt a sharp blow to the back of his head as the horsewhip connected. Then a hand reached in front of him and snatched up the key from the gutter.

He looked up to see the man holding the key,

scrutinising the naked woman on its side.

Carnarvon felt another sudden flash of pain, but this one came from deep inside his body and as he stared at the German's face he noticed the man's eyes change. Just for an instant, the man's eyes *glowed*, he was sure of it. He looked round to see if any of the others had seen but from their faces it was apparent they hadn't.

The man tore his gaze away from the key and he looked at Jacob. If his eyes had been the eyes of a madman before, they were now the eyes of the Devil.

He slipped the key into his pocket and turned his attention back to Jacob's wallet. Opening it, he took out the contents; a photograph of Jacob's late wife, a laundry ticket for a suit he'd left to be cleaned the day before, his identity card and finally his small, silver *Star of David* pendant.

The man laughed loudly. It was a mocking laugh, not the kind of laugh that indicated amusement but the kind that somebody produces when they have found something that they have been desperately looking for.

Without warning, the man suddenly lashed out at Jacob with the whip knocking him heavily to the floor.

Carnarvon began to protest but another blow from the horsewhip knocked him back and he fell against the wall. The madman stepped forward and placed his foot on Jacob's chest so that the toe of his boot was digging into the old man's throat. Jacob's head was bleeding and his eyes were watery but somehow he still managed to maintain a dignified countenance.

"Listen carefully, old man; explain to your friends at the synagogue that you have spoken with a man who has foreseen your future. You will no longer be the scourge of the Fatherland. The time has come to rid our great nation of the scum that clings to its belly like some dirty tidemark. We will no longer tolerate the inferior races that seek to drag us down into the mire of mediocrity. Make sure they listen carefully, Jew pig."

Carnarvon was shaking uncontrollably now, the bile in his throat seemed to be stuck like a thick immovable ball. Even if there were anyone about, to whom he could scream for help, he felt sure that he would be unable to utter a sound.

The madman spat into Jacob's face before removing his foot from his chest. He then used the whip to smooth the curious half cropped moustache that was still twitching from the force of the outburst. His expression became relaxed as he turned to face Carnarvon and he actually smiled.

"Gute Nacht, Herren."

The three men walked slowly away towards the beer hall as casually as if they had just been enjoying a breath of fresh air.

Carnarvon tried to stand but he felt light headed, then suddenly his vision clouded and blackness enveloped him.

Through the darkness he could see a faint light. It was slowly getting bigger.

As it grew, he realised a face was beginning to materialise, a face he recognised, a face that had haunted him in his dreams since the discovery of the tomb in Egypt.

He now intuitively knew that it was the face of something evil and monstrous.. The yellow eyes were wide with triumph and excitement. The mouth was set into a devilish grin and words were emanating forth, words spoken in some ancient language, yet somehow completely comprehensible to Carnarvon. The tone of the voice was warm in spite of to whom it belonged, almost conciliatory.

'You have served me well, Envoy. Now you may harvest the rewards that you deserve. You will be welcomed into my domain and live the rest of your days embraced as an immortal knowing that you played an implicit part in my

destiny and the destiny of those that we despise... we despise... .We despise.'

The face retreated into the darkness, the hoarse laughter echoing inside his head. Carnarvon's vision began to clear. His thoughts immediately returned to his friend Jacob and helping him to get to his feet. They would have to report the incident to the police. Wasn't there a police station in the next street?

As his eyes opened, he was surprised to see the pained expression of his daughter, Evelyn, staring down at him. She smiled, the relief apparent.

Carnarvon began to speak. "Jacob, is he..."

"Father, Jacob is fine." She touched his lips with a finger to quieten him. "You are fine too but you must rest, you've had a terrible experience."

"But I don't understand... how did you... how long have I..." There was a dull thudding in his temple now and he suddenly felt exhausted.

"Father, you must rest now. You have been unconscious for several days and the doctors were very worried. "

Carnarvon began to protest and tried to lift himself up but a sharp pain in his temple forced him back down.

Evelyn repeated her pleas for him to rest with tears in her eyes. "If you are well enough tomorrow, we will fly back to Egypt but it depends on what the doctor says this evening."

Carnarvon thought how much Evelyn resembled an angel as once more the darkness began to wrap itself round him.

It was a week later when Jacob read of his friend's death in the newspaper. The article said that Carnarvon had been bitten by an insect of some sort in Egypt and finally died in the grip of a terrible fever. Jacob knew differently.

The tears rolled onto Jacob's cheek and stung the scar that creased his face, the scar from the horsewhip of the man whose image was now imprinted onto his memory. A man whose picture he had since seen in propaganda leaflets that had been posted through doors all over Munich, the leader of the

'*Nationalsozialistische Deutsche Arbeiter Partei*'; Herr Adolf Hitler.

34

Bond Creek, Northern Territory Australia, 1997

Yabbie's was even quieter than usual, if that were possible. The dust storm that had been blowing the contents of the surrounding bush down Main Street was keeping the residents inside. Only the few hardened drinkers that had been propping up the bar on each of their previous visits now kept Steve and Kate company.

As it was impossible to sit on the veranda because of the swirling, red dust, they'd have to put up with the perpetual background noise of the television and the frequent drunken roars of laughter coming from around the pool table.

Kate looked at her watch again. It was ten past seven. They'd arranged to meet Brian at seven and she was getting impatient. Having spent another day wandering fruitlessly round more aboriginal sites, she was keen to question Brian some more about the pattern of visitations that he'd told them about the day before last.

Even more than before, she was convinced that the whole episode of the disappearances was somehow inextricably linked to the aboriginal sacred sites in some way. It was simply a matter of trying to discover what the link was. Kate looked up from her watch to find Steve looking at her.

"What?"

She wiped her mouth with the back of her hand self consciously in case it contained some remnants of the salted peanuts she'd been eating at the bar while they waited for their drinks.

Steve carried on looking and grinned.

"What? ...Steve you look like a bloody Cheshire cat, what's wrong?"

Steve took the top off his pint in an attempt to stop himself from grinning.

Wiping the froth from his lips, he put his pint down. Kate still stared at him with an expectant air.

"Well?"

"I'm sorry, Kate, it's nothing, really. I was just thinking how all this started and how we ended up sitting here in a middle-of -nowhere town waiting for an astronomer. Don't you think it's time to start thinking of getting back to London? You've tried your best..."

Kate's expectant expression had transformed into a resigned smile. He felt awful now.

"We've done as much as we could; maybe the whole thing *is* just a series of odd coincidences. I mean...we could be here forever trying to dig up another clue to a puzzle that doesn't even exist."

He was holding Kate's hand now, realising that he'd just probably stamped out the few remaining embers of her hopes.

He wasn't totally stupid; he realised the real reason why Kate was pursuing this thing so fanatically. He'd known more or less from the day she had suggested stopping on in Australia, back in Darwin.

Kate slid her hand from his and gave a huge sigh. "I suppose you're right. I just thought..." Her eyes were filling with tears. "I just thought that somehow I could ... do something."

The tears finally began to roll down her face. "I'm sorry

Steve, I shouldn't have dragged you into all this."

She reached into her pocket for a tissue and blew her nose.

Steve was still gazing at her and wondering how she even managed to look attractive blowing her nose.

He reached across for her hand again.

"All this, it's really about Edward, isn't it?" he whispered.

Kate looked up, her huge blue eyes filling with tears once more and nodded slowly.

Edward had been eighteen and had just started at college. He had come home for a long weekend for the first time since starting his course. He was so excited about everything; the new friends he'd made, the social life, his flat. He was simply overflowing with life.

Kate remembered feeling distinctly jealous when he was telling her all about the parties they had each weekend and the trips into the city to see rock bands at the Empire.

She was a year younger than her brother and would have to wait another twelve months before she could 'fly the nest' so to speak.

She and Edward had always been close and they spent the weekend together walking in the woods- Edward said he missed that, living in the suburbs.

For November, the weather had been unusually mild and on the Sunday he was due to go back, they were sitting in the garden waiting for their mother to finish packing all the washing he'd brought home with him before Kate drove him to the station. At least, that's what their parents thought.

In fact Edward had decided to hitch back and keep hold of the train fare that his father had kindly provided; a college social life required substantial funds.

He had persuaded Kate to drop him at the motorway

intersection where he could pick up a lift with a lorry driver or better still, an eligible, young, sex starved female executive commuting into the city in her company car. He always did have a good imagination.

When Kate had suggested that it might be dangerous, he had scoffed and produced a cardboard plaque with 'North, please' felt tipped on one side. When he flipped it over it had 'South, please' on the other. 'How do you think I got back here stupid?' he'd said affectionately hitting her over the head with the plaque: 'We poor students need every penny we can get.'

It was four o clock that afternoon when she dropped him off. He was wearing a huge grin, a green and brown combat jacket and had a stuffed to the top rucksack on his back.

'See you in three weeks, Sis', he waved as he walked away from the car.

It wasn't the fact that she or her parents heard nothing from Edward for a week that worried them; after all, he was enjoying himself too much to bother writing letters and had only been ringing home once a week, usually on a Saturday afternoon. It was the call from his Personal Tutor, Dr. Bell, enquiring why Edward hadn't attended any of his lectures all week. He'd asked round college and the students who shared his flat told him that he hadn't come back after the weekend. They had assumed he was ill.

Despite intense police enquiries over the next few months, neither Edward nor any of his belongings materialised. It was as if he had disappeared from the face of the Earth.

After a while the enquiries stopped and the police filed his name under 'Missing Persons'.

Her parents were distraught but entertained ideas that he had, for some inexplicable reason, gone abroad on some wild adventure. Kate was simply inconsolable. Deep down she knew Edward was not abroad somewhere. She knew in her heart that they would never see him again and it was all her fault. If only she had taken him to the station, persuaded him to catch the train...

Kate was dragged from her reverie by the sound of the door flying open. The dust storm was still raging outside and, as Brian entered, a cloud of whirling, red dust accompanied him. He reached behind himself and struggled to close the door, which was apparently about to be sucked off its hinges. Steve glanced at Kate who was rapidly trying to dry her eyes with a tissue.

Brian made his way over and Steve stood to shake his hand. "Glad you could make it. I thought you might decide to give it a miss with the storm and all."

"What, and miss out on a cold beer! Not to mention a bit of conversation, a man can go a bit strange having no one to talk to all day."

Brian smiled at Kate as he pulled off his coat and looked round for somewhere to hang it. Kate noticed he wasn't wearing his glasses; he looked even more handsome than he had at the observatory. She felt a tingle of excitement run through her as he turned to hang his coat on the back of his chair.

He sat down just as Steve returned from the bar with a fresh round of drinks.

"Aw, cheers mate," said Brian taking the heavy glass of beer from Steve and quaffing half of it in one go.

"Thirsty work, star gazing?" said Kate grinning.

"Sure is," said Brian downing the other half of his beer. He wiped the froth from his top lip and laughed. "Sorry about that, bloody mouth full of dirt from the storm." he explained.

"Do they happen very often out here?" asked Steve.

"Oh, once every couple o' weeks, I guess. Last one was

so bad, the north end o' town was almost buried, they reckon it took one bloke two days to dig his truck out."

Kate noticed Brian's eyes watering. They were a little red too and he kept rubbing them with the back of his hands.

"Dust got to your eyes, Brian? "she asked in a concerned tone. " I've got an eye bath in the first aid kit back at the motel...."

"No, they'll be fine in a minute. It's these new contact lenses; they're a bloody pain. It's only the second time I've worn them. I should've known better than to try 'em out whilst a storm was blowing. Anyone for another?" He grinned, holding up his empty glass.

Brian went to the bar to get another drink and Steve leaned forward conspiratorially. "So, he wore his new contacts despite knowing that the dust storm was coming? Obviously wanted to look his best tonight."

Kate's eyes met his. "Can't think why, can you?" he whispered.

Kate felt her cheeks redden and she kicked his shin playfully under the table. She looked round to the bar and she saw Brian looking their way. She thought of Michael thousands of miles away in England and a jolt of guilt ran through her. She cursed inwardly: '*No sign of a decent man for two years then two turn up within the space of a couple of months.'*

It was after eleven when Steve announced that he was 'bushed ' and was ready to hit the sack. Kate, frightened that it might signal the end of the evening and Brian's departure, tried to persuade him to stay for a nightcap, but it was to no avail.

Much to Kate's relief, Brian stood up and patted Steve on the back, "Righto mate, so I'll see you in the morning, bright and early for breakfast at seven."

Brian had explained earlier that he'd booked into the motel for the night and that he'd like to accompany them on their 'research trip' tomorrow as it would make a pleasant change from sitting alone in the observatory.

Although Steve and Kate agreed that it would be difficult to search the sites with Brian there, without revealing the real reason for the 'expedition', they decided for the time being not to tell him any more.

Steve looked at Kate and smiled. "Goodnight then ...I'll see you in the morning."

Kate once again found herself blushing as Steve left without looking back.

Now by themselves, there was silence for the first time that evening. They looked at each other, and then both began speaking at the same time. They laughed and somehow, at that moment, Kate knew she was infatuated.

"So, how about that nightcap?" said Brian, rising from his chair.

"If you like," Kate hesitated. "I've got a bottle of Scotch in my room back at the motel."

She looked up at Brian to gauge his response; she'd surprised herself by what she'd just said, so no doubt he would be a little shocked.

Brian smiled and nodded. "Sounds like a good idea to me. You can show me which sites you've visited already and which ones you want to see tomorrow." He turned to grab his jacket.

Kate's stomach lurched; looking at maps wasn't what she had in mind but she was sure she was reading the situation correctly. She thought back to Steve's words earlier, about the glasses and Brian wanting to look his best.

"Right, let's go." Brian said, zipping up his coat.

Brian's arms slipped round Kate's waist the second they were in the room. He spun her round to face him and their eyes met momentarily. The excitement that had been building up inside Kate suddenly overwhelmed any guilt that she had been feeling about her emotions and Michael, and she stretched up to kiss him.

His lips were warm and moist and his mouth opened slightly as the kiss became more passionate.

Kate was taken by surprise as an image of Michael's face popped into her mind. She squeezed her eyes tighter and tried to erase Michael's face and redraw Brian's in its place.

Brian lifted her up gently and her eyes opened for a second, although they were still kissing. Brian's eyes were closed. She tried again to free herself of Michael's face but she couldn't and she felt her gut tighten as the guilt welled up again.

Brian carried her forward towards the bed but Kate, realising that she couldn't go through with it, was about to pull away when she heard his feet connect with something on the floor and there was a loud 'pop'. She was thrown forward unceremoniously onto the bed as Brian struggled to keep his balance. She felt his body tumble over her and crash onto the bed beside her but he was too close to the end and his momentum carried him over the edge and onto the floor.

There was a loud thud as he landed heavily on the thinly carpeted floorboards.

"Brian, are you alright?"

Kate rolled across the bed and looked down. Brian was on his back holding in one hand the crushed map cylinder that had caused him to fall. It was crushed in the middle and the lid had been ejected as his foot had pressed down on it. The tops of the maps were sticking out of the end.

Kate giggled at the sight, and Brian grinned, half in amusement, half in embarrassment. Kate knew then that whatever romantic scenario she had envisioned earlier was not going to happen. The tightness in her stomach relaxed and she breathed a sigh of relief. She jumped off the bed and grabbed the bottle of whisky from the cabinet.

"Ready for that nightcap now? "

Brian smiled and nodded, and Kate knew that he understood.

She poured two measures of whisky into the tumblers and turned to find Brian spreading out the crushed maps out on the bed. Kate handed him his drink.

The top map was the one that Kate had marked to show the locations of the last known sightings of the missing persons. There were crosses spread out across it.

"Are these the sites you've been to already, or the ones you hope to visit?" asked Brian, rubbing his eyes.

" ... Er... not exactly " stammered Kate. " These are the location of the sites we hope to visit," she said lifting the top map away to reveal the one underneath. The marks on the second map were more or less identical to the first, the crosses just deviating slightly in position. The pattern was not lost on Brian and she could see the confusion on his face. He picked up the first map again and Kate realised that she would have to tell him the truth.

Brian listened to Kate's explanation for the next half an hour after which she poured them both another drink.

"Well, I can't deny that there does seem to be a correlation between the sites and the disappearances but apart from the cap and the watch, you don't really have that much to go on." Brian rubbed his eyes again.

"Do you mind if I use your bathroom? These bloody lenses are killing me."

Kate felt a stab of guilt remembering what Steve had said about Brian only wearing them in the first place to impress her.

"No, of course not. Would you like me to get you that eyebath?"

"No, that's okay, I'll just take 'em out to give my eyes a rest and I'll be fine."

He smiled through red, watery eyes and she felt flattered and a little sad that the evening hadn't quite gone to plan.

Kate stared at the map, looking for something that 'probably didn't exist' (Steve's words again). There was a thud and an "Ouch!" from behind her and she turned to see Brian clutching his knee and grimacing at the bowl of the toilet that stuck out a little from the wall.

"Shit, now my eyes feel better, I just can't see a bloody thing!" he laughed.

Kate grinned, "Never mind, I'll walk you back to your room later. Don't want you falling down the stairs and waking up all the guests, do we?"

"All the guests being Steve, of course."

Brian walked across to the bed and looked at the map again.

"I guess you think I'm mad then..." Brian didn't take her cue. "...Running round in the bush, looking for things that could belong to anyone..."

Kate looked up when Brian still didn't respond. He was squinting over the map, scratching the back of his head.

"What is it, Brian?" she asked realising that he was scrutinising the marks carefully.

"Kate, you're not going to believe this...in fact, I can hardly believe it myself...."

It was Kate's turn to look puzzled.

"These crosses you've made on the map are in the exact position of specific star constellations. Look...."

He pointed to a cluster of marks. " I didn't realise until I took my lenses out. Screw your eyes up, it helps get rid of the map detail. These marks here would be the Southern Cross and these here would make up the constellation of Centaurus. The aboriginal burial sites are a terrestrial representation of the stars!"

Although Kate didn't know much about astronomy, she was aware that several of the world's ancient civilisations had built temples and monuments, which mirrored the stars.

"You mean all the sites on the map are in line with a particular star in the sky?"

"Not exactly. The pattern is the same but presumably at some point in the past, possibly when the tombs were first used, they would have mirrored the pattern exactly."

"This is incredible. I knew that the Ancient Egyptians built the pyramids at Giza to represent the stars that make up the Constellation of Orion and that some people believe that there are lots of sites in South America that have close links to the patterns of stars and planets but this... I've never heard anyone suggest aboriginal burial sites have some kind of order. After all, most of the sites are natural caves, aren't they?"

Brian was rubbing his chin, caught in deep thought.

"I was just thinking ' *Skyglobe*' would tell us the date that the stars were in the position to align with the sites...."

"Sky globe?"

"I'm sorry; because of something called precession of the earth's axis, the positions of the stars, relative to the earth, alter slowly over thousands of years. '*Skyglobe*' is a computer program that enables us to 'wind back' time to any epoch and see where the stars would have been at any given moment in time"

"So you could use it to see when the stars would line up and maybe give us a date when the tombs might first have been used? "

"Exactly, I don't know what significance it might have to your *disappearances,* but it's certainly interesting, I've never read anything that has suggested a link between stars and aboriginal tombs before.

"Maybe we could have a look at it first thing tomorrow

before we set off," suggested Kate.

She looked at Brian's face. The look of excitement on his face told her that he'd have driven out to the observatory then if he'd not had too much to drink. She realised that whoever eventually became romantically involved with him would have a job competing with his passion for astronomy.

35

Munich, 10th November 1923

The yolk of the egg finally gave way after the third prod and Jacob pushed the piece of bread into the warm gooey liquid. He would have to have words with Elga, his housekeeper; a three-minute egg shouldn't take three prods.

As he lifted the bread to his mouth, he opened his newspaper out onto the table in front of him.

A photograph of the previous night's riots at the Odeonplatz dominated the front page. The picture showed apparent chaos with mass brawls taking place and bodies being carried head-high above crowds of what the paper described as, political subversives.

The article, which accompanied the photograph, described how the War Ministry offices had been the subjects of an attack by a large group of right wing militants led by someone called Ernst Rohm. They were demanding the resignation of major political figures and an end to the talk of Bavarian independence.

Apparently two nights previously, Gustav Ritter von Kahr, the leader of the Bavarian government had been forced to flee under armed guard from the Burgerbraukeller after a meeting he was speaking at had been stormed by members of the National Sozialistische Deutsche Arbeiter Partei. The riots at the Odeonplatz were seen as an escalation of the events there.

Jacob scanned the picture with interest; the NASDAP or Nazi Party as they were more colloquially known, had been gaining more and more support recently from the general populace who were becoming increasingly disillusioned with post war Germany and a government who were seen as impotent.

Jacob's heart suddenly missed a beat and he choked back the egg and bread in his mouth, coughing so violently that Elga, working in the kitchen, rushed in to check that he was all right. (She had been overly cautious about his health ever since '*the incident*')

She handed him a napkin and wiped off the spattered egg from the front of his newspaper. Jacob struggled to regain his composure and waved her away with a look that suggested he was embarrassed by her maternal concern.

As she closed the door, he looked back down at the picture. His eyes came to rest again on a number of men at the rear of the marchers, the brown shirts and black ski hats...

It was the first time since that night that he'd seen the uniform and it brought everything rushing back into his mind.

His hands trembled as he lifted the paper closer and scrutinised the photograph more closely, concentrating particularly on the faces of the men being carried: those obviously injured or possibly dead. It would be more than he could wish for. If only...

He suddenly became aware that he was tracing the line of the scar across his face with his finger; at least that wound was now healed. The psychological wounds would always be open as long as the vermin who were involved with the Nazi party were still alive.

He couldn't make out the features of most of the people in the photograph and a tear of frustration fell onto the newspaper. He had to wipe his eyes with the napkin before he could finish reading the report.

During the rioting, at least fourteen people were said to have been killed but the paper could not confirm any names. They could however confirm that... (The column was continued on the inside pages.) Jacob turned the page with frail, shaking hands. Another picture dominated this page. Staring up at him from the paper were the eyes of the madman that he hoped he would never see again. Eyes that were as black and evil as they had been nine months earlier when he and his good friend George Stanhope had been assaulted in the Karlstrasse. The small moustache was still there too; he remembered how he had been vain enough to smooth it down with his whip after he'd beaten them both to the ground with it.

Jacob tried to swallow but his mouth was devoid of moisture. He felt the bile rising in his throat and beads of perspiration rolled down from his brow stinging his eyes. He felt as though an invisible hand had squirmed its way up his anal passage and was pulling at his intestines threatening to tear them free at any moment. Then his eyes managed to re-focus on the entire picture.

Two armed policemen were forcibly restraining the man he knew as Herr Adolf Hitler. On the floor to the side of the three men was another man, lying in a pool of blood. He was either dead or seriously injured. Despite the man's eyes being closed, Jacob was sure he recognised him as being the man who had originally stepped out of the alley in the Karlstrasse to ask for a light for his cigarette. He was almost certain...

He closed his eyes and searched the recesses of his mind, trying to rekindle the embers of memories that he had spent the last eight months trying to stamp out. He was sure the man called Hitler had referred to him as Ulrich that night.

He opened his eyes again, the pace of his heart had

begun to slow, and the tears that rolled down his cheeks now were not borne of frustration but of hope...hope that the government would see the uprising for what it was: High treason. For Jacob knew that treason, if proven, was still punishable by execution. He pulled his silver 'Star of David' pendant from his waistcoat and began to pray.

36

Greenwich, London. 1997

Donovan added yet another crisp packet to the growing pile of debris in the footwell of the Mondeo's passenger seat. As well as crisp packets, the pile consisted of polystyrene coffee cups, empty plastic sandwich cartons and a variety of chocolate wrappers. He could now fully understand why so many of the American detectives in the fly-on -the-wall documentaries on satellite were three stone overweight and looked like they'd slept in their suits.

A stakeout was probably the quickest route to a heart attack that he could think of, especially with his penchant for illicit foods like salted peanuts and Twiglets.

He glanced down at his watch again; three and a half hours and no sign of anyone coming or leaving the offices. That in itself was strange; a company that could be commissioned for such high profile work as the Millennium Dome should surely be a hive of activity. This, according to Charlie, his friend at the DTI, was supposed to be their main office.

He checked his notepad again, the hastily scribbled address that Charlie had provided him with over the phone that morning stared up at him;

Beaumont International Construction, 146A Station Mews, Greenwich.

He looked across at the offices as if to confirm the

address; a pointless exercise really as he had checked a dozen times already. This *was* 146A Station Mews, although the offices themselves were totally anonymous from the outside. The offices were actually situated above an estate agent's called *'House busters'*. Predictably, there was a hand painted sign in assorted day glow colours stuck to the inside of the window exclaiming:

'Can't find the property you're looking for? Then who ya gonna call...? Ring now on 0171 289 6754

Above the offices on the second floor, there was no company billboard and no brass nameplate. In fact, there was nothing to suggest it was even occupied. It was a Tuesday morning, prime business time, and yet there wasn't even a light on inside.

Donovan tapped the dashboard agitatedly. Now that he'd polished off the last of his provisions, his hands were redundant. His lips were pursed as if he were whistling although no sound came out (something he always did when he was struggling to reach a decision.). Should he give it up as a bad job or should he take the dog by the bollocks and go and see if anyone *was* actually in the office?

He wasn't even sure what he had expected to find. It was just that journalist's itch that he knew he couldn't resist scratching.

Suddenly, the decision was made and he was out of the car and halfway across the road. He had to stop on the white lines in the middle of the road to allow a bus to pass in front of him. Through the windows of the bus he noticed a dark blue Range Rover pulling up outside the estate agent's. He recognised it immediately as Henderson's.

Before the bus had passed, he turned and scurried swiftly back to the Mondeo. Fortunately, the way he was parked meant that in climbing into the driver's side, he was obscured from view by the car.

He made a meal of getting his key into the lock whilst at the same time watching two men emerge from the Range Rover. Neither of the men, he realised, was Henderson but both were familiar to him. One was Henderson's P.A and chauffeur and the other was the workman he'd seen at the construction site talking to the Minister.

They disappeared, not into the side door, which Donovan assumed led up to 146A, but into the estate agents. Through the large front windows he watched as they made pleasantries with the two secretaries inside before going through a door at the back of the shop. A few seconds later, a light came on in the office window upstairs.

Why would the main offices of an international construction company be hidden away behind the facade of a small, backwater estate agent? Something wasn't right. Donovan knew that construction companies invariably had subsidiary companies, which acted as retail outlets for their properties but *'Housebusters'* - he didn't think so. It had all the hallmarks of a small independent: white woodchip wallpaper curling up at the joins to boot. Charlie hadn't mentioned anything about them having subsidiaries either.

He jotted down the number on the day-glow poster, not because a course of action was forming in his mind, but more because his hands were still short of something to do.

When he looked up from his pad, he noticed the light in the office had gone off. A few seconds later and the two men came back into the shop. Donovan noticed that Henderson's assistant was now carrying a suitcase that he hadn't had when they'd first arrived. They left the shop, climbed into the Range Rover, and drove off.

Before Donovan could even think of starting his car and following them, they were out of sight, swallowed by the morning traffic. He banged the steering wheel in frustration.

"Three and a half fucking hours for that," he whispered,

resisting the urge to rip the steering wheel from its column; after all it was only hired. He thrust his hand into his inside pocket searching for his mobile; he'd give Charlie another ring and see if he had anything else on Beaumont.

As he punched in the numbers on the keyboard, an idea jumped into his mind and he let out an involuntary giggle.

He looked across at the estate agent's office, and weighed up the two women inside who seemed to be doing more gossiping and laughing than attending to any business. They were both in their middle to late thirties, he reckoned. He tapped his bottom lip with an index finger, "You never know," he said out loud. "It might just come off."

He returned the phone to his pocket and started the engine. He drove round the corner into a narrow road and parked up out of sight of the office. Upon getting out of the car, he took off his jacket, loosened his tie, and rolled up the sleeves of his shirt. He extracted his Press Card from his wallet and slid it into his shirt pocket along with a ballpoint pen. His notebook and mobile in one hand and the final touch, ('You clever bastard, Donovan' he'd whispered to himself when he'd spotted this) the toolkit from the boot of the car, completed his transformation to an 'on-site technician.'

Angela and Marion were discussing the merits of the latest new under wire bra to hit the shops: the *Bioform Wonderbra,* when the little bell on the door indicated that they had a customer.

They both looked up as Donovan entered the shop, all smiles, and whistling (although he didn't realise the significance of it) the theme tune to *'Mission Impossible';* he was merely getting into character.

"Morning, girls," he said chirpily, leaning on the desk and chewing ostentatiously on an imaginary wad of gum (another prop designed to give him the appeal of the chirpy cockney, just- doing -my- job but -always on- the-pull - whatever -the situation type bloke.)

Marion and Angela traded glances for a millisecond. The telepathic message; *'I saw him first'*, relaying its way in both directions simultaneously.

Donovan pulled the Press card with his photograph on out of his shirt pocket, waved it vaguely in the girls' general direction, and replaced it before either could stand up to inspect it.

"Stone Security... annual inspection?"

He looked at Angela and then at Marion and back to Angela with a feigned look of puzzlement. Angela looked at Marion, her superior by approximately three months, as if to say: 'Well, go on, sort it out.'

Before she could speak, Donovan continued. "Don't tell me you've not had the notification..." He placed his hand on his forehead. "Bloody YTS, I told Trevor not to put 'em on the bloody phones... Makin' tea an ' brushin ' up, that's what YTS are for, not making bloody phone calls."

He pulled out his mobile and prodded a few numbers whilst shaking his head disparagingly and raising his eyebrows in what he hoped was a 'never mind they've got to start somewhere, I suppose' type expression. (He knew that women apparently found the traits of tolerance and forgiveness in a man very attractive).

Donovan heard the dialling tone finish and the click of an answering machine, then the sound of his own voice announcing that he wasn't at home at the moment.

"Wotcher Trev, yeah it's Dave. I'm at Station Mews in Greenwich...Listen mate they've not had notification again. It's the third one since yesterday...yeah, it's not on, mate, is it? Yeah okay... I'll complete this one but can you check they've notified Marylebone Street. It's bloody embarrassin' this...yeah, see you later."

Donovan held up both hands and shrugged his apology

before starting to unravel the hire car tool kit.

"Righto let's get started. Point me the way to the box."

He rubbed his hands together in a gesture that indicated he was keen to get started. "Any chance of a cuppa luv? I'm parched. Three sugars." *'Don't push your luck Donovan'* a voice inside his head whispered.

Marion pulled rank on Angela with a sideways glance and Angela stood up reluctantly to make the drink. Marion also stood and walked round the desk pointing to a cupboard by the door. "I take it, you mean the alarm?" she said smiling.

Donovan smiled back confidently and nodded. Despite the smile, his insides were knotted like an eel on a fishing line. With Marion sitting on her desk directly behind him, Donovan took out the smallest Philips screwdriver from the toolkit and began unscrewing the first of four screws on the box. He hoped Marion wouldn't notice that it wasn't really the right size.

As he struggled with the screws, he could feel Marion's gaze on his back. He was hoping she wasn't going to start quizzing him about the job when Angela returned from the back room with a tray of tea and some neatly laid out Digestives.

"Tea's up," she announced.

Donovan glanced round, thankful that Marion had moved away slightly "Thanks, I'll only be a second with this now, I'll just check the battery." Even though the last screw still hadn't come out he began to replace the others. "Great, everything looks fine in there. All done for another year." He replaced the screwdriver inside the roll and picked up his tea from the tray.

He tried to avoid wincing as the syrupy, sickly tea filled his mouth.

Three sugars? Where had that come from?

"Tea alright for you?" Angela asked, noticing his expression.

"Erm... yes, lovely, thanks. I just remembered that I've er.... got to test the alarm. Only I've left the bloody codes in the van. I'll have to nip out and get them." He looked at his watch and pretended to calculate whether or not he had time. Marion took the bait like a ravenous salmon and made an executive decision.

" 'Ere, that's okay; I know you're pushed for time. Save you going back out, the code's erm... 342...67...5."

Donovan looked at his watch again and smiled. "That's brilliant, thanks very much; I'll be coming here every week to check the system... now that I know what a great cup o' tea you make as well.

Angela blushed.

Donovan walked over to the box, praying that it was similar to his home alarm; a simple *Enter, Code, Set* procedure. He pressed the *'Enter'* button, typed in the code, and pushed the *'Set'* button. There was a slight pause then the staccato beeps indicating that it had been armed began. He let it continue for a few seconds before hitting the *'Unset'* button.

Relieved, he turned, gathered up the toolkit, and beamed a final smile at the two women before flouncing cockily out of the office.

Angela and Marion looked at each other and burst into a fit of giggles before Angela noticed with disappointment that he hadn't finished his tea.

Outside, on the way back to the car, Donovan quickly scribbled down the alarm code in his notebook before he forgot it whilst at the same time congratulating himself on his sterling performance.

37

Munich, Germany 12th November 1923

Jacob held the newspaper in a clenched fist high above his head. His prayers had been answered.

Tears of joy rolled down his cheeks onto his breakfast tray and the still intact three-minute egg in its cup.

"Elga, Elga, come quickly, woman!" he shouted to his housekeeper, who responded quickly to the uncharacteristic boisterousness in her charge's voice and rushed into the room.

"Elga, get my clothes ready! I must go to the Synagogue at once, I have some wonderful news..."

Elga began to ask what could be so important that it couldn't wait until after he'd eaten his breakfast but Jacob literally shoved her back out of the room to get his things.

He sat down again and smoothed the crumpled newspaper out onto the desk; he wanted to read it again...just to make sure.

As he 'ironed' it flat, the smiling face of Adolf Hitler beamed out at him. (The picture was one that was taken a few months before his arrest). Underneath were two smaller pictures of other Nazi Party members who had also been found guilty of treason alongside Hitler.

He looked closely at the picture of Hitler and for the first time he was aware that he could look at his face and feel no fear.

Although he hadn't been sentenced to execution as Jacob had hoped, five years in prison was a good start. The article also spoke of rumours that the Nazi Party was to be banned, which, if it were true would probably mean the end of Hitler's political ambitions; few parties could survive being without their leader for five years let alone being banned as well.

Jacob felt elated, he would go to the synagogue to share the news with his friends then, he decided, they would celebrate over lunch at his brother's restaurant. The smile on his face diminished a little, if only his good friend George had still been alive to experience this moment....

He stood up to telephone his brother and make the arrangements when suddenly a sharp pain shot across his chest and down his arm. He stumbled forward and managed to catch himself against the table before he fell. He stood still for a second, the sweat pouring from him, his lips dry.

He was breathing heavily now, sucking deep breaths down into his lungs. He didn't feel well; maybe the celebrations would have to wait until dinner.

He composed himself and turned to sit when another pain even more intense than the first gripped him. His chest felt like it was being forced between the giant rollers of a printing press. He began to feel faint and tried again to sit but he was too weak to pull out the chair and his own weight carried him backwards away from the table. He reached out clutching for the end of the table but his fingers only found the newspaper on top.

As he fell to the ground, it was as if his world had gone into slow motion. It took an age for him to fall and as he did so, the realisation that he was having a heart attack ran like the sand in an egg timer draining from top to bottom, into his brain.

He could feel every exaggerated, erratic beat of his heart pounding in his head and he knew then that he was going to die...

Bump, bump... the image of his adoring mother, crying on the day of his Bar mitzvah... Bump, bump ...his father placing his first bank account payment booklet into his hands and telling him to "trust no-one in business" ... Bump, bump...........his wife's beautiful smiling face on their wedding day...

Bump, bump... his employees' cheers when he opened his second factory just outside Munich and told them that they could expect more money in their pay packets... Bump, bump...His friend, George Stanhope dining with him at his club on finally realising his Egyptian dream, Bump....

His back hit the floor with a dull thud and literally knocked the last breath that Jacob would ever take from his body.

His eyes were still open as the newspaper that he'd grabbed at as he'd fallen, finally slid off the edge of the table and drifted slowly, gracefully down towards him.

As he lay staring up from the floor, the last face he ever saw before he finally succumbed to death was that of Herr Adolf Hitler.... smiling.

38

Landsberg Prison, Germany, January 1924

The key's appearance began to change.

The dull, murky green patina was replaced by a warm, vibrant umber that seemed almost to glow in the darkened room. The carved figure of the woman and the symbol underneath seemed to be raised even more from the surface of the key as if something were pushing them up from inside to highlight their significance.

Hitler was on his knees in front of the small wooden table on which the key lay. It had begun to tremble a few minutes ago and as he watched, it appeared to be getting more frenetic by the second. The tapping noises it made as it moved were almost hypnotic. His face was transfixed; a mixture of elation, terror and anticipation.

Ever since he had acquired the key from a degenerate Jewpig one evening after a rally in Munich, he had been waiting for *something* to happen.

From the second he had held it, he was sure it was special; the energy that surged through him whenever he held it, the overwhelming feeling of power, and most of all... the moulding of all the thought processes that had somehow been floating about without direction in his mind for the past two decades into something awesome yet incomprehensible ... incomprehensible, that is, until now.

As he stared at the key, it was as if his mind were being

sucked dry; all the troubled thoughts and malformed concepts that never seemed to grow into anything but tormented nightmares were dragged screaming from him to be replaced by clear, logical plans of action. They were essentially the same ideas and philosophies that he'd been nurturing since his early days as a struggling artist in Vienna but now they all made perfect sense.

Although it wasn't yet dark outside, the room was almost devoid of light.

He gradually became aware of a low-pitched humming that seemed to be filling his head. It felt as if the sound was emanating from inside him and dissipating out into the room, creating a direct link between him and the key. The figure on the key seemed to be growing larger as he watched, and the trembling made it look as though it were dancing.

In the blackness, the key was like a beacon, throbbing, beckoning. The warm umber had now become a burning intense red and the humming in his head surged louder with each throb.

Suddenly, there was a brilliant explosion of light and he felt an excruciating stab of pain in his temple. The humming noise had become louder and the entire room felt as though it were vibrating.

He squeezed his eyes shut as the pain gripped his brain. It felt like the top of his head had been flipped off as burning embers poured in. He tore at his head with his fingers trying to stem the relentless tide of pain, clumps of wiry, black hair falling to the floor.

The humming seemed to distort now into a cacophony of screams like the wail of a thousand lost souls crying out and he was aware of his eardrums stretching. Blood and plasma trickled from his ears and ran down his neck. A blinding light scorched his eyeballs even though his eyes were closed and his head was thrown backwards so violently that he was certain it would be torn from him.

As the sound round him reached a crescendo, the breath was forced from his lungs by an incredible blow to his chest. He forced open his eyes to see what had hit him but there was nothing there, just the key, still glowing on the table.

Then as suddenly as it had begun, everything stopped. He held himself rigid for a few seconds waiting for the pain to resume but nothing came... then he heard a growl... not a threatening growl, he sensed, but a low, satisfied growl, the kind a predator makes when it has finally made a kill after a long wait and is about to begin devouring the still alive flesh of the prey.

His eyes snapped open and he looked up towards the table. The eyes of the figure were open and staring at him with an intensity he could almost feel. The eyes were thin, yellow, and evil. The growl came again and once more it seemed to emanate from inside *him*. The growl gave way to a laugh and then a voice:

"You must listen carefully, disciple. I do not yet have the strength that I need.... You are the one for whom I have been searching. The time has come for you to fulfil your destiny. You can achieve everything for which you have strived ... not only will you rule the world but the people of the world will worship you as their saviour. You will be held on high as the new Messiah and all this in return for a small favour...."

Hitler was shivering now uncontrollably. Despite the intense heat coming from the key, he was freezing cold. The underside of his moustache was coated with a thin coating of frost as the condensation from his breath burst forth in erratic rasps.

His eyeballs were bulging slightly from their sockets,

the tiny blood vessels on the whites of them haemorrhaging one after the other and causing him to 'cry' tears of blood which dripped down his cheeks before freezing on his face. He was vaguely aware every so often of a snapping sound as his hands which were clasped together in front of him were squeezed so tightly together that the small bones in them gave way under the pressure and fragmented into a mush of flesh and sinew. His fingernails dug into the soft mush and threatened to emerge from the other side. Yet, he was oblivious to it all; the eyes on the engraving held his gaze.

"I need the souls of ten million...souls who are destined for purgatory because their time has come early ...souls I can harvest before they enter into the afterlife ...souls whose life force I can harness..."

The voice became quieter suddenly and sounded almost conspiratorial, almost as if it were suddenly aware that somebody might be listening.

"And if they happen to be ten million descendants of the so called... Son of God, then that will truly be a bonus that will make the Final Reckoning all the sweeter...You need to listen carefully."

39

Beaumont International Construction Head office, Greenwich , 1997

Donovan scanned the street in both directions. There was little traffic and, apart from the odd insomniac out walking their dog, very few pedestrians. He looked at his watch, the red digital display shone up at him: 00:05. He scanned the street again, all clear; it was now or never.

He pulled his coat round him checking that the torch and 'master key' were in the pocket and strode briskly across the road toward the *'Housebusters'* office.

Fortunately, the crime figures in this part of Greenwich were not high enough to warrant steel shutters on most small business premises. With another quick glance round, Donovan slid the 'key' into the lock and pushed open the door.

The familiar shrill warning beeps of the alarm sounded like an air raid siren and he was sure they were loud enough to be heard right along the street.

Flicking on the torch, he stepped quickly across to the alarm finger pad and typed in the code: 342675.

To his immense relief, the beeping came to an abrupt halt and he let out a lungful of breath that he hadn't realised he had been holding in for the last minute and a half.

"Thanks, Marion," he whispered, remembering the ease with which he had extracted the code from the gullible shop manageress.

He stayed perfectly still for a few minutes to make sure his entrance had not attracted any attention before walking to the back of the shop where he'd seen Henderson's P.A and the man from the construction site go two days before. He walked through a door, which led into a small kitchen area housing a kettle, a sink, and a microwave oven.

To his right was another door, the one leading upstairs, he assumed. He carefully closed the kitchen door thankful for the barrier it provided and turned on his torch again. Once again, the master key opened the door without so much as a click.

A steep flight of stairs led up into the office above and Donovan flicked off the switch of the torch and ascended cautiously. Even though he knew there was no one up there, his mind kept filling up with images of scar-faced henchmen and baseball bats.

He paused at the top of the stairs allowing his eyes to adjust to the dark. He could make out a desk and filing cabinet but apart form a telephone and what he assumed was a fax machine sitting on the desk, there was nothing. Once again, the ludicrous idea that this was supposed to be the main office of an international construction company brought an involuntary smile to his face.

He was silently congratulating himself on his ability to uncover a story when the silence was shattered by the telephone ringing. Donovan had instinctively turned to run back down the stairs before realising what it was and was stopped in his tracks by the sound of the fax machine engaging. He walked over to the desk and hunkered down beside the machine. He shone the torch onto the floor to minimise the glow and lifted up the thin paper that the machine had just spat out. The fax read:

Greetings Brothers,

'The Day of Atonement' is nearly upon us. (Daniel 8: 14)

The 2300 Day Prophecy will be realised and the work of the Messiah will finally be complete.

I have the key and look forward to the meeting on the Eighteenth. The details you sent regarding travel arrangements are fine. I will be arriving at Euston on the 09:15 from Birmingham New Street.

Winston.

Donovan read the message twice before the word 'key' slapped him in the face. That was the word that Henderson had used to describe the weird talisman that *he* had acquired from Brady several weeks before.

At the time, Donovan had wondered why he had kept calling it a key. When he had unravelled it from the grubby cotton handkerchief for the first time, it looked more like a small statue than a key. Donovan also recalled how having the key in his possession had given him an incredibly uneasy feeling. He had been relieved when he'd finally delivered it to Henderson.

Donovan looked at the fax again. Could there be two keys? And if so, why exactly was Henderson willing to pay so much to have them?

He reached inside his jacket for his pad and pen and jotted down the number from which the fax had originated. Donovan's mind was whirring now but he was aware that he'd been inside the offices for a good ten minutes. He made his way across to the filing cabinet and reached for the top drawer. It slid open with a slight grating noise. Inside were no more than a dozen pocket files. Donovan deftly flicked through them, looking for anything that might link the firm to Henderson or the Dome, or to anything for that matter. After several minutes staring at meaningless pieces of correspondence to manufacturing firms, Donovan realised he really didn't know what he was searching for.

It was only when he came to the next to last file that he found anything of interest. The first thing he found was a list of directors for the firm giving points of contact; the second was a series of site plans for the Dome. More interestingly for Donovan was the electrical schematic that was stapled onto the back of the plans. The previous seven site plans were obviously drawn up by the same firm; the style and format were all consistent. The schematic, however, was very different. It was incredibly complex and detailed; the circuitry that was to be laid down in the perimeter channel at the base of the Dome; the exact location where Donovan had seen the meeting take place between Henderson and the Beaumont people at the site.

Donovan laid out the plans and the list and took several photographs of each before slipping them back into the filing cabinet. Had Donovan not looked in the last pocket file, on reaching his apartment and examining all the material, he probably would have dismissed everything he had so far as elements of a simple business transaction. After all, what exactly did he have: A meeting at a construction site where a manila envelope changed hands (it might have contained the very plans at which he had been looking), a computer database listing frequent payments to an engineering firm, and a dodgy location for a main office of a supposedly international engineering firm. Not exactly Watergate was it!

As it turned out, the last file contained something that set Donovan's mind racing. There was a large, white envelope, inside of which, were a set of photographs, taken clandestinely with a telephoto lens. They were all of one man: Vernon Howell, aka David Koresh. Also in the pocket file was a dossier on a so-called Doomsday cult: the Branch

Davidians.

Flicking through it, Donovan was amazed by the amount of information it contained. There was a complete life history of Howells and his rise to become leader of one of the most infamous cults in America. Donovan was particularly familiar with them because the Waco siege had been one of the major events that occurred in his first year in London trying to get his foot in the door of Fleet Street.

What possible connection could Beaumont Engineering have with The Branch Davidians?

Something suddenly jumped into his mind. He turned and reread the fax... *The Day of Atonement.* He closed his eyes tightly trying to recall what he could about the sect. He was sure they believed in some kind of second coming; a day when the world would be cleansed of all evil...The Day of Atonement.

A noise from downstairs suddenly broke his reverie. Donovan cursed; he wouldn't have time to photograph any of the information. He slid the envelope and dossier back inside the file and slid the drawer shut. He could hear voices now, two men speaking. His heart was racing and he looked round searching for a place to hide.

"The alarm's been left off; we'll have to have a word with Marion about that."

"I wouldn't mind 'avin' a word with Marion full stop."

"Ah, she'd eat you fer breakfast, would Marion."

"That's what I'd be hoping for."

The conversation was followed by raucous laughter. Donovan, for the first time, noticed another door in the office. Of course: he'd noticed a side door when he'd first come to the shop. If it was that one, it led out onto the road.

He heard a key slip into the lock at the bottom of the stairs and the voices grew louder as the door opened. He was fumbling desperately in his jacket pocket now for the master key, the images of the scar-faces emerging once more in his mind. He heard the first footsteps on the stairs as his fingers clasped the cool metal of the master key. Carefully, he slid it into the lock praying that it wouldn't finally let him down. He twisted the key. Nothing happened and he cursed. Then he realised in his panic he'd twisted it the wrong way. Suddenly, he felt the door give and he gratefully pushed his way through and gently eased the door shut behind him.

In front of him was indeed a staircase leading down to the door at the side of the offices. It appeared to not have been used for some time judging by the variety of cardboard boxes that cluttered every step.

He contemplated staying put and listening at the door to see if he could glean any information but the images of the henchmen were too strong. He negotiated his way through the cardboard boxes and let himself out onto the street. He noticed a blue BMW parked on the double yellows in front of the shop. Thankfully, the driver had decided not to wait in the car. Considering his predicament, Donovan surprised himself by having the presence of mind to memorise the registration number before taking off at a brisk pace down the street.

40

Warranboola Observatory, Northern Territory Australia, 1997

Brian moved the mouse across the screen and selected another date. Immediately, the constellations altered their positions. Kate looked over his shoulder and waited for him to comment. They had now travelled back in time nearly twelve thousand years and the positions of the constellations were miraculously getting closer to the positions of the actual aboriginal sites.

"Can't be far off now, they're almost identical to the sites... let's try another...say... five hundred years," said Brian, not taking his eyes off the screen.

He selected the new date; it took them back to 10,500 BC. Once again the screen changed and the constellations reformed in a new position.

"I think that's it," whispered Brian, " I reckon that's it!"

He sighed and leant back in the chair almost as if he couldn't believe it.

"I'm telling you, Kate, there will be some people at my university who'd be amazed if they knew about this."

Kate was lost for words and it was Steve who spoke next.

"So, what now? We know the sites line up with the positions of some stars. How does that link with the disappearances?"

Kate shrugged her shoulders, "It probably doesn't," she said, "Just another remarkable coincidence, I suppose."

Brian had finished printing off the screen and walked over to a large easel that held a flipchart.

"Let's have a think for a minute. What exactly have we got?"

He began to write. "First, we know that at least eight people have disappeared in this area in the last five years, we know that they were all last seen in the vicinity of an aboriginal site, and now we know that the sites are linked to the position of celestial bodies." He paused for breath.

"We also have the hat and the watch from the cave in Arnhem land, and the link to Dave Ellis, the backpacker who had arranged to meet Ellen in Jabiru and never showed up," Kate added.

Steve had taken Brian's place at the computer and was studying the screen; suddenly, he spun round and studied the flipchart. Kate was wandering round the room trying to come up with a suggestion.

Suddenly, Steve spoke. "What about this?" He paused for a second, closing his eyes as if he were trying to work out how best to say whatever it was he had come up with. " On the way down here this morning you were talking about how other ancient sites exhibit this.... this erm... this astral link, like the pyramids in Egypt and some of the Inca and Aztec sites in South America. Well, it's just occurred to me that all those ancient cultures believed in Gods to whom they made sacrifices. The pyramids were kind of stairways to immortality, weren't they? The Egyptians sacrificed people to the Gods and for their Pharaohs so that they could become immortal in the afterlife. The Incas and the Aztecs were notorious for sacrificial rituals that kept their gods appeased, weren't they? Why shouldn't the ancient aboriginals have performed similar rituals?"

Steve had stood up now and was warming to his task. "And don't forget that Brian said that activity round the sites seems to increase in line with the lunar cycle."

Kate was rubbing her temple now as if she were trying to squeeze out some deeply buried information.

"There has never been any evidence of aboriginals making any sort of sacrifices to gods. In fact, it is the exact opposite, if anything. Their culture is based on looking after everything as a mark of respect for the gods that were responsible for creation," she said, finally sitting down.

"At least there hasn't yet," said Steve. "That's not to say we couldn't look for some."

"Look, let's not get carried away here before we've got more to work on. Let me just get this straight. Are you suggesting that the aborigines, based on some ancient belief that their gods, like the Aztecs and Incas, need sacrifices to be made to those gods, are kidnapping backpackers in order to kill them during religious ceremonies?" Brian was staring directly at Steve now.

"Well all the evidence fits, doesn't it! And who's to say they just sacrifice backpackers? Kate said there were over three hundred missing people in the Northern Territory alone. They could be taking anyone who is an easy target: the homeless, the drunks you see sleeping off a hangover in the park, anyone."

Kate had gone quiet again and Steve thought that perhaps she was thinking about Edward again. When she spoke, however, he realised she had been trying to work out what to do next.

"I've got an idea, it's a long shot but we've got nothing to lose, have we? Brian mentioned the activity increase on a full moon." She rummaged in her bag now for the diary that she'd bought a few days earlier. She flicked through quickly.

"There's a full moon in three days time, why don't we

wait till then, select a site, and wait? See if anything untoward happens."

"Yeah, but there are lots of sites within half a day's drive of here. It'd be too much to expect that we'd choose just the right one on the night it was selected for a sacrifice," argued Brian.

"Yes," said Kate, " but at least we can rule out some of them. Is it likely that they would keep using the same one? If people keep going missing from the same area each month, people would start to put two and two together. I reckon we can rule out all those that have a close proximity to a disappearance."

Brian poured out three mugs of coffee and handed them round. "Right then, I can cope with a day or two off from the 'scope. Get your maps out and let's decide where it's to be."

Kate pulled the maps onto the table and spread them out. "What about this one?" she suggested, pointing to a spot about forty kilometres west of the observatory. "Not too far and so far, no reported missing people."

They all looked at each other and nodded solemnly.

41

Munich, Germany 1929

The large double door swung open and a uniformed guard entered the room. He walked across the room to where Hitler was sitting at a bureau beneath a window overlooking the street.

The atmosphere was serene; a fire burned warmly in the hearth and a gramophone player filled the air with Wagner's 'Overture to Rienzi.'

"What is it?" he asked without looking up from the document he was studying.

"Herr Himmler, to see you, sir."

"Send him in at once," said Hitler, his voice betraying none of the tension that he could feel building up inside him. "And Gerhardt.... that will be all for today. We are not to be disturbed. I will see you in the morning."

With an almost imperceptible nod of his head the guard turned on his heel and strode out to see in the visitor.

Hitler stood and walked over to the fireplace. He had suddenly become very cold. Heinrich Himmler was the new head of the SS, but more importantly, he was the man whom the Master had decreed would enable them to fulfil their ambitions.

It had been a long five-year wait since Landsberg, but the Master had told him that he would need to be patient.

Patient he had been and despite many setbacks, the

Party was now stronger than ever. Each night, he took the key from the brown leather case that he'd had specially made, and stood it on a table in the middle of a darkened room, just like the first time in his prison cell. Each night he would speak with the Master who reassured him that the time was near, that other things had to be in place before they could forge ahead with The Plan.

The Master was right; of course, he remembered how difficult things had been at first when he was released from prison. How opposition had grown in his absence, even from within the party. Take Gregor Strasser, for example; if the Master had not guided Hitler in appointing Himmler as secretary to Strasser (who was at the time looking towards leadership of the Party) they would not be in the position to realise their ambitions even now. It was only Himmler's superb artistry in organising the public life of Strasser in a way that actually reduced his exposure to the very people he was trying to impress; the working classes, that ensured his downfall was inevitable.

Meanwhile, Hitler concentrated on wooing his favourite group of German people: the disenfranchised and the outcast military leaders from the Great War. Hitler had to be the Fuhrer if they were to succeed.

Good fortune also had a hand, of course; the depression that was just beginning to take hold in Germany gave everyone reason to start looking for strong political leadership again. The other thing that everyone also looked for when things went wrong was a scapegoat and that's where Herr Heinrich Himmler was going to be very, very important.

The door opened once more and Himmler stepped quietly into the room. Hitler had moved away from the fire and was standing by the drinks-cabinet pouring schnapps into two glasses. He looked up and smiled at the small, unremarkable looking man who had just entered the room.

Himmler was dressed in civilian clothes, the only piece of Nazi party paraphernalia visible being a small metal badge attached to the lapel of his jacket: a black swastika on a red background.

Hitler noticed that, as usual, he was immaculately turned out. The suit he wore was creaseless and his patent leather shoes were polished to an impressive shine. Hitler recognised this as an indication of the man's obsession with order and perfection; the very quality that made Himmler the ideal candidate for what he had in mind.

He looked at Hitler through small, round spectacles and smiled back; they were very comfortable in each other's company, having met on many occasions in the past. They also shared the mutual bond of having been part of the, now sacred, march on The Odeonplatz in 1924.

Hitler waved him over to sit in a leather armchair by the fire. They exchanged greetings and Himmler complimented Hitler on his choice of music; Wagner was a particular favourite of his. Hitler handed him a glass of schnapps before sitting down in the chair opposite.

There was a moment's silence as they both drank then Hitler placed his glass on the table and settled back into the armchair.

"Heinrich, I have something very special to show you. It is something that is going to change both of our lives forever."

He paused for a second to gauge his visitor's response. Himmler's eyebrows rose slightly but his expression remained the same. Hitler reached down to the side of the chair and picked up the small leather pouch that was lying on the floor.

Himmler swallowed back a slug of schnapps, nervously aware that the tone of the meeting had suddenly changed. The solemnity in Hitler's voice was a little unnerving.

"You see Heinrich, I am aware of your interest in the

purity of the Aryan race and your desire for the German people to become great again as they were when Heinrich the First fought off the Slavs in the Dark Ages."

Hitler knew all about Himmler's interest in Germanic chivalry. At a gathering of Party members a couple of years earlier, Himmler had spoken at great length about the deeds of the legendary Teutonic Knights and their crusade to defend the Fatherland against the Slavs of Poland, Russia, and Lithuania in the fifteenth century. Hitler also recalled how, that night's conversation had turned to the topic of genetics, another of Himmler's favourite interests. He was running a chicken farm at the time and claimed that through selective breeding he had managed to produce chickens that exhibited only desirable qualities. He had gone on to suggest that a similar thing could be done with the human population of Germany thus reversing the dilution of the gene pool that had resulted from hundreds of years of cross breeding with what he had called 'inferior races'.

Himmler felt himself begin to relax as Hitler spoke; maybe it was the schnapps or perhaps the feeling that Hitler was a kindred spirit. Whatever it was, the atmosphere in the room seemed to grow suddenly thick.

Hitler continued. "I too have a similar desire. There are too many non-Aryan races living amongst us, weakening our great nation, polluting our bloodline and holding us back from reasserting our greatness: the blacks, the Slavs, the Poles, the gypsies, the disabled...the Jews. The time has come, Heinrich, to put things right."

As he spoke, Hitler held the leather pouch in front of him as if it were a sacrificial offering. "Together, with this, you and I can make Germany great again. We can reunite our people and regain our living space. We can oust from our country the peoples who are unworthy of calling themselves German and ensure our heritage is maintained."

He untied the leather drawstring and the key slid out

into the palm of his hand. He placed it on the table in front of Himmler and twisted it round so the engraving of the figure and the symbol faced him.

Himmler looked down at the unusual metal key in front of him and immediately wondered what could be so special about it. Then, without warning, the hairs on the back of his neck stood on end. The eyelids of the figure on the key opened and out gazed two intensely evil yellow eyes.

Himmler sucked in his breath and instinctively pushed himself back into the leather chair. The eyes held his gaze and he felt his insides tightening. His heart was suddenly gripped as if a hand had physically closed itself round it and begun to squeeze. Beads of sweat began to form on his brow and roll down onto the small round lenses of his spectacles.

His first thought was that he was having a heart attack but there was no real pain, simply a feeling of pressure that frightened him yet somehow heightened his senses in an almost pleasurable way. There was something beyond the eyes now, a figure of some sort. He thought he could make out a face momentarily then it was gone. With it went the pressure and suddenly he was looking into the smiling face of Hitler who was holding out a glass of water.

Himmler held out his hand, amazed that he could even move. He looked down at the key. The eyelids were closed, the key looking as unimpressive as it had done a few minutes before. Had he imagined it? The look on Hitler's face told him that wasn't the case. He took a few sips of water before attempting to speak.

"What.... what is it? .... Where did it come from? How..."

Hitler interrupted by laughing loudly. "All in good time, my friend, all in good time."

Hitler picked up the key and returned it to its pouch. Himmler, still shaking slightly, took another sip of water.

Hitler was on his feet now leaning against the fireplace. He picked up a poker, poked the dying embers, and threw on another log. Fingers of blue flame immediately began to wrap themselves round the wood as if trying to physically drag it into the glowing embers beneath.

Himmler was suddenly aware that the temperature of the room had dropped by several degrees and an involuntary shiver ran down his spine. Hitler returned to his chair.

"If we are to achieve what we want, one thing is for certain: we need to ensure that the rest of the children of the Fatherland want it too. First of all, we need to gain power; unless we are in a position to control our opponents, we will not succeed."

Himmler had regained his composure now and was nodding in agreement.

"The SS will be the key to the first goal and to that end they must be totally dedicated to me. Not to the Party but to me. The SS will be the foundation of the building of the new German race. Every one of them will be of pure blood and every one of them will be proud to be part of the cleansing of our nation."

Himmler's mind was already beginning to formulate ideas about how to restructure the organisation now under his control. The excitement in his eyes did not go unnoticed by Hitler.

"Once in power, our goal will be twofold: the total elimination of non Aryan races from Germany and the recolonisation by pure Germans of territory that is theirs by birthright."

Himmler had stood up now and was pacing the room as if in deep thought. "This elimination process? I take it that you are not merely talking of selective breeding. That would take hundreds of years, if not thousands, to achieve."

Hitler picked up the leather pouch from the table and

held it in front of him. "The Master will guide us my friend. But it will not happen overnight; first we must gain power."

42

London 1997

Donovan looked at his watch for what seemed like the thousandth time. There were still five minutes to go before the train was due in. He cast another glance at the electronic notice board that announced information about arrivals and departures, keeping his fingers crossed that the *running on time* message referring to the 9.15 from Birmingham, didn't alter at the last moment to inform him that it was now delayed. He didn't think he could handle the suspense. He knew he was working purely on a hunch but instinctively felt he was really onto something.

Having narrowly escaped being caught in the Beaumont office two days earlier, he'd found that too much adrenaline was rushing round inside his body to allow him to sleep despite the fact that it was two in the morning by the time he arrived back at his flat.

With a million and one thoughts careering round his brain, he had abandoned the idea of going to bed and had logged onto the Internet, speculatively performing a search for *The Branch Davidians*. He wasn't surprised to find they had an official web site but he *was* overwhelmed by the amount of indoctrination that spewed off the pages.

He had spent an hour trawling through pages of doctrine and philosophy and re-familiarising himself with the man whom the Davidians genuinely believed was the

Messiah, David Koresh.

'Could there really be a connection between the fax he'd read in the Beaumont office and the Davidians? It had mentioned the Day of Atonement and from what he recalled of the cult he knew they had been a so-called Doomsday cult.

He typed in 'Branch members' and waited. The search yielded several results but unfortunately none of the pages he found listed the names of current members. But what about the survivors of the Waco siege?

He tried another search: *'Waco survivors'*

This time there was only one result. He double clicked and the page appeared on the screen.

The first few paragraphs described in detail the siege again and continually re-emphasised the view that the FBI were totally ignorant of something called *'The Seven Seals'* and were solely responsible for the murder of The Son of God.

Donovan pinched the top of his nose and screwed up his eyes as he slowly scrolled down; he was beginning to 'come down' now from the 'high' of his earlier encounter and suddenly felt very tired. Suddenly, a list of names appeared on the screen and he had to scroll back up until he reached the sub heading that he'd missed.

Apparently, it was a roll of honour to all the martyrs who had died for their beliefs during the tragedy. Donovan felt frustrated; if there were a connection between Winston and the cult, his name would hardly be on this list. He continued to scroll down.

There were ninety-five names in total, the last nine of which were in bold type; a legend at the bottom revealed that this indicated they were actual survivors. *Hallelujah!*

The last-but-one name brought a smile to Donovan's face: ***Winston F. Brown.***

He lit a cigarette and walked towards a newsagent's stand. The station clock read 09:17. He looked round as casually as possible for a familiar face; Henderson's P.A, perhaps, or the man he'd seen going into the Beaumont offices.

There were two men, wearing suits, leaning on the rail adjacent to the platform at which the train was due who could, in Donovan's mind, be the two 'henchmen' from the other night (even though he'd only heard their voices, his dreams that night had filled in the details of their faces!) but apart from them he saw no one he recognised.

As he picked up a copy of *'National Geographic'* and flicked through absentmindedly, he came across an article with the curious title:

'Travelling the Australian Dog Fence'.

It was about a fence that is actually longer than the Great Wall of China and was apparently built to keep sheep safe from dingoes. (Donovan wasn't quite sure how it could work unless it was a circular fence and all the sheep were on the inside.)

There was a picture of the fence cutting an immense scar across the unmistakable rust-red expanse of the Outback and he was suddenly reminded of Kate and her expedition. She had been there nearly a month now and although they'd talked a few times on the phone, he felt as though he'd almost imagined their few weeks together before she'd left. His heart sank for a second and his fist tightened on the magazine as the thought occurred to him. Then a smile crossed his lips as he remembered the night before she left and their lovemaking.

What would she make of all this cloak and dagger stuff? He wondered. If she were there, she'd probably laugh at the thought of him waiting for a person he didn't know to get off a train he probably wasn't on for reasons he didn't yet understand.

He was brought back to the present by the sound of an electronic chime and a metallic voice announcing that the train arriving at platform eight was the nine fifteen from Birmingham New Street.

He replaced the magazine on the stand, stubbed out his cigarette and made his way over to the platform.

The two men he had seen earlier were to his right, nearer to the exit barrier of the platform. Although he knew it was impossible that they could recognise him, even if they were who he thought they were, he still stood well out of their line of sight.

As the train drew to a halt and the passengers began to jump from the train and stream towards the exit, Donovan scanned the platform for a potential 'Winston F. Brown'.

There was the usual mix of commuters, tourists, foreign visitors and students all arriving in London for their own very important reasons. Donovan's perception of Winston was: a black male, mid thirties, possibly inclined to dress in a sombre fashion, no over the top jewellery but probably wearing one prominent piece of pseudo- religious paraphernalia.

Unfortunately, after about five minutes, as the stream of passengers dwindled to a trickle, he realised that either his imagined picture of Winston was way-off , or equally as likely, he simply wasn't on the train. After all, the fax had not actually specified the date of the train, simply a day and time. Apart from that it was quite possible that the arrangements had been changed since the night he'd read the fax.

The two 'henchmen' he'd noticed had met a small grey-haired lady, who, judging by the hugs and kisses bestowed on her by the two men, was either their mother or a cherished aunt.

As Donovan turned to leave the station and ponder over his next move, he noticed a woman waiting a few paces back from where he'd been standing. She was holding a piece of white card in front of her chest.

She was tall and slim, and wore a navy two-piece business suit. Her hair was long but gathered into a tight bun on the top of her head. Perched delicately on the bridge of her nose was a pair of half-moon glasses over the top of which she was looking questioningly at the last few remaining passengers from the nine fifteen.

Written on the white card were the words: 'Mr. Winston Brown'.

Donovan stopped in his tracks and turned to face the platform. There were only three people left: A middle aged man carrying a sleeping child in a papoose, a small, slightly confused- looking Japanese lady and a very distinguished looking business man type, slightly tanned, wearing a beige two piece cotton suit and a white open necked shirt. He was carrying a brown, somewhat tatty, leather briefcase.

Donovan looked beyond them all searching for his version of Winston Brown. Seeing nothing but an empty platform, he refocused on the lady with the sign who, having shaken hands with 'Beige Suit', was now guiding him towards the exit.

43

Northern Territory June 18th 1997

Steve squinted through the darkness: nothing stirred. It was a cold, clear night and the sky was a myriad of twinkling diamonds. The lack of a moon gave the landscape an almost ethereal quality and the shooting stars that left ghostly trails in the blackness reminded Steve of a story that he'd read in the news a month or so before flying out to Australia about a weird cult in America called *Heaven's Gate,* whose members had believed that they were destined to be transported to a heavenly world in a spacecraft. The sighting of the *Hale Bopp* comet supposedly signalled the arrival of the craft. Three days after the comet was sighted, about forty bodies were discovered at the cult's headquarters in California; all had committed suicide in preparation for the journey, suitcases packed by their sides: *'Weirdoes.'*

Steve shuddered involuntarily and pulled his thin, cotton jacket tighter round him.

"Chilly, Steve?" asked Brian who was sitting in the driver's seat next to Kate.

"Not bloody joking," shivered Steve, not wanting to admit to Brian that he was feeling a little uneasy about the entire escapade. To be honest, he'd had as much as he could take of what he now believed was a total waste of time and he wished Kate would simply let it go so they could return to England.

(He hated to admit it but he was also a little jealous of Kate and Brian's relationship, despite Kate explaining to him about the 'non event' at Dani's; he still felt a little pushed out.)

"What time is it?" asked Kate, for the hundredth time. They'd arrived at *Alde Hill*, a rocky outcrop about ten kilometres south of Sixteen Mile Creek, a little after ten o clock and since then they'd seen absolutely no-one. Brian's jeep was hidden behind a small cluster of bushes about two hundred metres from the opening of a cave that, according to the map, was designated a sacred aboriginal burial ground. They hadn't entered the cave when they'd arrived, unsure as to whether or not somebody might already be inside. Brian said that most of the activity he'd noticed at the sites close to Warranboola occurred round midnight so they'd opted to stake it out for a while.

"Ten before twelve," said Brian. "We'll give it another hour then if nothing's happened we'll take a look inside, eh?"

Kate looked over her shoulder to gauge Steve's response. She'd noticed he looked a little fed up and felt guilty at dragging him into all this. Steve raised a feeble attempt at a smile and nodded his agreement.

"Coffee, anyone?" asked Brian lifting a Thermos from under his seat.

Just as Brian had finished pouring the first cup, the low sound of an engine and tyres on dirt floated across the bush.

"Shit!" cursed Brian as some of the hot coffee spilled onto his hand as he hastily poured it back into the flask. Both Kate and Steve had wound their windows down and were peering through the dark at the rapidly approaching headlights.

The station wagon came to an abrupt halt outside the cave and the doors were flung open. It was difficult to see exactly what was happening, but there were loud shouts from inside the vehicle and at least two people appeared to get out from the side closest to the cave. The station wagon blocked out what was going on and although what they were saying to each other was clear, the words were spoken in aboriginal dialect.

"Why couldn't we have parked a little nearer to the cave," whispered Kate, her frustration now overcoming the immense feeling of excitement that she had, now that something was actually happening.

"And why can't they speak in proper bloody English," hissed Steve who was now as equally as excited as Kate.

The powerful beam from a torch suddenly lit up the cave entrance and then diminished as the two people disappeared inside. The driver of the station wagon remained inside the vehicle and appeared to be talking to someone although there didn't appear to be anyone else with him.

"Radio," whispered Brian, holding his hand to his ear to clarify his explanation.

"Who do you think he's talking to?" asked Kate.

"Maybe he's in contact with other cars that are headed this way," suggested Brian, shrugging his shoulders.

The driver suddenly opened the door and climbed out. He walked round to the tailgate and opened it up. Reaching inside, he drew out what appeared to be a long, thin stick and, judging by the way he let it fall to the floor, a rather heavy case.

He closed the tailgate and made his way towards the cave, struggling with the awkward objects.

Kate let out an audible hiss of air as if she'd been holding her breath.

"Right, what now?" asked Steve from the back, rubbing his hands together in anticipation.

"If he was in contact with others maybe we should hang

fire for a while in case they show up," said Brian.

"I agree," said Kate, "If they *are* up to no good we don't want to get caught in the entrance with no way of escape."

"Ok, let's give it ten minutes," said Steve firmly trying to assert himself a little. (He was getting a little weary of Brian making all the decisions.)

Inside the cave, the three men worked in total silence. Each knew exactly what to do. In the centre of the cave was a low, flat rock about two metres long by about a metre wide. One of the men was brushing the dust and sand from its surface. Another was piling bits of brushwood into a shallow pit at the rear of the cave and the third was lighting gasoline-soaked torches from a cigarette lighter and standing them upright in the sand at intervals round the cave. Two torches were placed at the head of the long stone creating the effect of an altar.

The paintings on the walls of the cave seemed to come alive as the torches spread their light. The images were mainly patterns; swirls and dots, which represented the tracks of different animals. Above the 'altar' though, one image stood out plainly as being different. The image was much larger than the rest and was quite clearly the figure of a woman, her eyes closed in tranquil repose. Beneath was a symbol, which had more of a hieroglyphic quality about it; it was an inverted arc with six points sticking out from the top at regular intervals.

As the flames from the fire in the pit began to grow, the two men who had entered the cave first sat cross-legged, one on either side of the altar. The third man lifted the lid from the wooden case and took out a large knife and a metal platter. He placed them on the rock and then stood between the two torches facing the cave entrance, the long sacrificial spear by his side. They were prepared.

"Come on," said Steve. "No-one else is coming. I say

we go and take a closer look."

"What do we say if they see us?" asked Kate realising that they hadn't actually discussed a plan of action.

"I don't suppose we can walk in and say we're tourists just passing through," suggested Steve flippantly.

"And if they are in the middle of disposing of the odd abducted backpacker, we'll ask can we take a few souvenir snapshots," added Brian, joining in the black humour.

"Would you please stop it?" hissed Kate, suddenly feeling as if they had both been humouring her all along.

Steve suddenly remembered Edward and felt guilty. "I'll go and take a closer look. You and Brian stay here and keep a look out. If anyone comes before I reach the cave I'll hit the deck, no one will see me in this light. If I'm not back in ten minutes, send in the cavalry."

Before Brian or Kate could say anything, Steve was out of the car and running towards the cave.

Steve was out of condition and was breathing heavily by the time he reached the relative security of the station wagon. He rested there in the lee of the vehicle listening for the sounds of footsteps or voices. His heart was racing and he could literally feel the adrenaline pumping through him. Cautiously, he rose up to peer at the cave through the windows of the station wagon. There was just a deeper blackness indicating the position of the entrance. No sign of the three men.

He crouched down again and tried to compose himself. Thinking quickly, he took off his shoes and jacket so that he could move more stealthily and pushed them beneath the station wagon, out of sight. With a last glance round, he scurried across the last twenty feet or so to the cave.

He paused for a second to catch his breath and then he entered.

His eyes took a few moments to make the adjustment to the almost total blackness; *almost total blackness* because about fifty or so metres in front of him, there was a kind of intermittent flickering of light. He reached out until his fingers touched the cold but reassuring cave wall and then slowly he began to walk towards the light. His mind began to fill with awful images of decapitated people wandering aimlessly, clutching at him in the dark. All the while the light ahead grew brighter.

He realised he was creeping more slowly as he got closer, reluctant to see what lay beyond the darkness and wondering why on earth he hadn't let Brian volunteer. He could be sitting in the relative safety of the car now instead of feeling like the principal character of a Dean Koontz novel. The tunnel opened up slightly now and he caught sight of a burning torch; *Shit, it is a Dean Koontz novel!*

He dropped to his knees and forced himself to crawl the last few feet. There was, conveniently, a large rock directly in front of him, behind which, he now cowered almost not wanting to look into the chamber.

He counted to ten then slowly lifted his head so that he could see over the top of the rock.

Kate forced herself to look away from the window. "How long has he been in there?" she asked.

"Seven and a half minutes and counting." said Brian.

"Jesus, is that all! It feels like an eternity." Kate was rubbing her temples now, aware that if anything happened to Steve it was all her fault.

"He'll be okay," said Brian reassuringly. "He's probably having a right laugh with whoever is in there as we speak. Remember it's not unusual that these ancient races have religious rituals that are synchronised with astrological events. You know that better than I do. It doesn't mean there's anything sinister going on, despite our suspicions concerning the disappearances.

Kate turned to stare back out of the window.

Steve breathed a sigh of relief as quietly as he could. To

the rear of the cave he could see one of the men, nearly naked except for the leather thong round his waist, holding what was quite clearly a spear. His eyes were closed and his paint smeared face twitched as he chanted some kind of incantation. His feet stamped the dusty earth rhythmically. It was as if he were in a trance.

One of the other men was hitting a long, low rock in the middle of the cave with a club-like object in time to the incantations whilst the third aborigine also in a trance-like state scooped up what appeared to be still-hot ash from a fire, throwing it forcefully against the walls of the cave. Each time he scooped, he moved along the wall of the cave so that the dust stuck to a different section of the rock. Steve was aware for the first time that the walls were decorated with traditional aboriginal paintings. He noticed that they were quite different from the style of the paintings that he and Pippa had photographed at the sites further north. (He felt a sudden, unexpected but pleasant tingle in his groin. It was the first time he'd thought of Pippa for a week or so. He'd give anything for her to be there right now. Perhaps they'd make out clandestinely behind the rock as the aborigines performed the ritual. It would be quite erotic; right up Pippa's street).

He had just begun to relax and was beginning to enjoy the ritual taking place before him when he suddenly felt a hand on his shoulder. His bladder instinctively began to empty and his heart stopped as a warm hand closed around his mouth. He froze and waited for the feel of cool steel to cross his throat or slide between his ribs. Instead, his head was slowly turned round and he stared open eyed into the face of...Brian.

"You fucking dipshit!" he squealed. "Are you trying to give me a fucking heart attack?"

"Calm down..." began Brian.

"Calm down? Calm fucking down? ..."

"Shhhhh," said Kate, "for God's sake, they'll hear us."

Both men were silent. The three of them turned to watch the scene unfolding before them.

They watched for over half an hour as the aborigines performed more complex rituals, the incantations becoming louder and more desperate; the movements becoming more erratic, almost convulsive.

Finally, as all three men knelt down before the largest painting on the cave wall, heaving and panting from their exertions, Kate gestured to Steve and Brian that they should leave. Steve could tell even in the flickering light that the adventure was at last over and Kate had decided that enough was enough.

"We'll call the airport first thing tomorrow morning and arrange the flight home," said Kate, putting an arm round Steve who had joined her and Brian in the front for the drive back to Warranboola.

"And Steve, thanks for sticking by me for the last week or so; I know you thought I was nuts all along."

Steve just smiled, he was still recovering from the shock he'd had in the cave when Brian grabbed him.

"You never know," said Brian, "Just because we didn't find anything odd going on tonight doesn't necessarily mean that somewhere, at another site…"

Before he could finish, Kate interrupted; "Thanks, Brian, but I suppose I'm quite relieved really that we found nothing untoward. I suppose I realise now that I was just chasing something that only existed in my mind because of my brother's disappearance all those years ago. I guess I always felt…I don't know… responsible."

Steve squeezed her close to him and kissed the top of her head. Kate closed her eyes and relaxed for the first time in as long as she could remember.

The jeep pulled off the dusty bush track and turned left onto the metalled State Highway for the forty kilometre drive back to the observatory.

Had they turned right and driven for five kilometres or so they would've passed a pick up truck with four male aborigines struggling to mend a punctured tyre with a broken jack. On the back seat of the pickup lay the body of a twenty-year-old hitchhiker from Hamburg in Germany. Her throat was sliced from ear to ear.

44

Poznan, Poland. 4th October 1943

The small, round lenses of his spectacles misted over as he climbed out from the relative warmth of the car and stepped into the bitterly cold autumn afternoon. His black leather boots struggled to gain purchase in the four inches of snow that carpeted the ground and the freezing air burned his lungs as he inhaled.

He turned and looked back inside the car where the Fuhrer still sat, flicking through the thirty page document that they'd spent the last hour discussing.

The Fuhrer was pleased with the progress that had been made since the Final Solution had begun in earnest eighteen months earlier. Over three and a half million Jews had been liquidated already in the death camps alone, not to mention another half a million in random cleansing missions in hundreds of villages in the Baltic States. He was well aware, though, that there was still a long way to go to reach the ten million which the Fuhrer had decreed was necessary in order to satisfy the Master.

Himmler removed his spectacles and wiped them clear with the handkerchief given to him by the driver who had opened the door.

"Remember, Heinrich, there must be not a single German who doubts that our work is necessary. I demand total loyalty."

Himmler smiled but did not turn round to look at his friend and mentor. He was busy scanning the ranks of the three hundred or so SS Group Leaders assembled in front of him.

"Do not fear mien Fuhrer, I guarantee it. Mien ehre heisst treue."

Inside the car, Hitler was caressing the key in his lap. The engraving felt warm and he sensed the power that was slowly growing inside. It had been a long struggle since Landsberg and the night The Master had first appeared before him. Twenty years of painstaking preparation was finally beginning to bear the fruit that would feed the immortality he had been promised.

He would let nothing stand in his way, hence why meetings like this were essential. Rumours of unease had been drifting back from the death camps for the last few weeks and it was important to sustain the discipline if the Final Solution were to be carried to its conclusion.

He could of course address the men himself and convince them that the extermination of the millions of *untermensch was* simply a means by which the Aryan race would achieve supremacy but he also knew that by limiting his appearances and only giving the occasional oratory, his almost god like persona would be further embellished.

The key was getting warmer now and he sensed, rather than felt, the slight pulse emanating from deep within. He closed his eyes and immediately the Master's face filled his mind.

When he had first seen the face, twenty years before, it had been vague and wispy; there for a second then gone the next, almost like heat rising from a hot surface. As time passed, however, he had noticed that the face was becoming more detailed, more vivid, and more real with each new appearance, particularly since the death camps had begun to operate. It was as if the deaths of the thousands of Jews were somehow providing a life force that enabled his face to materialise.

The yellow eyes bore into his soul and the fingers that ended with long, black talons, reached out towards him tracing a line from his temple to his chin.

"Your time is near disciple, do not fail me now...The Messiah will soon be ready and you will become all that you have ever desired."

The tone of the voice was threatening, yet somehow sensuous, the type of tone he himself used when manipulating people whom he knew could wield power on his behalf; people he realised who could in fact pose a threat to his own dominance given half the chance. Deep in his mind an alarm bell began to ring but the seduction overwhelmed him and he felt the excitement beginning to rise. A warm glow began to spread itself upwards from his feet, into his thighs, centring on his groin. Despite the fact that his eyes were closed, he could see Himmler standing in front of the SS leaders, his fists tightly clenched, his intense eyes holding the gaze of all the men he surveyed. He had not yet started speaking.

Almost imperceptibly, he felt the key rise in his hands as though a force was pulling it upwards, then without warning, the warmth that had embraced him so beautifully just seconds before, disappeared. His eyes snapped open and for a fleeting second he thought he saw a figure rising from the key. He gripped it more tightly as it rose higher in front of him and he struggled to hold onto it. He felt a chill run through him and suddenly felt extremely vulnerable, as if he were naked and a warm blanket had been violently pulled from him.

Without warning, the key dropped into his lap and there was a deafening crack as the car window exploded outwards.

Himmler was surveying the faces of the men before

him. Some looked strong and confident, others looked anxious, one or two even looked afraid. He began to doubt whether even the Fuhrer could deliver a speech that would convince all of them that the unearthly crimes that they were all committing on a daily basis were justifiable.

Judging by the haunted look behind the eyes of several of the men at the front, it appeared that the reality of exterminating thousands of men, women and children, even if they were sub-human, was taking its toll. He deliberately focused his eyes on those that he perceived to be struggling with their consciences.

"One principle must be absolute for the SS man...we must be honest, decent, loyal and comradely to members of our own blood and to no-one else. The Russians, the Czechs, the Poles; they are useful only in helping us to purify the bloodline. We are the result of thousands of years of natural selection. The weak; the deformed; the sick of mind...they have all fallen by the wayside, as nature intended. It is our duty to ensure that this process is not reversed; that the evolution of the perfect society is not threatened by individuals who seek to interfere with what is right..."

He paused for a moment to give them time to think about what he had just said and he caught the eye of a man on the front row who was whispering to the man beside him. He was about to continue when the man shouted something out.

"But still, they are children just like mine. It cannot be right to kill them like cattle. They have done no wrong."

Himmler was startled at first but he maintained his composure. He had been prepared for someone to respond like this. He asked the man to step to the front so that the rest of the men could see him. (He would use the man's own psychology against him; if he was so worried about his own children, what would happen to them when the Jews ruled the world and there were no jobs for them and they were thrown into ghettos.)

The man nervously stepped forward and Himmler turned him to face the men.

Himmler was about to speak when something hit him hard at the base of his spine. His first thought was that he had been shot, but instead of falling to his knees, he felt a surge of energy well up into his torso. The uneasiness he had been feeling moments ago was replaced by an overwhelming hatred for the man in front of him. The man was facing the crowd now, smiling, proud that he had spoken up. Himmler calmly reached down, unclipped the gun from the holster at his side and shot the man in the back of the head. The man fell forward, blood spurting in a crimson arc onto the snow.

A deathly silence fell over the crowd of men. Then Himmler bent down, put his hand into the man's tunic, and pulled out something from round his neck; something shiny. He held it up to show the men. Slowly, one by one, the men began to applaud as they realised, what was in his hand: a Star of David pendant on a silver chain.

When the applause subsided, he continued his speech. "I shall speak with frankness of this grave matter. Among us it should be spoken of openly yet publicly it should not be mentioned. Most of you know what it is like to see a hundred corpses lying together, five hundred or a thousand. To have stuck it out and remain decent is what makes us special. This is a page of glory in our history which has never been written and will never be written."

The applause rang out once more and Himmler felt the power, deeply entrenched inside him, surge once again.

The men before him were now rapturous, screaming loudly, 'Zeig Hiel' and slapping each other on the back. Only one man wasn't joining in; the man who had just seen his brother shot in the head. Even though he too saw the

Star of David like everyone else, he knew that his brother was not a Jewish sympathiser, just someone who could no longer live with the guilt of supervising the cold blooded murder of innocent people. As he stared at the face of the man standing on the ridge in front of him, he noticed something strange. It could have been his imagination but the features seemed to change momentarily. One second they were the round-faced features of Heinrich Himmler, the next they were harder, more angular, the nose seemed to stretch and the teeth became more prominent and just for a second the face became his brother's, wide eyed and terrified. He looked at the men round him to see if they had noticed it but they were all engrossed in the celebration. When he looked up again, Himmler was walking back towards the sleek black car from which he had stepped twenty minutes earlier.

Himmler brushed a few shards of glass from the seat before sitting down. He didn't ask what had happened to the window. As he approached the car, the power that had somehow entered his body and taken control of his actions suddenly drained from him. His knees buckled making him lurch forward into the snow and he had to reach for the car to stop himself from falling. As he looked up through the broken window, he saw a shimmer of ethereal light as it transferred back into the key resting on the Fuhrer's lap. He took a deep breath and closed his eyes, trying to make sense of what had happened.

When he opened his eyes, he found his friend staring down at the silver chain that still dangled from his closed fist. Blood was trickling out from between the fingers and he became aware of the intense pain. Slowly, he unclenched his hand to reveal the pendant inside... It was a silver crucifix.

45

Epping, London 1997

The Mercedes pulled into the narrow driveway and paused momentarily as the huge cast iron gates opened automatically. The car swung through the gates and disappeared.

A few seconds later, a black cab drove a short distance past the driveway before pulling into the side of the road. "Thanks mate," said Donovan looking wistfully at the meter. He opened his wallet and extracted four twenty pound notes, "Keep the change,"

The driver smiled and nodded, it was the first *'follow that car'* he'd ever done.

Donovan suspected that the driver quite enjoyed it really. He'd have something to tell his mates in the pub later and of course he would embellish the details slightly to make it sound like a scene from *'The Thirty Nine Steps.'*

Donovan jumped out and made his way slowly back towards the drive.

It was well protected from snoopers; the walls that surrounded whatever was inside were a good seven feet tall and several signs warned trespassers that Alcatraz Security protected the property, twenty-four hours a day. He walked past the gate noting that the house couldn't be seen from the road, the drive swinging to the left behind a bank of trees.

Following the wall for another sixty metres or so, Donovan was surprised to find another smaller drive leading into the grounds. Behind the gates on the right was a small, squat, sandstone building.

Donovan assumed it had probably been the lodge in days gone by. It was most likely used as an entrance for deliveries and such. He was pondering his next move when he heard a loud click and the gates began to swing open. His first instinct was that he had somehow activated a remote sensor and he started to move away lest a large hairy canine rush out and grab him by the throat, but a few seconds later, a small, green, three wheeled van pulling a trailer laden with gardening tools emerged from the drive. The driver was speaking into a mobile phone that he'd wedged between his shoulder and chin whilst he negotiated the corner. As Donovan watched it drive past he heard the click again and turned to see the gates slowly closing. Without hesitating, he ran towards the narrowing gap and just managed to squeeze through before they closed.

He scurried past the 'lodge' as quickly as he could, despite the fact that the dust on the windows suggested that it was no longer in use, and pushed his way in between the rhododendron bushes that lined the drive. He waited momentarily to catch his breath and to make sure that Alcatraz Security hadn't been monitoring some well-positioned CCTV system that had captured his furtive entrance into the grounds.

After a few minutes, he felt confident that he hadn't been spotted and began to look round. Although he couldn't see any sign of buildings, he began to make his way through the woods towards where he assumed a house might be.

Henderson strode excitedly towards the car as Winston Brown stepped out onto the gravel drive. He had good reason to be cheerful. If his research was accurate, this man had in his possession the second of the four keys.

"Good morning, Mr. Brown and welcome to Harlington. My assistant will take care of your bags." He nodded to the small, balding man beside him who had followed him out from the hall.

"I hope your journey was a pleasant one," continued Henderson, looking Brown up and down and wondering where the key was. He was sure he would have it on his person somewhere; most likely in the brief case. The man was not quite what Henderson had expected; despite his intense research, he had failed to acquire a photograph of Brown prior to this meeting. The man was a bit of a disappointment. He imagined someone with an aura, someone with charisma. Brown was about as inconsequential as one could imagine.

"Thank you, most pleasant," answered Brown.

Henderson noticed that Brown had developed a slight Texan drawl despite the fact that he knew the man was born in Wolverhampton and had only spent the past six years in the States.

"I have taken the liberty of having a light lunch prepared for us. Then, this afternoon, after you have settled into your room, we will make the preparations in readiness for this evening's ceremony."

Brown smiled and patted the battered brief case that swung from his shoulder. Henderson returned the smile, holding back a fierce urge to snatch the bag from him to examine the key; he knew he would have to be patient.

Donovan crouched down further into the bushes as the Mercedes drove past him back towards the road. He had just managed to catch sight of the two men before they walked up the steps and disappeared into the house.

"I knew it...Henderson!" he whispered to himself. He looked across at the mansion. It was a Georgian affair with huge windows and white marble columns everywhere, typical of the style. He noticed that despite the assurances of Alcatraz Security, there appeared to be no cameras; none that he could see at any rate.

He pondered his next move, settling on his haunches. Should he try and nose around now or wait until dark? He looked at his watch. It was only ten past one; it wouldn't be dark for ages.

The sound of tyres on gravel indicated more visitors and he pushed himself further down into the undergrowth. A blue Range Rover pulled up the drive and stopped in front of the house. Donovan recognised it as the one he had seen at the Beaumont offices. The two men who stepped out though, he didn't recognise, but it would be reasonable to suggest they were the two henchmen he'd narrowly avoided meeting when he'd fled down the stairs. Neither of them, he noted, had any traces of facial scars. In fact, they looked like your average politician types; conservatively tailored suits and leather brogues.

A small, balding man opened the door for them and they went inside. Donovan decided that as the men inside were now probably greeting each other this might be his best chance of getting closer to the house without being seen. He bolted across the drive and took cover behind the Range Rover before creeping the last few metres to a spot beneath one of the large windows that ran along the front of the house. He was thankful for the cover, albeit slight, afforded by the vegetation that clung to the walls of the house.

He took a deep breath then cautiously pulled himself up to peer through the window. Inside he saw the two men who had just arrived being shown into the room. Henderson stood up from the dining table at which he was sitting and walked over to them. Unfortunately, the thick walls and double-glazing prevented Donovan from eavesdropping but it was evident that neither of the men had met Winston

Brown before as he also rose from the table and shook hands with them both.

Henderson said something to the men and they sat down, apparently to join them for lunch.

Donovan watched in frustration for a few more minutes but could glean nothing from the conversation that was taking place. He hunkered down again. Apart from the four men now in the room, he had seen only one other person: the butler. The lack of security he'd so far witnessed made up his mind for him. He decided to have a quick look round then head for home and come up with a plan of action to somehow get closer to Donovan so that he could delve further into what was going on.

He crept along the front of the house, sticking close to the wall, before he came to an arch that led into a courtyard. He could see a long out building to his right. He guessed it had once been a stable, judging by the horse-riding paraphernalia that still adorned the outside walls. It must have been converted recently for other purposes; what had once been windows and doors were now slabs of thick opaque glass.

The only entrance to the building was beneath a porch at the far end of the courtyard where two sliding doors made of the same black glass as the windows barred the way. The style was in complete contrast to the main house and Donovan wondered if it perhaps contained a swimming pool or a gymnasium.

With a quick glance around, he scurried across the courtyard half expecting a voice to halt his progress. To his relief, it didn't come and in a few seconds he was standing in front of the doors. He could see his reflection in the glass and the thought suddenly occurred to him that although he couldn't see in, if there were anyone inside, they could probably see out.

There were no handles on the door and he sighed in

frustration. He started to feel very vulnerable and took a step forward to be closer to the building. Suddenly, the doors slid open. It took him by surprise and he nearly bolted before he realised that there must be a pressure pad beneath the mat on which he was now standing. He scurried quickly inside. The doors slid shut behind him.

He was now standing in a small anteroom. In front of him were two more doors, this time made of heavy wood of the non-electric variety. The anteroom had a stone floor and the walls were painted a deep crimson. The atmosphere was not warm and humid as a swimming pool would be but cold and dry like a church on a non-service day. Donovan was not prepared for what he saw as he opened the inner doors and he couldn't help whispering out loud *'Fuck Me!'*

The door closed quietly behind him and he looked round the room in disbelief. The inner walls were also painted in the same deep crimson as the anteroom but every two or three metres huge tapestries adorned the walls. Each one had a kind of runic quality but the symbols portrayed on them were all clearly from different cultures.

He scanned across them looking for a common theme. Although some of them looked kind of familiar, he couldn't place them. The first three symbols looked distinctly hieroglyphic, whilst the next few had an aboriginal feel to them. There were a couple at the far end that depicted people with distorted features: eyes that were oversized, hands with six fingers. He took a few steps forward so that he could see ones on the walls immediately to the side of him and his gaze fell on a symbol he did recognise. A shudder ran through him. The black swastika looked out of place amongst the other symbols, probably because he knew what it symbolised. Maybe the other symbols also had something to do with evil too. He wished he had his camera with him. Kate would be back next week and she might recognise some of them.

He looked beyond the swastika and his eyes rested on the tapestry that was the focal point for the room. It was twice as large as the others and he realised for the first time that there were, beneath it, some semicircular benches set out to form a small amphitheatre.

The low stone table set in the space in front of the benches was about two metres long and a metre wide. The two candles that stood on tall metal stands at either side of the table gave the scene an almost religious feel.

Sweat rolled down Donovan's temple despite the coldness of the room. He looked once more at the tapestry above the altar and stared for a minute trying to make sense of it. The main symbol was a little like the canopy of an umbrella with six points coming from it. Above the canopy was a kind of undulating line that suggested something was emerging from the canopy and disappearing skywards. Finally, he noticed that at the base of the canopy there were elliptical lines, several of them crossing over one another but circling the base of the canopy. It reminded Donovan of the diagrams his physics teacher used to draw at school to represent electrons flying round the nucleus of an atom.

He scanned the room again, still trying to piece together what it could all mean.

Firstly, Henderson pays him a fortune to extricate a weird statue from Ian Brady. Secondly, there were the dodgy accounts and payments to Beaumont (which, to all intents and purposes, was a ghost company).

Henderson passed suspicious brown envelopes to workers at the Millennium Dome site and now he invites a man who has connections with one of the most infamous cults in America to visit him at his mansion. There must a common thread.

Perhaps this room was it; perhaps Henderson was a fucking loony who was setting up his own cult. It wouldn't be the first time somebody as powerful as Henderson had become involved in a pseudo- religious organisation, one in which he could wield the power that he so obviously craved and would massage his massive ego.

Donovan looked up at the tapestry again and, for the first time, realised what he was looking at.

"Jesus Christ, it's the Dome."

The canopy was the Millennium dome! The six spikes were the spires that supported the roof, of course there were twelve really, but from the side...Thoughts were coming fast and furious now.

The trench he'd seen round the perimeter of the base of the Dome, was that what the lines were at the base of this picture? The electrical schematic that he'd photographed at the Beaumont offices!

Were these lines supposed to represent a flow of electricity? And the book he'd seen in Henderson's study ...what was it called? ... Something about a stone... it had something to do with ancient civilisations, for it had pictures not dissimilar to some of the tapestries that were here!

His head was spinning now trying to piece it all together. He needed time; time to think; time to look at everything he had uncovered so far.

He looked at his watch and realised with horror that he'd been inside for nearly twenty-five minutes, lunch might have come to an end. He turned to leave and nearly walked straight into the figure standing directly behind him. He registered the face of the butler momentarily before he felt a massive blow to the back of his head, forcing him to stagger forward onto the stone floor. He felt the chill of the hard stone on his cheek and then there was nothing but darkness.

46

Chust, Czechoslovakia. November 1943

The sound of the gunshot was deafening.

Kristina's mouth dropped open; the vomit rose uncontrollably and burst forth making a slapping sound as it fell onto the cobbles below. Some of the thick, biley liquid splashed onto her tiny, bare feet and she dropped to her knees unable to catch her breath.

Her father tried to reach down to her but the sharp blow to the back of his neck with the butt of a rifle knocked him into the gutter.

As Kristina retched again, through the tears, she watched as the stream of dark crimson blood from her dog, Boombi, trickled between the cobbles towards the steaming remnants of her last meal.

She was vaguely aware of a moaning sound behind her then the loud, angry voice of one of the men in uniform who had forced them to leave their grandmother's house so suddenly and without warning, broke the silence.

She understood a little German, enough to understand what he was shouting:

"You have three seconds to stand otherwise you are a dead man."

Kristina lifted her head; everything seemed to be happening in slow motion. Boombi lay on his side a few feet in front of her, his eyes closed, his tongue protruding, like a pink slug, from his mouth. *Who could have done something so terrible? Just because he wouldn't stop barking.*

Behind her, the man had begun to count out loud. His tone was sharp and threatening

"Eins!"

Kristina wiped her hand across her mouth, pieces of half digested food sticking to the sleeve of her woollen cardigan.

"Zwei!"

She pushed herself up into a standing position. Bile rose up into her throat again.

"Drei!"

Kristina turned round as the storm trooper lifted his pistol higher and pointed it towards the prostrate figure of her father. She screamed "Noooooooo!"

The bullet slammed into the nape of his neck and threw his head violently to the side. Kristina, who was only two feet from her father, blinked as flecks of blood, flesh and small jelly-like pieces of his brain splattered her face.

Stunned, she turned round, searching for a familiar, comforting face; a face that would smile and tell her to wake up; that it was just a nightmare and everything would be all right.

In front of her were five people: the man who'd just killed her father, another guard who held back her grandfather with both arms round his chest; her mother and grandmother.

Her grandmother, who was pushing her daughter's face into the pleats of her dress to muffle the screams, was holding up her mother forcibly. The look of terror on her grandmother's face told Kristina that this wasn't a nightmare. Something suddenly caught Kristina's eye. Beyond the small group of people waiting in the road which ran to the side of their house, was a car. It was a large, sleek, black car with huge wheel arches and an enormous grille at the front.

She recognised it as the kind that made her parents uncomfortable when they were walking home from the Synagogue on Sundays. She had noticed that whenever one passed them, her parents seemed to quicken their pace and encourage her to walk more briskly.

The movement that had attracted her attention was the rear window sliding down. Inside, she could make out the dark shape of a man. The window didn't slide all the way down but stopped short so that only the man's eyes and nose were visible. Through small, round spectacles, the eyes locked onto Kristina's.

Despite just witnessing the death of her father, the terror that now filled her was unimaginable. The yellow eyes bore into her soul and she knew, even though she had never seen him before, that he was somehow responsible for the terrible things that were happening to her family.

As Kristina watched, unable to tear her eyes away, the face seemed to fade in and out of focus. With each fade the features appeared to alter slightly; the nose became more pronounced and slightly hooked; the cheekbones lengthened; the yellow eyes darkened to become brown; even the hair began to lengthen until it came below the ears.

Tears slowly began to trickle down Kristina's cheeks and she finally managed to avert her gaze and look back to where her father's body lay in the street. *How could it be possible?*

She turned back to look at the car only to see it moving off up the road. The window was slowly rising, but she could still make out her father's face smiling at her from inside.

47

Donovan half opened his eyes and groaned. His head was throbbing and he could taste blood at the back of his throat. He was disorientated and intuitively reached out for his alarm clock to check the time. Instead of the alarm clock, his fingers closed round something unfamiliar. He turned his head to look at the object and was surprised to find that he was not actually in his own bedroom. The object he held in his hand was a book. He turned the book the right way up to read the title on the spine: *The Holy Bible*.

His first thought was that he'd been on a bender and had spent the night in a B&B and then it began to come back to him: the mansion, the strange outbuilding, the tapestries and then the butler standing in front of him.

He rubbed the back of his neck realising that he must have been clobbered.

He climbed off the bed and looked round the room. It looked just like any hotel room except for the wrought iron bars that covered the windows. He looked across at the door; no doubt that would be locked too. Before he had the chance to try it, he heard voices outside. They were approaching the room. He took a few paces backwards and waited. He recognised one of the voices as Henderson's and he took a deep intake of breath. How was he going to explain this?

The voices stopped outside the door and the sound of a key in the lock confirmed Donovan's earlier thoughts. The door handle turned and Henderson walked in followed by two men: the butler and one of the men whom he'd seen arrive earlier. All three were dressed in long, purple robes and despite his predicament, Donovan struggled to keep from smiling; images of the Ku Klux Clan springing immediately into his mind.

"Well, Mr. Donovan, I see you have recovered from Jonathon's little welcome. Now perhaps you would kindly explain exactly what you were doing skulking round the grounds of the Hall this afternoon."

Donovan's mind was racing, he hadn't been conscious long enough to think of a plausible excuse for being there.

"I was trying to locate you as a matter of fact. It's about Brady and that key thing I got for you..." he began before being swiftly interrupted.

"Don't underestimate me, Mr. Donovan. I think you'll find that it would be a rather costly mistake."

The look in his eyes was the same Donovan had seen when they'd met at the party at Maisie Howarth's house: cold and threatening.

"Well, actually, it wasn't so much Brady as the Millennium Dome..."

He looked up at Henderson to gauge his reaction. He was smiling. "The fact that you seem to be paying some ghost company a lot of money to undertake work which is not actually part of the 'official' construction plans kind of attracted my attention. And you know me, once I get a sniff of a story..."

"Very good, Mr. Donovan. And what other snippets of 'information' have you managed to uncover?"

Donovan had already realised that his chances of bluffing his way out of the situation had disappeared when he had been caught in the 'temple'.

"Only that you have connections with the Branch Davidians and that, judging by the contents of your 'stables', connections with one or two other odd organisations as well."

The three men looked at each other and smiled. Henderson walked past Donovan and looked out of the window. He paused for a moment as if contemplating something. Then he turned around.

"You are quite correct, Mr. Donovan. Our connections spread wide and far. Further in fact that you could ever imagine. Have you managed to work out what the electrical installation at the Dome is actually for?"

This was a rhetorical question as Henderson was in no doubt that no one but he could possibly understand the way in which the Dome was going to work. He looked directly at Donovan and laughed. "Sit down, Mr. Donovan, and let me explain. Since you will not be leaving us again, I don't see why your curiosity cannot be satisfied."

Donovan wasn't shocked by this revelation; he had already realised that Henderson was up to something so fundamentally corrupt that he wouldn't be allowed to simply walk out of there and be trusted to keep things to himself.

He sat down on the edge of the bed.

"You see, the Dome is not merely a tourist attraction, Mr. Donovan. It is in fact an electrical generator. The electrical installation that you spoke of earlier will be capable of producing an enormous electro-magnetic field.

The twelve spires on top of the dome are locating beacons and the dome itself is nothing more than the world's largest parabolic dish. For the last ten thousand years, the souls of ten million people have been harvested and interned in the nether regions of the heavens. They are now ready to fulfil their destiny."

Donovan realised that Henderson was now trembling as he spoke. His eyes looked glassy and there was an odd smile behind his words. His eyes were half closed as if he were mentally visualising something.

"The Dome will provide the channel through which The Master will return and with him will come the souls of the ten million. You see, Mr. Donovan, David Koresh was merely a small cog in a very large machine. You might say he was an envoy, responsible for keeping a key, identical to the one that you yourself, in fact, brought to me a few days ago, safe until it was ready to be used. When four of these keystones are placed in the 'Stone' and the 'Stone' is set in the exact centre of the Dome, all will be complete. The life force will be harnessed and The Master's return will be realised."

Henderson's head dropped forward and his eyes opened fully. He smiled at Donovan before signalling to his associates that the meeting was at an end.

The bald-headed man turned and opened the door. Donovan remained on the edge of the bed as Henderson walked past. As he reached the door, Henderson suddenly turned round.

"Oh, there is one last thing you need to know, Mr. Donovan..."

Donovan stood up, he felt vulnerable now somehow.

"You will be pleased to know your efforts will not have been in vain. You will join us this evening for... Mass."

The door closed and the key turned in the lock.

The slight hesitation in Henderson's voice before he had said the word 'Mass' left Donovan in little doubt what they had in store for him.

48

Auschwitz. (Birkenau) Poland. January 1944

Kristina laid the knives and forks carefully on the long wooden table. The visitors were apparently very important and everything had to be just right. A knife placed upside down or a wine glass placed on the wrong side might result in a severe reprimand, putting her privileged position as a trustee in jeopardy. She looked along the table and salivated like one of Pavlov's dogs, even though no food had yet been served. Her mind was filled with images of steaming mashed potato and her grandmother's homemade kugel.

The thought brought an immediate tear to her eye as she remembered the day they had arrived at the camp. Her grandmother and grandfather had been ordered into a different line from her and her mother as they stepped off the train. It was the last time she ever saw them. Later, when she discovered where they had been taken, she had vowed that she would do everything in her power to keep herself and her mother alive so that they might somehow find a way to avenge their deaths.

It was her mother's idea to gain favour with the guards and the officers in order to be considered for the job she was now doing. She had been fervently opposed to it at first but as her mother had explained, if it provided them both with a greater opportunity for survival, it also gave them hope of retribution when it was all over.

A tear dropped onto the napkin that she had just laid out and she hastily turned it over. She wiped her face on her sleeve and continued with the job.

The pallid cloud of grey smoke billowed ominously from the stark brick chimneys of the crematoria and seeped like a watery stain into the lifeless wintry sky. Despite the location of the camp, deep in the heart of a thick pine forest, no birdsong disturbed the eerie silence.

The small group of men standing beneath the chimneys studied the cloud as if it were an impressive piece of architecture or perhaps a famous work of art.

Although the tour had been arranged for the benefit of the Fuhrer, to illustrate the efficiency of the implementation of the Final Solution, he was only vaguely aware of the conversation taking place round him; questions about the capacity of the crematoria and how long it took to process each cohort of prisoners.

The Kampkommandant was very nervous, knowing that the Fuhrer demanded absolute efficiency in order that as many Jews be liquidated in as short a time as possible. He was determined to illustrate that he was carrying out his duties effectively. Beads of sweat were forming on his brow as he realised that despite his best efforts at impressing his visitors, Herr Hitler appeared to be unmoved.

"Our processing rate here is one of the highest in Poland," he said, turning to face the Fuhrer. He paused, scrutinising the Fuhrer's face, hoping to see even the slightest raising of an eyebrow to indicate that he was pleased.

Hitler remained silent. He was in deep thought. As he watched the smoke slowly rise, he became aware of an almost pulse-like sensation deep within his body. He recognised the sensation as the presence of the Master manifesting himself within *him*. Even though the key was safe inside a locked drawer over seventy kilometres away, the Master was able to enter him and be present wherever and whenever he chose. Ever since the day that Heinrich had addressed the Extermination camp Kommandants at Poznan, the Master seemed to have grown in strength to such an extent that he was now able to move around at will.

The smoke continued to rise and he began to feel faint. The pulse inside him was now so strong that his eardrums felt as if they were stretching. He had a sensation of rising up from the ground and he looked round to see if the officers around him were aware of what was happening. Apparently, they were not; they were still engrossed with the discussion about the gory details of the camp.

He looked back up towards the chimneys, towards the hypnotic tower of smoke. It appeared to be changing. As it rose higher into the sky, he noticed that it became wispier and almost translucent before mixing with the blanket of cloud that hung over the camp.

The pulsing inside his head was now almost unbearable and he had to clench his fists tightly in order to remain in control. Suddenly, he felt a colossal blow to his chest and as he looked up, he saw something dart towards him from the top of the tower of smoke at an incredible speed. There was another massive blow to his chest and he felt a surge of power run through his body. Before he had chance to recover, there was another blow, then another. They continued coming until they became so frequent that each new hit became indistinguishable from the last. There was no pain, just a sensation of warmth flowing through his veins and arteries at an incomprehensible speed.

He lifted his head again and looked up. His eyes grew wider at the sight before him. From the top of the cloud flowed a continuous swathe of wispy mist. He looked down at his chest where the mist seemed to be concentrating and penetrating his body. Then he became aware of something else; something frightening and overwhelming. Inside the mist, he could make out faces. They were not faces he knew but he was in no doubt to whom they belonged. The heads were shorn, the cheeks emasculated and the eye sockets sunken. Some were faces of the very old, some very young; some were women and others, children. There was, however, one thing they all had in common: the haunted look of having been taken before their time.

He didn't know how long he had been looking up (it felt like hours), when he felt a light pressure on his elbow. He turned to see Himmler looking directly into his eyes. He looked concerned.

"Are you alright?" he asked.

Hitler composed himself before answering. "Yes, I'm fine. I just felt a little faint for a moment."

He looked round at the others to gauge their response. They were all clearly waiting for their Fuhrer to pass a comment of some sort before moving on.

"Splendid. Now I believe we have a fresh consignment arriving this afternoon," he said, finally smiling at the Kamp Kommandant.

"Yes, indeed we do Mein Fuhrer, in just over an hour. In the meantime, may I suggest we return to the main camp where I have arranged for us to take lunch."

He held out his arm to indicate the way back and as the Fuhrer strode in front of him, he breathed a sigh of relief. If everything went smoothly this afternoon, a bottle of his favourite Cognac might be in order tonight.

Kristina was trembling. She was staring at her feet, convinced that her expression would betray the hatred and loathing that felt as if it were burning a hole in her chest. She suddenly realised that her hands were knotted into fists and she flattened them and pressed them against her thighs.

The Kamp Kommandant led the visitors to their places,

passing in front of the eight girls who had been trusted with the job of waiting on them. Although they had all been told to smile politely as the visitors entered, Kristina dared not lift her head and she prayed that the Kommandant wouldn't notice it. Fortunately, he was so wrapped up in ensuring that his visitors were seated and content that he wouldn't have noticed if the girls had been stark naked.

As soon as the entourage had appeared in the dining hall chatting and laughing, she had recognised the small man with the round glasses. Without warning her legs turned to jelly and she had to support herself against the edge of a table to prevent herself from falling over. She had quickly managed to regain her composure and now, despite the trembling of her knees and the thumping of her heart against her ribs, she felt back in control. The men sat down and the two girls at either end of the line peeled away and began serving the wine. Kristina and the other girls filed into the kitchen to fetch the first course. The chef was adding the final touches to three trays of smoked salmon and behind him steam rose from an enormous platter of roast beef. The girls stepped forward to take the trays. Kristina's eyes were drawn to the platter of beef. At its side lay a long carving knife.

The girl in front of her stepped forward and picked up a tray. The chef was muttering things under his breath as he checked that everything was in order. Kristina stepped forward and suddenly lurched to one side and fell heavily to the floor. She clutched her ankle and cried out, feigning pain. The chef instinctively reached out to try and stop her falling but then realised that the visitors would now be waiting to begin their meal. He urged the next girl in line to take the tray and only then did he kneel down to help Kristina to her feet.

He lifted her onto a stool and she reassured him that she would be fine after a moment's rest. He turned to check on the sauce that was simmering on the stove. He plunged his index finger into the brown, bubbling liquid, closed his eyes, and tasted it before wiping it on his trouser leg and tutting. He turned and strode towards the larder in the far corner of the kitchen. Kristina waited until he had disappeared inside then darted forward, picked up the carving knife, and slid it quickly inside the pocket of her apron. She was about to sit back on the stool when the chef stepped back out from the larder. She smiled nervously and he took it as an indication that she had recovered from her fall. He smiled back but it quickly transformed into a scowl as he noticed two baskets of bread that hadn't been taken through.

"Come on, quickly, take the bread!"

Kristina turned and scooped up the baskets, relieved to get out of the kitchen. She glanced down at her apron to make sure the knife was concealed then took the bread out to the table.

As she leaned forward to offer the bread to the Fuhrer and then to Herr Himmler, she had no trouble smiling politely.

49

Epping, London 1997

Donovan stood up from the bed as the door opened. Two of the men who had accompanied Henderson earlier entered, followed by another man whom he hadn't seen before. He was dark and swarthy with bad skin. Donovan thought he wouldn't have looked out of place in a Turkish medina selling camels. All three were wearing purple robes.

"Mr. Henderson requests your company in the dining room. If you would be so kind." The man spoke with an accent that Donovan guessed was Southern European or maybe North African.

Donovan looked at his watch. It was six thirty. He hadn't eaten since breakfast but somehow he couldn't imagine Henderson wanting to provide him with a *Last Supper* so to speak. (He had come to the conclusion as the afternoon had wore on that the Mass Henderson had spoken of was nothing but a crude euphemism for a funeral ceremony.)

As he was led down the huge wooden staircase onto the ground floor, he casually glanced round weighing up the possibility of escape. He was trying to cast his mind back to when he'd first sneaked a look in through the window; maybe he could work out the plan of the house.

The stairs gave way to a shabbily carpeted hallway that was lined with wood panelling and all along the hallway, oversized watercolours set in ostentatious gilt frames hung from the wall. They looked dusty and neglected, as if the person who had lovingly collected them had died and forgotten to bequeath them to anyone.

To the left was a set of double doors. They were half glazed and he could just make out through the stained glass the outline of another door. It was wooden-panelled and the dark rectangular shadow about half way down suggested a letter- box. *The main entrance?*

To the right, the hallway opened up and led to a number of doorways. The sound of voices engaged in conversation, and light classical music, floated out from the second door, along with the smell of roast lamb.

Donovan stopped at the bottom of the stairs, more in an effort to buy time to look round than to be told which way to go. The man with the foreign accent touched him lightly on his arm and gestured to turn to his right.

As he looked over his shoulder, Donovan noticed for the first time the pendant that was hanging round his neck. It looked like an amulet of some description. It appeared to be made of gold and was shaped like an almond. Set in the middle was a huge, green gemstone giving it the appearance of an eye. The man nodded to his right impatiently and Donovan stepped into the hall. He took two paces forward then a dull thud behind him followed by a yelp made him turn round. The man with the pendant was bending down picking up several letters from the carpet with one hand whilst rubbing his shin with the other. Donovan hadn't noticed the Queen Anne bureau at the bottom of the stairs; he'd been too busy looking for a means of escape.

The man pushed shut the bottom drawer that had caught his leg as he'd passed, and replaced the letters back on the bureau next to a pile of white vellum envelopes and a writing pad. Donovan noted the address on the top wasn't

Harlington Hall and that the letters had no stamps. *Outgoing mail, waiting to be posted?* An idea flashed into his mind but before it was fully formed, Bad Skin prodded him, less gently than before, and he walked toward the dining room.

As he entered the room, Henderson stood to greet him.

"Ah, our special guest; glad you could join us, Mr. Donovan." Henderson beamed at him like a long, lost friend and for a minute he thought the other people sitting round the table were going to applaud. They didn't, though; most of them just smiled and nodded politely.

The room was bigger than Donovan had imagined and beyond the dining table there were French doors leading to a lounge area set on a slightly lower level. Two huge, leather Chesterfields faced each other and in between them sat a large glass coffee table. Donovan noticed the drapes were half drawn in there, presumably to keep out the early evening sun. In the dining room, there was nothing besides the table and a cabinet housing a music system. The flickering green light of the graphic equaliser seemed curiously out of place.

The table, he noticed, was set for eight but only six people were seated. It was also apparent that they had not begun their meal. Three large, silver platters adorned the centre of the table and all were still covered. Two bottles of sparkling wine fizzed beside them.

Henderson stood up and held out his arm towards the top of the table where there was an empty place. "Please sit down, Mr. Donovan. The first course will be served in a moment."

Bad Skin seated himself directly opposite Donovan at the top end of the table in the last remaining seat and, with an almost imperceptible nod of his head, Henderson dismissed the two men who remained standing.

There was a moment's silence before the butler

appeared carrying a basket of bread rolls and everyone round the table began making preparations to eat. Donovan was beginning to doubt his sanity as the surrealism of the situation began to sink in and for a minute, he began to question his mental state. It was as if he had imagined the whole of the last ten hours and he was now settling down to a pleasant evening with friends.

The soup was served and, as they ate, Donovan studied the faces of the men round him. As well as Henderson and Bad Skin, there was Winston Brown, the man he'd followed from the station, two men who looked like magistrates (worryingly, both of whom looked familiar), a man who Donovan guessed was from somewhere east of the sub continent, and finally, someone whom he recognised immediately as the man he'd seen taking envelopes from Henderson at the construction site.

For the next thirty minutes, the strange dinner proceeded in the same manner as it had started. The men made polite conversation about the stock market, world oil prices and the NATO air strikes in Kosovo, whilst more courses were served and eaten. No one made any attempt to include Donovan in the small talk, (for which he was glad; his mind had begun to drift back to how he was going to get out of the house). Occasionally, Henderson smiled at him in between mouthfuls of lamb and glazed carrots but apart from that, he might have been invisible.

Donovan was deep in thought when the classical music halted abruptly and he became aware that everyone had stopped talking. He looked up to find the others looking at him. Henderson got up from the table and walked slowly round the table until he was standing in front of the French doors.

"Gentlemen, I think we are now ready to retire to the lounge."

Although Henderson smiled as he spoke, Donovan

detected a tenseness round his mouth that made his top lip quiver involuntarily. He sensed that he was about to discover what all this was about.

50

Auschwitz (Birkenau) Poland 1944

Himmler wiped his mouth delicately with the napkin before folding it neatly and placing it on his side plate.

"Excuse me, gentlemen," he said, looking toward the Kommandant for a clue as to the whereabouts of the lavatory. The Kommandant took his cue and pointed to the door through which they had entered, making it clear that it was a few yards across the compound.

Himmler smiled at the girls as he passed them. Each smiled obediently back in return.

Kristina watched the door close behind him then looked desperately around for the opportunity she needed. There was a small amount of wine left in one of the bottles on the table. She scurried over to the table and poured the remnants of the wine into the Fuhrer's glass. The Kommandant indicated with a wave of his hand that she should bring some more and she hurried into the kitchen with the empty bottle. The chef was busy arranging cheese onto a board and didn't turn around as she made her way out of the door at the back of the hut.

As soon as she had pushed the door gently shut, she lifted the hem of her dress and broke into a run. She knew that, at best, she might have a minute to fulfil her plan.

Himmler watched the steam rise from the river of urine that trickled down the yellow-stained ceramic gutter. He

290*Alexander James*

belched loudly and excused himself despite the fact he was alone. He had enjoyed his lunch immensely and the three glasses of wine had not only helped wash the sour taste of death out of his mouth, but left him with a very pleasurable light headedness.

A spider had built its web on the wall just above the gutter and he was torn between watching it cocooning a fly in silk and aiming a jet of urine at it.

The twisting motion of the spider's prey as it was quickly mummified was almost hypnotic and a sudden wetness on the side of his leg brought his attention back to the task of relieving himself. He cursed out loud when he saw the stain appearing on his trousers and in anger lifted his boot and squashed the spider into the wall.

He buttoned his fly and turned round looking for somewhere to wash his hands. There was a china bowl and a jug sitting on a crude wooden table by the door and he walked across hoping that there was water in the jug.

His mood improved as he realised that in addition to water, there was also a small bar of soap and a hand towel. He poured water into the bowl and deliberately splashed a little onto the dry trouser leg in an attempt to disguise the stain (he could say he'd been over zealous whilst washing his hands.)

He picked up the soap and lathered his hands in the water relishing the feeling of cleanliness that it gave him. He hated the thought of germs hiding insidiously under his nails and he forced the soap under them. His thoughts turned to the crematoria that they'd visited that morning and he likened the Jews to the germs he was washing from his hands. The crematoria were just like enormous bars of soap cleansing the world of filth. He smiled to himself and he picked up the towel to dry his hands. As he did so, he heard the door click open behind him and turned to see who had entered. He was surprised to see one of the girls who had been serving lunch in front of him.

She looked wide-eyed and she was panting heavily.

"I think you have made a mistake, I believe..." he began, then he realised that she was holding a carving knife. His hand fell instinctively to the holster at his side but he knew that in the time it would take to unclip his gun, she could have killed him. The look in her eyes left him in no doubt that that was her intention. He thought of shouting for help but his mouth had suddenly gone dry and he licked his lips nervously. He glanced at the door urging it to open. The girl realised what he was thinking and took a step forward, the knife raised in front of her. He tried to step back but the table prevented him from retreating any further.

"Look ... I can get you out of here. I can get you a passport and arrange for you to be sent wherever you wish...you could go back to your family."

She was only a foot away now and he could see remains of roast beef stuck to the blade.

"My family!" she whispered. "My family can never be a family again because you..." She pressed the knife to his throat so that the tip disappeared into a fold of skin. He could feel it pressing on his Adam's apple.

"...because you had them murdered. I watched you drive away after my father was shot. You even smiled, you evil bastard. Well, this is for my father and my grandfather and my grandmother and for Boombi."

Himmler could feel blood now running down his neck onto his shirt.

The girl's eyes were crazed and she was speaking through clenched teeth.

Once more he glanced over at the door. He felt the knife pull away and he realised she was drawing it back to achieve momentum to stab him in the throat.

Suddenly, he felt warmth rising up from his feet and his

first thought was that he had finally lost control of his bladder. Ridiculously, he visualised his bloody corpse being discovered later by the guards and them discussing the piss stains in his pants. He closed his eyes and waited for the blade to strike.

When nothing happened, he opened them slowly. The girl was staring at him, tears welling up in her eyes. The knife, he noticed, was now at her side dangling from her hand. Her mouth was moving but no sound came out at first. Suddenly, her mouth began to move: "Papa?"

Himmler was aware that the warmth that had begun at his feet was now washing over his whole body. He was also aware that he was no longer trembling. In fact, he felt unnaturally calm and relaxed. It was only after he had spoken the first few words that he realised *he* hadn't actually thought of the words, and even stranger, that the voice that spoke was not his own.

"Kristina, my beautiful Kristina. Come to Papa."

The girl didn't move, so he stepped slowly forward and reached out to embrace her. She bowed her head and he closed his arms round her. He kissed her on the forehead and whispered her name again.

She looked up at him through her tears and he smiled down at her.

"Papa, I missed you so much, but how…"

Himmler's hand slid down her arm and gently prised her fingers from round the knife handle.

"My angel, I missed you too," he said, kissing the tears from her cheeks.

Her hand had fallen away from the knife now and he brought it round so that it rested level with her crotch. He lifted his free hand to her chin and lifted it slightly so he could look into her eyes. He stared into them deeply as he pushed the knife up to its hilt, into the soft flesh above her pubic bone.

She gasped in horror as she realised what he'd done and he felt her nails digging into the flesh on his upper arms. He felt her body begin to sag and, as it did, he drew the knife upwards sharply. The blade snagged as it bit into her sternum and her weight became too much for him to hold. He pushed her away from him and she slid slowly to the floor, her gaze still rooted firmly onto his face. Her mouth twitched as she tried to speak again but bubbles of crimson-coloured sputum prevented the words from forming.

In the back of his mind, a voice was telling him to unclip his gun and shoot her, to end her misery, but it was as if there was another, stronger voice controlling his actions.

Instead of unclipping his gun, he found himself leaning over her. Grasping the handle of the knife, he twisted the blade so that the flesh below her torn dress gaped open. He could see her heart beating erratically, desperately trying in vain to pump blood that was no longer coursing through her veins and arteries but trickling toward the gutter on the other side of the hut.

He slid his hand inside her chest, noticing for the first time that his nails were long and brown; more like talons than nails.

Her heart made a squelching noise as it was wrenched from her insides and he had to use the knife to sever the last few blood vessels that remained intact. Incredibly, her eyes were still watching him as he lifted her heart to his mouth and bit deeply into it.

51

"Sit here, Mr. Donovan. I think this position will provide the best view."

Henderson was pointing to the leather sofa which faced away from the dining room.

"View of what exactly?" thought Donovan, squeezing himself awkwardly into the narrow space left in between the two 'magistrates'. Had the curtains not been almost completely drawn, he would have been dazzled by the sun which was currently perched on the crowns of the plane trees that lined the drive outside. As it was, only a few rays penetrated into the darkened room, cutting a laser-like path through the floating dust that had filled the air when the three men had sat down.

Donovan noticed, for the first time, that there was a box sitting on the glass coffee table in front of them. He also noticed that the rays of light from the sun seemed to be trained directly onto it.

Winston Brown and the other three men stood behind the sofa also facing the table. To all intents, it looked like they were preparing to have their photograph taken.

Henderson walked round the sofa opposite and made some minor adjustment to the curtains.

Donovan was beginning to become agitated now as he sensed that the moment of truth coming. He was hot and uncomfortable, and the sweat on the back of his legs was making them stick to the leather sofa. He squirmed a little, then whispered an apology as the two magistrates turned their heads and stared at him as if he'd farted in a sauna.

Henderson finally appeared to be satisfied with the brightness in the room and he turned to face the seven men. He rested his hands on the backrest of the other Chesterfield and closed his eyes momentarily as if he were composing himself. The light rays were now directly behind him and only the glow from the lights in the dining room illuminated his face. The effect was quite theatrical and his face seemed almost to be suspended in mid air.

"Now gentlemen, before we enlighten Mr. Donovan as to why we are all here, I need to show you all something very special."

His eyes fell onto the box on the table.

"Mr. Finnegan, would you do the honours, please?"

There was movement behind Donovan and the man from the construction site stepped forward. He hunkered down beside the table and carefully lifted the box. Apparently, the 'box' was actually a cover because as he lifted it, something remained on the table. Finnegan placed the box on the floor and resumed his position behind the sofa.

Although it was dark in the room, the object on the table was quite visible due to the fact that that it seemed to contain a light source of its own. It was only after a few seconds that Donovan realised that he'd seen the object before or at least he'd seen pictures of it before. After he'd visited the construction site in Greenwich, he'd been curious as to what the Millennium Dome was going to look like when it was finished so he'd accessed the official web site on the Internet. The object on the table was a scale model of the Dome! He remembered thinking at the time that it was nothing more than a glorified tent but seeing this model made him realise what a feat of architectural engineering it was. The model was maybe forty centimetres across and twenty centimetres high and had twelve spires sticking out of the top. The canopy was suspended by cables attached to the spires and the cables formed a huge symmetrical pattern which, when seen from above, drew the eye into the exact centre of the Dome. Donovan couldn't help but think that it resembled an inverted satellite dish. The light seemed to emanate, not from beneath the canopy, but from beneath the glass table and Donovan realised that the Dome was not resting on the table but was in fact built into the glass. The glass was maybe five centimetres thick and he noticed that embedded into the glass was a complex arrangement of wires.

There was now total silence in the room, lending an almost churchly reverence to the proceedings, and Donovan half expected them to start praying. He looked at Henderson who was now grinning like the proverbial cat.

Finnegan hunkered down beside the glass table and lifted the 'roof' gently from the Dome. The inside of the model was empty except for what looked to Donovan like a small pebble located in a recess in the centre. There were four small protrusions on top of the pebble and Finnegan appeared to press down on each one before replacing the roof. All the men were staring at the model as if it were the Apollo Eleven and they expected it to lift off at any second. Finnegan moved away from the table and returned to his position. Henderson was still standing in front of the windows.

"Gentlemen, you are about to witness something that no mortal has seen for over ten thousand years. Enjoy!"

Henderson bowed his head and took two paces to his right. The light beams shone through the window striking the dome precisely on the spires. Immediately, a low hum filled the room. It was similar to the sound a stereo speaker makes when it is at full volume though no music is being played. Donovan twisted his head slightly to look at the other men. Despite the fact that nothing much appeared to be happening, the model transfixed them. A sudden loud crack brought his attention back to the table and the low hum became much louder and more resonant. Donovan felt the soles of his feet begin to tickle as the floor of the room began to vibrate.

There was another loud crack then a finger of electricity spiked between the spires, momentarily lighting up the room. The sound in the room became even louder and Donovan tore his eyes away from the model to glance round the room. The walls appeared to be vibrating now and the reflection in the mirror hanging from the picture rail to his left was becoming distorted as if the glass was stretching and contracting.

Another loud crack made him jump and this time the flash of electricity danced between the spires creating a fiery circle of blue. It reminded Donovan of a Frankenstein film he'd seen once with Bella Lugosi. The mad doctor was trying to revive the monster using power from an electrical storm. He glanced up at Henderson who, like the others, was totally entranced. His eyes reflected the electrical charge jumping across the spires and made him look like some kind of evil android from a cheap science fiction film.

Donovan turned his attention back to the table and noticed that the wires beneath the model were beginning to glow red and like the mirror, the glass seemed to be shimmering, creating a kind of hologram effect beneath the Dome. The other curious thing was that from the ceiling of the room, tendrils of fine mist seemed to be spiralling down towards the centre of the Dome as if they were being drawn into it. The ceiling itself, like the mirror and the table, also seemed to be moving. Worryingly, the movement seemed to be predominantly inwards towards the Dome. He looked at the walls again and realised they too looked as if they were being pulled inwards. The hairs on the back of his neck stood up involuntarily as a piece of plaster fell from the ceiling, landing not two feet away from Henderson. Unbelievably, Henderson didn't flinch; he was too engrossed in what was happening on the table.

Another chunk of plaster hit the floor, this time narrowly missing the small Asian man. Donovan looked up at the ceiling again; cracks were appearing by the second and he could see wooden rafters through the holes from where the plaster had fallen. They, too, appeared to be bending.

"Fuck me, the whole fucking ceiling is going to come down at this rate," he thought. He suddenly noticed something else, something that bothered him more than the walls caving in or the ceiling collapsing: when he opened his mouth to breathe, swirls of vapour trailed away in front of him, joining the growing stalactite of mist disappearing into the centre of the Dome. Frightened, he looked round the room at the others. He could hardly believe what he was seeing. From each person's mouth or nostrils, trails of muslin-like vapour snaked towards the centre of the room. Donovan was reminded of a video that had once been sent to a newspaper he was working for. Someone had claimed to have photographed ectoplasm emanating from a dead relative and wanted ten thousand pounds for the pictures.

He didn't know whether or not it was his imagination but he suddenly began to feel weak and the thought that somehow the Dome was draining all his energy away jumped into his mind.

From the corner of his eye, he noticed that the Asian was swaying from side to side. His eyes were half closed as though he were about to pass out and a small trickle of blood ran from his nose. Winston Brown also appeared to be losing it and his head kept falling onto his chest as if he were desperately trying to stay awake.

'This is fucking madness,' thought Donovan. *'We're all going to be killed.'* He glanced over at Henderson who still seemed oblivious to anything other than the Dome. He decided that if someone didn't do something soon, they'd all be sucked dry. The police would discover their bodies congealed to the furniture like empty, blood-drenched pillowcases. He pushed his hands into the leather sofa and tried to stand but he was a dead weight. Henderson had spoken of explanations after they'd witnessed the spectacle so surely he expected them to survive it. Donovan wondered if he had underestimated the power of the thing on the table.

He tried again to rise from the seat but quickly realised that it was futile.

Surely the others felt the same as he did; why weren't they trying to do something? Maybe they were, but like him they were powerless to move.

Suddenly, without warning, the electrical discharge across the spires died and the humming abruptly stopped. It was as if a tremendous weight had been lifted from the room. Donovan could actually hear the walls creaking as they returned to their normal state. The Dome was still and lifeless except for the dull glow that had been there at the beginning.

A bead of sweat rolled down his cheek and he became aware of a dull ache in his teeth caused by the vibrations and the fact that he'd been grinding them together for the last ten minutes. He looked at the Dome, then at the gap in the curtains. There were no light beams now entering the room and it dawned on him why Henderson had been so confident· they would survive. He had timed the demonstration perfectly, in the knowledge that the sun would dip behind the trees after a few minutes and cut off the power source to the machine. He wiped his forehead with his shirtsleeve and took a deep intake of breath.

Henderson laughed loudly and Donovan looked up to see him smiling in his direction.

"Impressive stuff, eh, Mr. Donovan?"

"I think you could say you managed to attract my attention,"

"I think you are now ready to appreciate the enormity of what we are trying to achieve here, but first some refreshment. Gentlemen, drinks will be served in the dining room."

52

The Fuhrerbunker, Berlin April 30th 1945

General Helmuth Weidling, the Commander of the Berlin Defence Area, raised a handkerchief to his brow and dabbed away the beads of perspiration that had suddenly formed there. He had just been given the news that the Soviet army had now advanced within five hundred yards of the Reich Chancellery.

In the bunker, buried twenty feet beneath the Chancellery, Hitler awaited the latest news of the Allies' advance. His only companions were Eva, to whom he had been married for less than forty eight hours; the Goebbels family and Martin Bormann-his private secretary.

Despite Helmut's fervent appeals over the last two weeks, imploring him to leave the bunker and go into hiding, possibly even exile, Hitler had stubbornly refused to admit that the great dream was over and insisted on issuing orders that were not only futile, but were a stark indication that his grasp of military strategy had completely deserted him.

Now, Helmut felt that he had no choice but to request permission to break out from the bunker in order to give his men the opportunity to flee before the Red Army finally broke through. The other option was... he looked down at the pistol resting on its side on the table.

In his private chamber the Fuhrer was slouched in an

armchair. His usually immaculately combed hair was dirty and unkempt, and his eyes looked heavy and glazed over. Although he gave the appearance of looking toward the dog that lay in deep slumber on the couch opposite, in reality, he was focused on the small key-shaped object on the coffee table before him.

The only clues that the dog, Blondi, was not asleep were the absence of the rise and fall of the chest and the black tongue that hung lifelessly from the mouth. The cyanide had been quick and he now knew that his physician, Werner Haase, had been accurate in his estimate of the potency of the poison. He couldn't bear the thought that his bride might suffer.

He closed his eyes and tried to recall the first time he had encountered the Master and the promises that had been made -the power, the adulation, the wealth but most of all, the immortality. Now he knew the truth. The promise had been nothing but lies designed to seduce him from the start. Everything he had worked for during the last twenty five years was worthless. He simply existed to help free the Master from the purgatory in which he was incarcerated. And now that he had outlived his usefulness, he had become as expendable as the millions he had killed – just one more soul to be sacrificed for the Master.

He opened his eyes wearily and they came to rest on the key. The eyes of the figure through which the Master had spoken to him just a few hours before were now closed, the girl an embodiment of serenity. He rose to his feet and reached forward for the key expecting some reaction, some resistance, but there was nothing. It felt cold and metallic, not warm and comforting as it had always been in the past. Even now, he craved for the Master to come to him again and tell him that his immortality was assured.

He was standing now and as he looked up from the key, he saw his reflection in the mirror on the wall, staring back at himself.

Eva was the first to react to the sound of the breaking glass and she jumped up from the chair where she had been sewing. Magda Goebbels, who had been sitting opposite her, looked across to her husband. He had just taken a call from the General Wiedling in the *Benderblock* and the expression on his face told her that the news was not good. She stood as if to follow Eva to the door of the room from where the noise had come, but he shook his head and gestured for her to come to him instead.

Eva reached the door and tried the handle. Although it turned slightly, she immediately realised it was locked.

"Adolf, Adolf , mein liebe. Open the door. Please. Are you alright?"

Although she spoke in a whisper, her voice cut through the silence, her concern obvious. The Fuhrer had not been himself for several days now. She tried again whilst at the same time tapping on the door. "Please, Adolf, let me in. Are you alright?"

A few tense moments passed, then the handle clicked and she pushed open the door. Hitler was standing a few feet inside, and although the room was dimly lit, she could see the broken mirror behind him and the reflection of light from the shards of glass the on the floor. Amongst the glass was a small, dark object resting on its side.

Her husband was smiling at her despite the tears that rolled down his face and he beckoned her to come into the room. She walked forward into his arms and he embraced her tightly. She could feel the beat of his heart as he bent to kiss the top of her head. She opened her eyes and looked across to the table in the middle of the room. It was bare except for three items: a framed photograph of the two of them enjoying a weekend at the Eagle's Nest in Berchtesgaden, her husband's pistol, and a small glass vial containing a single black capsule.

53

"Of course, the real Dome will not require the rays of the sun to provide it with the power to restore the Master. The Stone will generate enough energy to create a huge electro-magnetic force strong enough to open the portal through which the souls can travel and allow Him to be reborn, as foretold by the Seventh Seal in the Book of Revelations. But I am getting ahead of myself, Mr. Donovan..."

Henderson sat down next to Donovan and placed his glass gently on the table.

"My associate, Mr. Aziz, will explain." He smiled at the man who had escorted Donovan from his room earlier.

Mr. Aziz returned the smile and cleared his throat. The pendant that Donovan had noticed earlier was resting in a fold of the purple, satin robe that he wore, staring out at him like a huge, unblinking eye. The gemstone in the centre shimmered like firestone, creating the illusion that it was alive. When Aziz started to speak, it was almost in a whisper, as if the words were held in great reverence.

"Thousands of years ago in my country, Mr. Donovan, there were many Gods. The Gods moulded the world and the people who worshipped them. There were Gods who provided sustenance; Gods who gave comfort to those in need; Gods who healed the sick and so on. The greatest God of all, however, was Osiris. He was a mighty God who ruled the kingdom with wisdom and compassion. He civilised the people and gave them a code by which to abide. Every one of his people loved him and lived by his words. Unfortunately, Osiris had an evil, jealous brother, called Seth, who secretly wished that Osiris were dead so that he could rule in his place. To this end, Seth tricked Osiris into lying in a decorated box that he had commissioned to exactly Osiris's dimensions on the pretence that whoever fit the box exactly could claim it as a prize. Once Osiris was inside, the lid was nailed down and molten lead poured into the seams. The 'coffin' was then thrown into the River Nile and Osiris was never seen alive again."

Mr. Aziz closed his eyes as if it pained him to continue. Donovan took the opportunity to glance round the room at the other men. Each one of them was engrossed. He noticed that the Asian hadn't bothered to clean the blood from his face after the 'light and sound show' and his shoulders were coated with a fine layer of dust from the fallen plaster.

Mr. Aziz cleared his throat again. "Isis, the wife of Osiris, eventually tracked down the coffin, which had washed ashore in the land of Byblos. It was so admired by the king that he had ordered it to be made into a huge pillar to support the roof of the royal palace. When Isis explained to the king what Seth had done, she was allowed to take the coffin back to Egypt. Unfortunately, one evening whilst Isis was away, Seth discovered the corpse of Osiris. He was so enraged that he ripped it up into fourteen pieces and scattered them throughout the kingdom."

Aziz paused for breath. The room was deathly silent. Donovan was beginning to realise that his suspicions about Henderson and his 'weird cult' theory were not very far from the mark. Mr. Aziz was definitely a potential contender for 'Wacko of the Week' in his purple robes and his cyclopean pendant. The others weren't far behind. The thought of escape entered his mind again and the seed of an idea began to form. *The letters he had noticed on the bureau earlier had had no stamps on them. Surely that meant they were waiting to be posted. If he could write a note to Kate and secrete it amongst the letters on the bureau...*

His thoughts were interrupted by Aziz continuing with his fucking Jackanory performance.

"Many years later, Osiris was resurrected as King of the Dead in the underworld known as 'The Duat'. One day, he appeared to his son, Horus, who by now had grown to manhood. Osiris commanded him to avenge the wrongs committed by Seth. A great battle ensued and eventually Horus was victorious despite having one of his eyes plucked out. Seth was banished from the earth and forced to live in purgatory."

Mr. Aziz slowly raised his head and looked directly at Donovan. "You see, Mr. Donovan, Seth has been waiting patiently for many thousands of years- a wait that is almost at an end."

His hands closed round the pendant hanging from his neck as if it were of importance to his tale. "Seth plucked out one of Horus's eyes, giving him a tangible link back to Earth- he also had the knowledge of 'The Stone.'

"Thank you, Mr. Aziz," said Henderson, rising from his seat.

Aziz bowed slightly before sitting down.

"From our earlier conversation, Mr. Donovan, you will recall that the Millennium Dome is in fact the portal through which Seth will be resurrected as Lord and Master of the Earth. Our little show tonight was merely an inadequate demonstration of the power that has been harvested over the last ten thousand years in order to provide the Master with his life force. The ancient scriptures decree that Seth will return because ultimately he has the knowledge and the power."

Henderson smiled as though he had just answered the question about the meaning of life.

"So let me get this straight," said Donovan. "You're telling me that The Dome is not really an architectural symbol of the Millennium but a giant generator designed to suck this Ancient Egyptian pariah from the realms of purgatory so that he can rule the earth? And the power to do this has been harvested from the souls of humans who have been sacrificed over the last ten thousand years?"

Henderson continued to smile. "I suppose that's one way of putting it, Mr. Donovan."

"And these sacrifices, when exactly have these been taking place? You'll forgive me for being obtuse but I think someone might have noticed if ten million people suddenly went missing."

"I think you will find, Mr. Donovan, that over ten thousand years, ten million is not a substantial figure. Adolf Hitler, remember, managed to murder six million in a little under three years."

Donovan sat back in his chair and sighed. "So, you're saying that Hitler was part of an ancient religious sect intent on resurrecting this Seth character and that was his sole purpose for the near extermination of an entire race? Come on, Henderson, surely…"

"Mr. Donovan, cast your mind back to when you visited Mr. Brady at my request. I seem to recall that you bought him some books as a sweetener to help you extricate the 'key' that I paid you handsomely to get for me. Do you remember the nature of those books?"

Donovan's mind was racing. Of course he remembered; he had done his homework thoroughly, as always. He knew Brady had an interest in… Hitler. His throat suddenly felt dry and he had to take a sip of his drink before he could speak.

"I'm sorry, is there something I'm missing here? Because Ian Brady was an admirer of Hitler and they shared a penchant for killing people; that means they were both sacrificing people to gather up souls for Seth?"

Although he was managing to maintain an air of incredulity, Donovan realised that the more he heard, the more curious he was becoming.

"That is exactly what they were doing. Let me explain further, Mr. Donovan. As you are now aware, the Dome itself is purely the machinery. When Seth was banished, he was astute enough to leave behind the tools needed to generate the Life Force. You may have heard of the Lanzon Stone, Mr. Donovan-it was recently shipped over to London from Peru. The Peruvian authorities have been kind enough to loan it to us as part of the exhibition which will be housed in the Dome when it opens on New Year's Eve in a little over two year's time. The Stone, however will not be returned to Peru when the exhibition ends-it is far too important for that to happen. Instead, a perfect facsimile will be sent back in its place. Seth also left behind four keystones that were scattered across the earth. Seth knew that they would eventually be found by mortals who could easily be influenced. Through the keys, he could manifest himself, and in return for the sacrifices, promise immortality to whoever held the keys. The keys were scattered worldwide and history reveals where they emerged. Take the Aztecs, Mr. Donovan. They sacrificed hundreds of thousands. The Egyptians performed exactly the same kinds of sacrifices as did other civilisations throughout history. Coincidence? Coincidence, that despite being separated by thousands of miles and, in some cases, thousands of years, they performed identical rituals at sites almost identical in their construction and geographical orientation?

Mr. Donovan, archaeologists have been telling us for

years that these sites all over the globe were built to mirror the heavens. In actual fact, they were all built on a celestial template recorded at the time Seth was exiled from earth. In July 2012, the stars will come to the end of a ten and a half thousand year cycle of precession. They will once again realign with the temples and the portal will be ready to open. Are things becoming clearer, Mr. Donovan?"

Donovan was amazed at the extent of Henderson's delusions.

"My associates in this room have worked tirelessly in the past four years to trace the keystones that will complete the machinery, Mr. Donovan. You, yourself, unwittingly brought one of them to me when you agreed to see Brady."

"You were explaining about the Hitler connection, I seem to remember," replied Donovan, eager to see how he could weave him into his conspiracy theory.

"Mr. Aziz was responsible for tracking down that particular key. You see, it was common knowledge that during the excavation of the Tomb of Tutenkhamun in 1922, Lord Carnarvon, along with Howard Carter, entered the tomb before the Egyptian authorities. There are several photographs of Carnarvon clearly showing that he later had in his possession one of the keystones. A little research revealed that just before his death in 1923, he visited an old friend in Munich. I don't know how good your grasp of European history is, Mr. Donovan, but you may recall that 1923 was the year that the extreme Socialist parties came to the forefront of German politics."

Donovan suddenly became aware of Mr. Aziz standing by his side.

"It wasn't difficult to track down the whereabouts of the keystone, Mr. Donovan," he said.

He walked across the room, bent down and picked up a battered, brown leather briefcase that was lying by the side of the music system. He reached inside and pulled out what appeared to be a scrap of paper and passed it to Donovan. Donovan realised it was a photograph. It was old and faded, and the edges were tattered but there was no mistaking who the subject of the photograph was. Sitting in a leather armchair, casually posed and apparently relaxed, was Adolf Hitler. Beside him on a wooden table was something that Donovan recognised immediately; It was the key that had been given to him by Ian Brady.

Aziz delved into the case again and drew out another photograph. This one was much better quality and showed some soldiers standing on top of a pile of rubble. They were sticking out their chests and smiling, posing for the camera. Donovan scanned the picture. After a few seconds, his eyes froze on the fourth soldier from the right. In his hand, he held the keystone. He looked up enquiringly at Aziz.

"Russian soldiers standing on the ruins of the Fuhrerbunker-Berlin 1945," he explained without prompting.

"Okay, so Carnarvon discovered the key after it had been influencing the Egyptians for a few thousand years. How come he didn't turn into a raging psychopath and start killing people whilst it was in his possession?"

Donovan couldn't help smiling. *"Go on, Henderson, explain that one."*

"Think about it, Donovan," Henderson whispered in a slightly irritated tone. "How many souls could Carnarvon have harvested in what was left of his natural life? He was old and weak. He was, however, still useful as an envoy. And who better to hand over the key to than to someone who had the power and charisma to control an entire population and convince them that what he was doing was in their best interests? Are you aware that the literal translation of the Hebrew word 'holocaust' is *'totally burned sacrifice'*?

"And Ian Brady; so he had an interest in Hitler. How did he come to be in the possession of the key?

Mr. Aziz smiled knowingly and once more reached into the briefcase. This time, the piece of paper he lifted out was not a photograph. Before showing it to Donovan, he explained that the soldier holding the key in the previous picture was a *Piotr Demanovic.*

"After the war, Demanovic settled in a quiet northern town in England called Middleton where he opened up a small business. It was a pawn shop, Mr. Donovan."

He passed the piece of paper over. Donovan examined it closely and surmised it was a receipt. It had a legend: *'Peter's Place'* at the top and beneath it was handwritten:

'War memorabilia. Received with thanks- £14s'

The receipt was signed at the bottom: *Piotr Demanovic and Ian Brady.*

Donovan looked up from the receipt. Both Aziz and Henderson were smiling. He shivered involuntarily as he looked back down at the evidence.

Henderson walked across the room towards Winston Brown. "Let me introduce you to Mr. Brown. He was one of the few survivors of the Waco siege in Texas in 1993, an event with which I am sure you will be familiar, Mr. Donovan."

Donovan didn't respond but Henderson continued anyway.

"Mr. Brown brought the second key along with him this morning with some very important documents written by none other than David Koresh-the so called Messiah and leader of the Branch Davidians." Brown seemed to grow several inches taller, relishing the limelight. "Perhaps you would be interested to hear about how he came to have a keystone, Mr. Donovan?"

Brown almost began speaking before Henderson had completed his rhetorical question. "Apparently, it was

David's grandfather who originally acquired the key. He had a brief affair with a woman called Eleanor Harvey. They were very close but before they could marry, she met her death inexplicably in a freak accident whilst they were holidaying in France. She fell from a second floor balcony and impaled herself on the iron railings that skirted the building. The key was part of her estate which she had bequeathed to David's grandfather prior to her death."

"And how did she come to be in possession of the keystone?" asked Donovan "...no, don't tell me, let me guess: she was a relative of Genghis Khan."

"Very droll Mr. Donovan, I can see your predicament has not suppressed your sense of humour," interrupted Henderson. "How she acquired the key is open to speculation but if I tell you that she was one of the few survivors of the sinking of the Titanic and that she recovered the key from the ocean before she was rescued, maybe you can come up with a few suggestions... bearing in mind that over fifteen hundred people lost their lives on a ship that was said to be unsinkable."

Donovan looked directly at Henderson and for a second he could have sworn he saw a darkening and narrowing of his pupils. Henderson didn't appear to be annoyed at his sarcasm but nevertheless, he felt threatened.

Brown coughed falsely to regain Donovan's attention before continuing. "Koresh's grandfather unwittingly secured the key in a lead safe along with other mementos of Eleanor and it was twenty years before David's father inherited it. David knew very little of his father because he disappeared when David was very young. Before he did, however, he passed the key on to David. Being a carpenter, his father had made a special wooden case for it. It remains in the case even today. The Davidians believed David was the messiah, Mr. Donovan. What they didn't realise was that he was planning their deaths in return for his place in the Kingdom of Immortality." He paused for breath as a tear rolled down his cheek. "In the end, he knew he could do no more for The Master and he sacrificed not only his followers but himself as well."

Donovan turned to Henderson when he realised Brown had finished speaking. "You said there were four keystone; so what about the other two?"

"Don't concern yourself, Donovan. I myself discovered one of the keys several years ago on a visit to South America. Or should I say, it discovered me. Who else should the Master choose to do his bidding now that he has nearly enough life force to return but someone in a position to sanction and oversee the construction of the Portal?"

Donovan looked into his eyes as he spoke and this time he was certain of what he saw; the pupils definitely narrowed.

He stepped closer to Donovan and lowered his voice to whisper. "Let me assure you, it won't be long before I have the final keystone. At the present time, it is in good hands somewhere in the antipodes-most likely Australia. My sources tell me that they are very close to discovering its exact whereabouts. Unfortunately, Mr. Donovan, you won't be around to witness the resurrection-you will just have to be content with the demonstration you were party to earlier this evening. Mr. Aziz, I think it's time Mr Donovan returned to his room. We have things to prepare."

Donovan looked up at Aziz who was standing menacingly beside him. The two henchmen suddenly appeared at the door and he realised he desperately needed a plan.

54

Heathrow Airport, London 1997

"Hi, I can't take your call right now, please leave a message after the tone."

Kate smiled as she listened to Michael's answering machine message again and a warm tingling sensation ran through her body at the thought that she might be seeing him in a few hours-that is, if she could ever get hold of him. She had tried to contact him a dozen times in the last twenty four hours to let him know she had finally given up on her wild goose chase and was returning home immediately. She couldn't understand where he could be and why he wouldn't have gotten in touch when he had listened to all her previous messages.

The beep of the answering machine dragged her mind back to the call.

"Hi Michael, it's me –again- where are you? We've just landed at Heathrow. I'll be home in an hour. Can't wait to see you..." She paused, hoping he was actually in the flat and was hurrying from his darkroom to pick up the phone. After what seemed like an eternity, she said goodbye and placed the phone back onto its cradle.

"Well, any luck?"

She turned around. Steve was smiling at her through a mouthful of cheeseburger. He had a tray laden with cartons of fast food and plastic cups full of soft drinks. He was wearing a baseball cap which was on back to front and with his dark tan and blue eyes, he looked more like an errant teenager than a university postgraduate.

"No. Maybe he's on a stakeout or something-he told me that he had once spent a week in his car trying to get a shot of a cabinet minister entering a massage parlour in Essex."

Steve grinned. "Could do with a visit myself, after a month nookie-free, chasing you all over the Outback. Don't suppose you've got the address?"

Kate laughed, wearily picked up her backpack, and followed Steve to an empty table. She would just have to seek solace in saturated fat for half an hour until it was time to catch the train.

55

Epping, London 1997

Donovan was now sitting at the table beneath the bedroom window rapidly scribbling information down on the notepaper as quickly as he could.

When Bad Skin and Aziz had pushed him from the dining room and out into the hallway fifteen minutes earlier, the seed of an idea that he'd had earlier suddenly grew into a full blown plan.

About three metres along the corridor was the bureau that Aziz had fallen against before dinner. The envelopes and stationery were still there. Donovan made his mind up. He stood still and braced himself for the next push that he knew would come if he didn't move. He wasn't disappointed, firm hands planted in the centre of his back pushed him forward. He let out what he hoped sounded like a convincing squeal of surprise and launched himself forward, falling against the bureau and knocking the letters and everything else on the bureau onto the floor. He feigned an attempt to keep his balance then swirled round before falling on top of the stationery. He heard Aziz mutter something angrily under his breath. Then, an argument broke out between the two men. Donovan didn't hear what they were saying to one another as he was desperately concealing envelopes and paper inside his shirt.

Having deposited Donovan back in his room with

orders to shower, undress, and replace his jeans and shirt with the white robe that had appeared on his bed during his absence, the men had left informing him they would be back in fifteen minutes.

He read what he had written so far, hoping that Kate would understand his shorthand. He had explained about his dealings with Henderson and acquiring the keystone from Brady; how he had uncovered the connections to the Branch Davidians at the construction company's 'offices' and he even tried to explain Henderson's deluded rantings about the Dome and someone he called 'The Master.'

He wrote the address of Harlington Hall, the time, and date and finished by explaining that he feared the worst. Should she never see him again, he urged her to take the letter to the police. Underneath the writing he drew, as accurately as he could from memory, a picture of the keystones and a diagram of the stone into which the four of them would be fitted to activate the 'Resurrection' as Henderson had called it. He closed his eyes and tried to form a picture of Kate's face in his mind. He whispered, *"I love you, Kate."* before folding the paper and sealing it inside the envelope he had already addressed. His only hope now was that he would be accompanied to wherever he was being taken via the hallway and could somehow secrete his letter amongst the others.

It was exactly eight o clock when the door was pushed open and Aziz and another man, who hadn't been at the dinner table earlier, appeared wearing the same purple robes as before. Donovan was sitting on the edge of the bed now wearing the white robe. He nervously clenched his left fist into a ball, hoping that the muscle on his forearm would press the envelope against the inside of the robe sleeve and prevent it falling to the floor. Aziz nodded and motioned Donovan towards the door. He rose and the men stepped aside to let him past. Again, they followed a few metres behind as he walked slowly down the stairs. As he reached the bottom step, he paused, willing the men to guide him to the left and down the hallway. Right would take him out to the main entrance and scupper any plans he might have of depositing the envelope on the bureau.

Even if he was successful, he knew his plan depended on Henderson's secretary or butler stamping the envelopes automatically without looking closely at the handwriting or addresses before posting them, and although in his heart he knew that would be unlikely, he had no other options.

He stifled a gasp as he heard Aziz mutter, "Back down the hallway."

Turning left, he knew his timing would need to be perfect. He took three paces then reeled round to face the men. They both came to a halt and seemed to brace themselves, thinking that perhaps he was about to try and get past them to the main entrance. Donovan smiled and with a wave of his hand he pointed up towards a picture on the wall to the right, slightly behind the two men, and said, "I don't suppose you know, but is that a Turner or a Constable?"

The two men automatically turned to look, and Donovan flicked his wrist sharply, allowing the envelope to drop into his palm. He was now resting against the bureau, facing the men, his left hand at his waist concealing the letter and his right on his chin as if he were contemplating the answer to his question. With another flick of his wrist, the envelope slid onto the top of the bureau.

Aziz and the man turned back to face Donovan and through gritted teeth, the man snarled, "Who am I - Vincent Van fucking Gogh!" He stepped forward and grabbed Donovan's shoulder, spinning him round and pushing him forcefully down the hallway.

Donovan passed the dining room on his left and noted it was now empty. At the end of the hallway, he was told to take a short flight of steps, which circled round on themselves. He came to a small porch with a stone floor and a large pair of arched wooden doors.

Aziz pushed past and opened the doors. As he turned, Donovan noticed that he was now holding a gun.

"No heroics, Mr. Donovan. I shall have no hesitation in killing you if you feel the need to run," Aziz whispered.

Donovan had a mental image of the three of them hurtling across the drive in their robes, each taking turns falling flat on their faces.

Aziz gestured with the barrel of the gun for Donovan to step outside. He stepped past Aziz and realised they were in the courtyard where he had discovered the 'temple' earlier. His mind flashed back to the weird tapestries and strange altar.

They crossed the courtyard in silence and as they entered the temple through the electric sliding doors, Donovan immediately became aware of a low humming noise. At first, he thought that it was perhaps a generator but then the sound became more irregular and he realised it was the sound of voices chanting. The doors to the ante room suddenly swung open; two more men in robes stood on either side of the entrance and the long narrow carpet that ran the entire length of the room was illuminated by the glow of candles that also ran the length of the room at metre intervals. The carpet drew Donovan's eyes towards the altar that lay beneath the huge tapestry of the Dome that he'd seen earlier.

Henderson stood with his back to the tapestry. He was dressed like the others in a robe but his was green and gold. He also wore a strange headdress which was tall and white. He was holding in one hand some sort of staff and in the other, a large golden cross with a loop at the top.

There was movement to Donovan's left and, from the darkness created by the pillars that rose to the ceiling of the temple, a dozen or more robed figures stepped into his view, skirting the carpet. The low chant that he noticed before suddenly became louder; then, louder still, as the same thing happened to his right. Robed 'worshippers' now formed a human tunnel leading to the altar.

Henderson's head was bowed as if in prayer. The voices grew louder still and Donovan gradually became aware that the chanting consisted of two words, long and drawn out *"Nun"* followed by *Atum."*

A dig in the small of his back from Aziz's gun encouraged him to move forwards toward the altar. Henderson's head was still bowed. Donovan tried to make out the faces of the people that lined the aisle on either side of him, but each wore a hood and their features were hidden in shadow.

As he approached the altar, Henderson lifted his head and raised the staff abruptly. Donovan stopped in his tracks. Suddenly, his arms were grabbed firmly from behind and a kick to the back of his knees forced him into a kneeling position. The chanting suddenly ceased. Henderson's head was now raised, eyes closed as if in meditation. After a few moments, he raised the staff then brought it down firmly, with a loud crack onto the stone floor. This, it seemed, was a cue of some sort as two robed figures appeared from the shadows. One was carrying something in front of him that he held out with both hands, almost like an offering. Whatever it was, it was long and slender and wrapped in some kind of cloth. He gently laid it down at the head of the stone table, bowed his head, and finally retreated back into the shadows. The other man also carried something- a dish-shaped metal container. He carried the dish forward and carefully placed it into a circular frame that sat on a stand at the foot of the table.

Donovan knew already what was inside the cloth-he had known since Henderson had entered the bedroom before dinner that there was no chance of him being allowed to leave. He scanned the room immediately in front of him and on either side of the altar, desperately seeking a way out. The darkness made it impossible to know what was beyond the final two pillars on either side. He guessed that there must be some recess or passageways at this end of the temple because the two robed men had appeared from either side. He looked up again at Henderson, who now seemed to be in a trance-like state. His mouth was moving and, although Donovan could hear no sound, it was clear he was delivering some kind of incantation. Donovan allowed his upper body to slump a little to gauge the reaction of the men behind him. He expected some response but, as he stooped further, nothing came. He had nothing to lose.

Almost imperceptibly, he began to curl his toes and lift the soles of his feet beneath the robes. As he rose slightly onto his knees and moved his weight over his feet, he expected strong arms to pull him back down. He paused, but again, no response. Perhaps they were too engrossed in watching Henderson's performance to notice.

It was now or never. With all his strength, he lunged forward, aiming his grasp at the staff at Henderson's side. As his fingers curled round the shaft of the staff, he twisted onto his side and rolled away to his right. He managed to use the momentum to regain his feet and as he rose to an upright position, he came face to face with the man who had brought the dish to the altar. The man's eyes were half closed, not taking in what was happening. Donovan slammed the end of the staff into his midriff and the man instinctively doubled up. As the man's head came down, Donovan brought his knee up swiftly, catching him in the centre of his throat. Donovan heard him gurgle then fall to the ground. He leapt over him and sprinted into the darkness ahead.

All hell let loose behind him in the temple and he could hear Henderson screaming orders. He had given himself a head start but he had no idea what lay ahead. He dropped the staff and pulled the robe up round his waist to make running easier. In the darkness ahead he saw some stone steps leading up to a doorway. Although he had never been in the back of the temple he thought it might lead out to the woods at the front of the house. If he could just get outside maybe he could lose them amongst the trees. He launched himself up the steps. There were two doors, each with a huge brass knob in the centre. *Please, God, make them open.* He reached forward and twisted the one on the right. It turned then gave way under his weight and he gasped with relief as he fell forward through the door and light dazzled his eyes. His relief was short-lived, however, as he realised he had fallen into another corridor. Unlike the temple, this was completely different. It was hospital-like, with brightly lit, tiled floors and the smell of disinfectant. It was the most bizarre thing he had ever seen. He looked back from where he had come. The large wooden doors that he had burst through were painted a clinical white on this side and attached to the middle of each door was a sign announcing:

'*Nursing Staff only-strictly no admittance*'

Donovan's mind was racing now. *How was this possible?* Still aware that Henderson's men might be seconds behind him, he picked himself up, slammed the door shut and began to run. About fifty metres ahead was a set of half-glazed double doors. Through the glass he could see a man and a woman dressed in white coats. They were in deep conversation and clearly hadn't noticed his presence. Glancing round, he saw a door to his left and he ducked inside quickly before they had chance to look up and see him. He leaned with his back to the door trying to gather his thoughts and it was a moment or two before he realised that the room he had entered was more like a gallery. It was dark and long and very narrow. All along the left hand wall were windows at three metre intervals. Light emanated from each one into the gallery and he sensed, rather than saw, movement beyond the glass. He moved forward cautiously and hunkered down onto his knees, trying to see through the first window but at the same time, remain out of sight. He craned his neck forward to look and was caught completely off guard as he came face to face with a young woman. He fell backwards waiting for a scream of alarm but was amazed when she simply carried on staring 'through' the window. As she began brushing her hair, he realised that she was actually staring at herself.

The 'window' was a one-way mirror. He scrutinised the face in front of him and noticed that the eyes were ringed with red. The dark circles underneath them gave her face a haunted look. From her figure and the clothes she wore- a white t-shirt and faded denims- he guessed she could be no more than mid twenties. As she pushed her lank hair behind her ears, he noticed something else–track marks. The unmistakable telltale signs of a drug addict; small red pinpricks running all the way from her wrist to her lower arms; puncture wounds not quite hidden by bruising. *What was going on?*

Suddenly, there was movement in the room behind the girl and a door opened. The woman he had just seen in the corridor talking to the man stepped into view. She was holding a silver tray. The girl whirled round and the woman said something to her. The woman laid the tray on the bedside table. The girl seemed to skip over to the woman and sat on the edge of the bed like an eager child. She lifted her arm up toward the woman who produced a tourniquet from the pocket of her white coat. She looped it round the raised arm and pulled it tight. Donovan could see the vein filling with blue blood. He looked on aghast as the 'nurse' picked up a syringe and a vial from the tray. She carefully located the vein with the needle and injected the clear liquid into the girl's arm. The girl's head shot back and she took a deep breath. Then she appeared to breathe out a deep sigh before slumping forward. The nurse withdrew the needle and supported the girl with her lower body before gently rolling her back onto the bed.

"Ah, Mr. Donovan, I see you have discovered our little 'annexe.'"

The sound of Henderson's voice made Donovan spin round and instinctively spring upright, ready to run. Two men flanked Henderson, one of whom Donovan vaguely recognised, but from where he didn't know. He glanced quickly towards the other end of the gallery, once more searching for an escape route. Aziz and another man were walking along the gallery and Aziz was still holding his gun.

"Don't bother, Mr. Donovan, you have run out of time. You see, like the junkie in our 'rehabilitation centre', when you disappear no one will notice. You are just like them really; you came here seeking answers. Well, now you know. It's very simple all in all; London is full of people with problems, most of whom, jump at the chance of being 'helped'. And the best thing is, Mr. Donovan, that we are actually doing society a favour. As well as having a limitless supply of 'offerings', we manage to cleanse our streets of scum at the same time-a beautiful trade off, don't you think?"

Donovan's fists clenched in anger as the full realisation of what was happening dawned on him. Behind him in the room, a movement caught his eye and he turned to look. Two nurses were removing the girl's clothes.

Laid out beside her was a white robe, identical to the one he was wearing.

56

The Reckoning

Sydney Opera House, Australia. July 24th 2012

"Ladies and Gentlemen, it gives me great pleasure to introduce the Chief Executive of 'The O2' and Chair of the British Olympic Committee-Mr. Simon Henderson."

Henderson rose from the dining table and made his way onto the stage accompanied by a gentle patter of applause. He shook hands with the Australian Prime Minister and as their eyes met, he could hardly contain himself. In a few short moments he would have the final key. He turned and walked forward to the lectern and bank of microphones.

"Thank you ladies and gentlemen. I am delighted to be here in Sydney this morning, to collect, in person, the final piece of art for our opening ceremony. As you are aware, the Olympics this year will be used as a vehicle to promote peace and unity across the globe. For the last twelve years, we have been collecting iconic pieces of art from every culture on the planet. Last week, for example, I met with the president of Polynesia, in Greenwich, as two giant Moai were craned into position in the Dome. Today, I am here to formally say thank you to the Australian people for allowing us to borrow some of your most valuable and precious national treasures. As I speak, paintings by

Clifford Possum Tjapaltjarri and Kathleen Petyarre are being displayed alongside artefacts from Ancient Egypt and the Inca civilizations. We have gathered together all these artefacts to illustrate mankind's innate need to communicate and leave a lasting impression on his environment. Regardless of which language we use, every person on the planet can appreciate the rich tapestry of cultures that make our world a unique and awe inspiring place. In the true spirit of the Olympics, we hope these Games will bring nations and cultures together to celebrate the achievements of mankind and the importance of working together to make the world a peaceful and harmonious place in which to live. Thank you, Australia!"

Henderson's speech was greeted with cheering and enthusiastic applause. Mr. Nagarra stepped forward holding a small wooden case. He leaned forward to the microphones so that the gathering could hear his words.

"Thank you, Mr. Henderson. To commemorate your visit, we have one final piece to present to you. This one, however, isn't a loan. It is a gift to your country from ours."

He flicked open two clasps on either side of the wooden case to reveal the keystone. Henderson couldn't take his eyes from it. It was identical to the other three in every way.

Out of earshot of the microphones, Nagarra whispered quietly to Henderson, "I trust this is what you were hoping for."

Henderson smiled from ear to ear and shook Nagarra's hand firmly. "The Master will reward you handsomely, my friend."

57

London, July 24th 2012

"Please be very careful with that- it's very precious to me," Kate pleaded as the burly removal men brushed past her on the stairs. They were carrying the mirror that her mother had given her two weeks before she finally succumbed to the cancer that had blighted the last three years of her life.

The younger one nodded, mumbled a reply, and carried on down the stairs and into the hallway.

Kate reached the top of the stairs and turned to survey, possibly for the final time, the flat that she had called home for the last sixteen years. She cast her mind back-it would have been 1996 when she'd moved in. She had just completed her Degree and had decided to apply to do a Masters the following year. It was October and the leaves on the sycamore trees, that lined the street outside, had just turned a beautiful autumn red and begun to fall. As she waved her parents off, having helped her unpack, she kicked her way through a pile of leaves and skipped up the steps.

The return of one of the removal men brought her back to the present. "Are you ready for a cuppa yet?" she asked." I'm just about to put the kettle on."

"Thanks love, that'd be great. I don't suppose you've got a biscuit as well; all this lugging about doesn't half give you an appetite."

His smile completely transformed his features and Kate, for the first time, realised that he was actually quite attractive. His eyes twinkled and, although they were not quite as strikingly blue as Brian's, she guessed that he probably used them to full effect when he needed to.

She walked downstairs and into her kitchen. The removal men hadn't started in there yet and everything was as it had always been. She filled the kettle from the tap and plugged it in. As she was putting the Earl Grey tea bags into the cups, she flicked on the television with the remote. It was just after one o clock. She could listen to the news whilst she made the tea.

The screen came to life immediately. Fire crews were busy fighting the latest explosion in Leeds. The race riots had flared up again and the target for the hatred was once again the Polish contingent.

The kettle beeped and she turned to fill the cups.

The newsreader's voice became background noise as she fished out a packet of digestives from a carrier bag containing the last remnants of her food cupboards and emptied them onto a plate.

The mention of Sydney on the news drew her attention back to the TV. Brian was out there at the moment completing a two-week lecture tour in New South Wales. He would be back on Thursday just in time to help with the move into their new house in Richmond. She could hardly believe it was nearly five years since they had married; the time had flown by so quickly.

On the screen, the reporter was standing in front of the Opera House. He was explaining that, inside, a ceremony was taking place to celebrate the final completion of all the preparations for the 2012 Olympics in London. Several dignitaries from London were attending to 'officially' receive Australia's contribution to the Opening Ceremony. The Chief Executive of 'The O^2' (as the Millennium Dome was now called) was due to arrive at any moment to meet with the Australian Prime Minister-Alan Nagarra.

Nagarra was shown waving and signing autographs when he had arrived himself some twenty minutes earlier. As Kate watched the first ever aboriginal Prime Minister of Australia, smiling and chatting to the crowd, she was reminded of Reg and Peter-the two men who had been the guides on their expedition to Australia in 1997; the expedition she had been on when she had first met Brian.

"Right love, that's the upstairs done, mind if we have that break now?"

The two removal men appeared at the kitchen door. Kate clicked off the TV and turned to pass them their tea. The one with the nice eyes smiled as he took the cup before noticing the tear rolling down Kate's cheek.

" 'Ere, are you all right love?" he asked, placing a hand on her shoulder.

Kate wiped the tear away and smiled, "Yes, I'm fine, thanks-just memories–you know how it is when you've lived in a place for so long?"

Kate excused herself and went out into the garden. She sat on her battered garden bench and chided herself for getting upset again. When would she ever get over what had happened? It was, after all, twelve years ago for God's sake! The article on the news had not only brought back memories of meeting Brian but it also resurfaced what had happened when she returned to England all those years ago. If only she could have discovered what had happened to Michael. That was the worst- not knowing. At least, had he died she could have let him go. He had simply vanished from the face of the earth. She remembered the months of trying to get the police to do something –start an enquiry, anything. Because Michael had been an only child and both his parents were dead, she was the only person who was trying to find out what had happened. In the end, the police finally agreed to make an appeal on the television programme, 'Crimewatch UK'. Apart from one caller who claimed to have seen someone matching his description getting into a taxi outside Euston Station, the appeal had been fruitless. How could something like that happen to her twice? First Edward, then Michael!

She stood as the tears welled up once more and turned to go back inside. Hopefully, the move to Richmond would finally help her move on with her life.

58

London, July 24th 2012

Kate gazed through the window as the final few remaining pieces of her furniture were loaded into the back of the removal van. The moment was tinged with sadness but she knew deep within her heart, had known it for a long time really, that it was time to let the past go and focus on her future. Moving to Richmond was almost like a new start for her and Brian. The last five years had been good but the ghost of Michael would stay with them until they made a completely fresh start.

There was a shout from below. "We're ready for the hallway now, love. Is it all ready to go?"

Kate moved away from the window and walked onto the landing. "I've emptied everything out of the cupboards and taken the drawers out to make it a little lighter for you," she called down.

Both men were examining the huge Welsh dresser that she had inherited along with the flat. Originally, she had planned to move it into the dining room but once she had moved in, she realised why the previous occupants had chosen to leave it in the hall. It was perfect as a telephone table, great for storing shoes and wellies in the bottom cupboards, and the drawers were handy for car keys, address books, telephone directories and other assorted sundry items that she knew she would spend all her time searching for unless they were there, immediately available when she needed them. So, there it had stayed, in all its glory.

The men were debating the easiest way to get it through the front door and from their puzzled expressions it was clear that there was some doubt as to whether or not it would actually fit through. The older man was scrutinising the shelf above the drawers. He ran his finger along the back where it met the top section of the dresser. "There you go!" he exclaimed as he drew his finger away. The dust that now coated the end of his finger had been concealing two small, brass screws. "We can do it in two pieces," he grinned, giving his mate a high five, delighted with the discovery.

Kate could understand their relief; they had been there all day and it was nearly seven o clock. Both the men looked hot and sweaty and in need of a cold beer. If they hadn't loaded up her refrigerator and its contents earlier, she'd have rewarded their efforts. Still, only the dresser and a few bits and pieces and they'd be done.

The men worked well together, almost without effort or the need to communicate verbally. As one withdrew the second screw, the other positioned himself at the other side ready for the lift. The top section slid away from the bottom with a low groan and the men carried it away with ease through the front door. Kate made her way downstairs and into the kitchen where a couple of dishcloths were soaking in a bowl of warm water. She lifted one of the cloths out and wrung it out. Returning to the hallway, she swept the cloth across the back of the shelf, a little embarrassed by the accumulation of dust.

She pulled the bottom section away from the wall, to get at the line of damp dust that was now clinging to the wall and was surprised at how heavy it still felt, even without the top section and the drawers. As she leaned forward, to get at the dust, something caught her eye behind the cupboards. It looked like a piece of paper resting against the skirting boards. She stood on her tiptoes and stretched over to see what it was but she couldn't quite reach. Although she couldn't be sure, it looked like a letter.

At that moment, the removal men appeared at the front door and she moved aside to give them room to work.

"Last but not least, eh love," the younger one said, with relish in his voice. The arrangement was that the van would be driven to the warehouse and remain there overnight before being taken to the new house in the morning. The pub was beckoning.

As they heaved the cabinet away from the wall and struggled with it towards the steps beyond the front door, Kate knelt down to pick up what she could now clearly see *was* a letter. Judging by its colour and coating of dust, it had been there some time. She turned the envelope over and drew her palm across the top to reveal the address. Immediately, her heart missed a beat and a chill ran through her as she recognised the distinctive scrawled handwriting that could only belong to one person. She rubbed her thumb over the stamp and the postmark stared up at her- July 1997!

59

London, 26th July 2012

Brian looked up from the computer screen and swivelled round to face Kate. He could see the anguish in her eyes.

"Well?" she asked when he didn't say anything.

"Look Kate, don't you think all this is a bit far-fetched, I mean…"

Before he could say anything else, Kate grabbed his shoulders and swivelled him round on the computer chair to face the screen once more.

"Far fetched it might be, but look at the date - it can't be a coincidence. Even if Henderson just *believes* that this resurrection thing can happen and it's all a figment of his warped imagination, according to Michael's letter, he has managed to convince an awful lot of people, some of them very powerful people by all accounts, to go along with him. There could be hundreds of people's lives in danger."

Brian scanned the dates on the web site again.

When Kate had picked him up from the airport an hour ago, she'd been ranting and raving about having finally discovered what had happened to Michael and how there was a conspiracy going on involving a lot of important people. It had taken fifty minutes to drive back to the flat, during which time she had filled him in with all she knew. Only now though, having read the letter and looked at her Internet research, was he beginning to realise the extent to which she completely believed what sounded like a plot from a Dan Brown novel.

"Look," said Kate pointing to the screen. "I simply typed in the word 'Seth' into the search engine and a whole load of websites came up. Most of them were about Ancient Egyptian myths but a lot of them, like this one, were about the Apocalypse. When I looked at the links, one of them was for the Branch Davidians. Remember Michael mentioned them in the letter! Then this one came up. According to the Mayan 'Long Count' calendar, the date of the apocalypse is July 27th 2012."

Brian was scratching his head and trying to stifle a yawn, the jet lag was kicking in now and he was finding it hard to concentrate.

"And to top it all off, when I typed in that date - guess what came up!"

She moved the mouse and clicked on another tab. A fresh web page popped up: the home page of the official web site for the 2012 Olympics. Smiling up from the main photograph on the page was Simon Henderson, holding a strange looking object in one hand and shaking the hand of the Australian Prime minister with the other. Above the picture, a digital clock was counting down and the legend beneath read:

'...To go to the official opening of the Games'
The clock read 14 hours and 51 seconds.

Kate slid Michael's letter across the desk for Brian to see. Beneath Michael's scribbling was a drawing of the object that Simon Henderson was holding and beneath that, a drawing of the Millennium Dome.

60

The O2 Dome, Greenwich, London. July 27th 2012. 6pm

Henderson was staring at his reflection in the mirror. He was recalling his visit to South America eighteen years earlier. A shiver ran down his spine as he remembered looking into the eyes of the engraved figure on the stone and seeing the Master for the first time. Two hours and he would finally see the Master again - this time in his earthly form.

He turned round as the door to his office opened and Aziz stepped inside.

"All the preparations have been made. Lord Coe will be arriving at 7:15 pm exactly."

His voice quivered and his eyes revealed a nervousness with which Henderson could empathise. Henderson stepped towards him and took hold of his shoulders with both hands.

"Mr. Aziz, we have waited so long for this time to come. Our destiny is nearly upon us and we need to stay calm," he whispered.

Aziz looked up and nodded solemnly. Henderson guided him back towards the door.

"Come, we must get the keystones."

In the main arena of the Dome people were filing in from the outer building and taking their seats for the opening ceremony. There was a buzz of anticipation, even

336

though the arena was only a fifth full.

According to the media hype, the ceremony was going to welcome in the Games in an *'Awe inspiring pyrotechnic televisual fantasia'*.

The theme of the ceremony was focused on celebrating the variety of cultures throughout the world and hanging from the ceiling of the Dome, emulating the circular shape of the arena, were a dozen aboriginal paintings, each the size of a tennis court. Right in the centre of the arena was an enormous obelisk-type stone. Positioned round the stone were four huge Polynesian Stone Heads – Maois. Each one scrutinised the crowd from a different direction. Dividing the floor space into triangular sections were carpeted pathways, which would presumably guide all the athletes into position for the ceremony. Interspersed between the Heads, and in each triangular section, were incredibly beautiful sculptures of all shapes and sizes: a gigantic sphinx, several carved totem poles and a huge variety of other artefacts from all round the world.

There was a red carpet winding its way round the circular periphery of the arena and at the far end was a stage. On the stage was a lectern standing behind a bank of microphones and above the stage was a gigantic forty-metre television screen. The screen displayed an enormous virtual flag bearing the five rings of the Olympic emblem, which rippled gently in a virtual breeze. From the centre of the ceiling of the dome, a fantastic, blue laser beam of light shone down onto the obelisk giving the impression that the beam of light was actually emanating from the obelisk. Transposed on the ceiling of the Dome was a hologram of the earth spinning in the black void of space. As the laser beam 'collided' with the earth, it was deflected off into space in a million tiny pinpricks of light that eventually became distant stars and constellations.

Aziz and Henderson were now in the security vault of

the Dome. There were three other men with them, all dressed in purple robes. Henderson placed his palm on the scanner pad that was embedded into the front of the safe then tapped a six figure security code into the keypad-270712. There was an audible hiss and the steel wheel on the door of the safe rotated through ninety degrees. Henderson pulled the door open and smiled.

61

6.15pm

Outside the Dome, swathes of people were making their way towards the security checks at the main entrance. There was a police helicopter hovering high up above the Dome, its light sweeping the murky waters of the Thames below. Two hundred metres up and down-river of the Dome were police launches effectively providing a security cordon round the area. Floating in the middle of the Thames immediately between the Dome and the Canary Wharf complex was a barge. It was essentially a launch pad for some of the pyrotechnics that would greet the crowd as they exited the Dome later.

Brian and Kate were on the very edge of the crowd, scanning the periphery of the Dome trying to locate a potential way in. With no tickets, there was no way they would be allowed entry through the main entrance. There were doors *(fire-exits?)* located every fifty metres or so round the sides of the Dome but each one was securely closed.

Kate examined the security fencing that had been erected to guide the crowds towards the main entrance and keep them from wandering round the back of the Dome. It was the modular mesh type that was basically inserted into portable concrete bases and secured together with steel clips. She pressed one of the clips together and it sprung open, releasing the two retaining posts. She and Brian stood with their backs to the fence giving the impression that they were waiting for someone. *If ever they needed a diversion.*

Suddenly, there was a high-pitched whooshing sound followed by an incredibly loud bang. The crowd turned instinctively at the unexpected sight of fireworks rising into the still blue, early evening sky. Kate and Brian took their chance and slipped through the gap in the fence. They sprinted the thirty metres towards one of the fire exits and hid in the recess. Looking back towards the crowd, they could just make out the barge on the river. There were several men remonstrating with one another, obviously trying to work out how the firework had accidentally been ignited.

Kate smiled at their good fortune and then turned her attention to the doors behind them. There were no handles on the outside and the gap between the doors was too tight to consider trying to lever them open. The sound of laughter close by surprised them both and they instinctively hunkered further into the recess. After a few seconds, Brian poked his head round the corner of the recess and looked further down the side of the Dome. About fifty metres along was a blue glass structure adjacent to the Dome. Two men stood, chatting and smoking beside the next fire door along. They were, Brian guessed, mid fifties and dressed in some kind of ceremonial robes. Brian turned and gestured to Kate to take a look.

"Don't exactly look the types who would be involved with the cabaret, do they!" she whispered.

"Maybe they belong to one of the visiting nation's entourage or something. These types of ceremony are always way over the top," he whispered back.

Suddenly, another person came into view. This one wore the same type of robe but the hood was up so there was no way of determining whether it was a man or woman. Whoever it was said something that appeared to mobilise the two men as they stubbed out their cigarettes and disappeared quickly inside.

Kate and Brian nodded to one another and slipped out from the recess.

62

6.35pm

"... And remember, once Lord Coe's speech is concluded, the doors are to be locked and the arena sealed. No one gets out. If anyone asks, tell them there has been a temporary malfunction of the security software, the system is re-booting and, for their own safety, they are to be kept inside until the system has been re-set. Everyone must remain in a calm state of mind. Is that clear?"

Henderson scanned the faces of the men before him. Over two hundred followers of the Master were nodding in unison. He turned to the four men who were standing on either side of him, each holding a keystone.

"Then, we are ready," he said, his eyes glistening with excitement.

He raised both his hands to the heavens and closed his eyes. The followers turned and began to file out of the room in silence.

Henderson became aware of a tingling sensation that seemed to emanate from the ground beneath him then he felt a surge of power course through his legs and into his torso. The ends of his fingers suddenly felt as though they had been slit open and his bodily substance was being sucked upwards towards the ceiling of the room. Feeling suddenly uncomfortable, he opened his eyes and was amazed to see thin, snake-like tendrils of vapour swirling slowly upwards from his fingertips. He blinked, unsure of what he was seeing, and when he opened his eyes again, the vapour wasn't there anymore. For a second he was grasped by an almost overwhelming feeling of insecurity and glanced at the four remaining men to see if they were aware of what he thought he had seen. Each of them was still watching the others as they were leaving the room to take up their positions around the exits of the arena.

He looked towards his fingers again then drew his arms slowly down to his sides. Beads of sweat formed on his brow then trickled down the sides of his face. Taking a deep breath, he stepped forward towards the doors that led out to the waiting area behind the stage. The four men with the keystones followed.

63

6.40pm

Brian and Kate were now in the next doorway along where they had seen the robed figures disappear ten minutes earlier.

"Why couldn't we just go to the police as I suggested?" whispered Brian.

"What, and have them look at me again like I was a basket case. I hassled them about my brother's disappearance when I thought they weren't doing enough, then again when Michael went missing. They already think I'm a serial *schizo* with nothing better to do than invent crackpot scenarios for them to investigate."

Brian looked at her sympathetically.

"...And then of course there was the month I spent chasing shadows across Australia trying to solve the missing backpackers mystery. Really Brian, if this is just some huge figment of my imagination and tonight is really just about the opening of the Olympics then I..." she faltered, tears welling up in her eyes.

Brian turned and drew Kate towards him, holding her to his chest whilst over her shoulder he examined the hinges on the door in front of him. He was amazed to see the door had been left ajar. It seemed whatever orders had been issued had been important enough to make the last man through careless.

"Shit, Kate, look!" he said spinning her round to face the doors.

Kate gasped, stepped forward, and then cautiously peered through the small gap between the doors. Beyond, there appeared to be a concrete stairwell leading upwards to a pair of white double doors. The steel bar across the back of the doors that Kate was now opening further confirmed that they were indeed at a fire exit.

There was no sound coming from above but they both suddenly became aware of a strange vibration emanating from beneath their feet that was accompanied by a very gentle, almost rhythmic hum. They looked at one another.

"Sounds like someone's turned on the electricity supply, said Brian.

Kate scanned the stairwell, trying to decide their next course of action. The men they had seen could be just behind the doors, lying in wait. Then again, if she was wrong about everything, the chances were that they had gone to join in with the ceremony and no one was guarding the fire exits-*why would they?*

She was reminded of her youth when she and her friends used to run a scam to get in the local Odeon. One of them would pay to get in then release the bars on the fire doors which were opened at the end of the film to allow everyone quicker egress. When the lights went down for the film to begin, they would sneak in quickly in the darkness and find a seat as quickly as they could. They had been successful every time and not once was there ever an usher waiting to pounce on them.

She moved inside, having made her decision and began to climb the stairs. Brian followed close behind. Although he was still very sceptical about everything that Kate had told him, he now knew that she was determined to bring everything to a conclusion one way or another, whatever the outcome. Nothing he could say to her now would make any difference.

Half way up the stairwell, to their left, were two huge steel doors. The sign on the doors made it clear that to enter was to risk death. The symbol: a man with a fork of electricity apparently frying him was accompanied by the legend:

'Extreme Danger 500,000 volts'

They climbed up the remaining steps to the white doors and waited for a second. They looked at each other momentarily before Kate grasped the handle on the door and gently eased it open. Immediately, the sounds of people moving round and chatting excitedly filled the air. To her relief, there was no sentinel guarding the doors that led out onto a carpeted landing. About five metres beyond, she could see the back of a row of seats. Clearly from the view that Kate now had of the ceiling of the Dome rising upwards and the huge paintings that were suspended from it, the seats were up in the heavens. Despite the fact that people must have been entering the building for at least half an hour no one appeared to have made it up there so far. They crouched down on their haunches and, keeping their heads below the height of the seats, crabbed their way across the floor to peer over the top of the seats and into the arena below them.

People were flowing through doors into the arena and the bottom tiers of seats were rapidly becoming occupied. Brian noticed that, as people came into the arena, they were being ushered into their places by people wearing the same purple robes that the men had worn outside earlier. He also noticed that there were more of these attendants on the move round the walkways that punctuated each new tier of seats. Although he was no expert with regard to event security, he couldn't help feeling that there were a disproportionate number of them inside the arena. It also now became apparent that there were at least two of them standing by each entrance and a further two at the end of each complete row of seats. Brian winced as he received a painful dig in the ribs and it was all he could do not to yelp in pain.

"Brian, look –there!" Kate was gesticulating at something on the floor of the arena.

Brian gazed down, taking in for the first time the huge array of cultural artefacts that lay below. *What was she pointing at?*

Kate could hardly contain herself now and her gesturing became more frantic.

"What is it, Kate? What am I supposed to be looking at?"

Kate, now in a kneeling position behind the seats, began scrambling round in her pockets for something. Retrieving what appeared to be a piece of paper, she flattened it out in front of her.

"That!" she announced, with a look of triumph.

The paper was the letter that she had discovered in her flat-the one allegedly from Michael. Halfway down the paper, beneath the scrawled handwriting, was a drawing- a drawing of the huge obelisk that was centre stage in the arena.

64

6.45pm

"I'm telling you Brian, this is it. It all fits together. Michael explained in his letter that Henderson planned to resurrect this 'Master' character using the Dome, a huge electrical power source and some sort of stone. Don't you see, the Mayans predicted the end of the world –TODAY July 27th 2012-it can't be a coincidence!" Kate was flailing her arms round in agitation now.

"But why would anyone want to be involved in helping something happen that would ultimately destroy themselves?"

"Maybe because they have knowledge that we and all the other soothsayers don't. Remember, there are thousands of theories about the apocalypse and when it will happen. Most of them don't predict what will be left afterwards; they just predict the date. Nostradamus, the Mayans, even the Greeks came up with 2012!"

"What are we going to do now?" hissed Brian, "Find a security guard; inform the police?"

"Have you *seen* any security guards since we got inside? The ones doing the organising all appear to be wearing those robes." Kate hissed back. "We need to get closer to the floor of the arena and that stone. Remember what Michael said in his letter? Four, what was it…keystones, have to be placed in locks that are recessed within the stone itself in order to initiate the resurrection."

At that moment, there appeared to be an increase in the activity from down below. They peered over the back of the seats. People were beginning to stream up the stairways now, randomly selecting rows to sit in, rather than being directed to seats row by row. Brian noticed that on the stage was a man holding a radio handset to his mouth. Although he was wearing a robe, the hood was down and he appeared to be shouting into the radio with some urgency. A glance to the back of the arena told Brian with whom he was speaking. One of the men shepherding the crowds through the main entrance was speaking into his radio whilst encouraging the people to find seats quickly. Brian guessed they must have been taking too long and were behind schedule. No doubt SKY coverage was dictating when everything had to happen so it was crucial that things ran to time so as not mess up the rest of their programming. Either way, Plan B would be to his and Kate's advantage. Grabbing Kate by the elbow, he marched her quickly down the steps towards the floor of the arena. Within ten steps they had become part of the milling crowd and, although they were in the minority heading down, they wouldn't draw too much attention from anyone.

65

Henderson peered through the gap in the curtains at the back of the stage. In front of him, just behind the lectern, he could see the silhouette of Aziz and beyond that, the followers frantically guiding people to their places. In thirty minutes, their world would change beyond belief.

Behind Henderson, Lord Coe, the Chair of the British Olympic Committee was having a microphone attached to his lapel in preparation for his opening speech. Although there were perhaps twenty people backstage, most of whom were part of Henderson's technical staff, there was no conversation and an almost tangible tension filled the air.

Lord Coe was ready and nodded towards Henderson who had now taken his place in the wings to stage left.

With a gesture towards one of his technical staff, all the lights were extinguished and there was a collective gasp from the crowd as the arena was plunged into total darkness. There was a short pause then the nearly inaudible sound of music began to drift into the arena. The sound was almost ghostly in the sense that it was impossible to gauge from where it was coming. It grew gradually louder and after a few seconds, the melody became recognisable, as the sharp stabbing thrusts of the violins gave way to the unmistakable brass section instrumental of Wagner's 'Ride of the Valkyries'. The music became all consuming as it completely filled the arena and seemed to overwhelm the crowd.

In the bottom tier of the seating some thirty metres to the left of the stage, Brian and Kate sat tensely waiting for what was going to happen next. As the music became recognisable she turned to Brian and whispered in his ear; "Brian, this is Wagner-oh my God, Brian, do you remember the film, Apocalypse Now? This was the soundtrack!"

Brian, who had spent most of his spare time at the observatory in Warranboola listening to any type of music he could pick up on the long wave radio recognised it immediately; he had become a bit of a fan of classical music as testified by the play-lists on his Ipod.

"It's also the part of the opera where Odin's spirits of War, the Valkyries, are welcoming the dead soldiers to Valhalla-the resting place of the dead," he whispered back.

Kate's eyes widened further. "The resting place of the dead? In the note, Michael said the resurrection depended entirely on the harvesting of souls!"

As the music became louder still, Kate once again sensed a vibration that seemed to be coming from beneath the floor. Suddenly, the doors at the back of the building opened and a dazzling blue-white light flooded the arena. Kate was reminded of the scene from the film 'Close Encounters of the Third Kind' when the aliens finally emerge from the mother ship.

Vaporous trails of mist began swirling in through the doors sweeping like a tidal bore across the floor of the arena. Then, emerging from beyond the light came the silhouettes of hundreds of people. As the people stepped into the arena it became clear they were the athletes representing the nations. Each carried a candle-like light and, as each team entered, they followed a different pathway into the arena. For ten minutes, the athletes made their way along the red carpets, accompanied by the powerful, pounding, almost gladiatorial music. The crowd seemed almost awestruck.

The teams were choreographed to perfection and as the final note of the music rang out, the doors slammed shut, leaving the arena once again in darkness. The result was mesmerising; the lights twinkling from the floor of the arena created a geometric pattern; two vast overlapping pentagrams that surrounded the obelisk in the centre of the arena. This pattern was mirrored in the ceiling of the Dome.

Kate stole a glance at Brian who, like the rest of the crowd, seemed to be mesmerised by the scene before him. The effect was hypnotic. The obelisk appeared to be floating amidst a constellation of stars, the mist swirling upwards creating the impression of far off galaxies and star clusters. To the crowd, and particularly Brian, who had studied the universe for most of his adult life, it was almost like floating in space. The moment lasted for only a few seconds as the athletes, as one entity, covered their lights, once again returning the arena to darkness.

The doors, from where the athletes had emerged, opened once again, and this time, through the mist, four horsemen appeared. Although they had an almost medieval appearance, instead of lances, each one carried a flaming torch. Each horseman came to a halt beside one of the Maois as the entire tableau on the floor of the arena was cast in a purple patina of light from above.

The crowd's attention turned to the stage now where spotlights suddenly illuminated the heavy curtain as it rose upwards revealing a solitary figure standing behind the bank of microphones.

For the first time, there was an empty pause and the crowd was unsure whether to applaud or cheer or simply wait. Before they had the chance to decide, Lord Coe spoke. "Athletes of the World-Welcome to London 2012!"

Spontaneous applause broke out and people began standing in appreciation of the spectacle they had just witnessed.

It took about five minutes before the applause ceased and people took their seats once more.

"It gives me the utmost pleasure to welcome all the nations of the world to London for what will undoubtedly be the greatest celebration of sport in the history of the modern world. I take great pride in…"

As Lord Coe proceeded with his speech, behind the scenes things were moving quickly.

Brian nudged Kate and nodded his head in the direction of the upper tiers. Beyond the highest row of seats where they had originally gained access to the arena, an unbroken line of robed men stood. Their hoods were round their heads and Brian had the uneasy feeling that the crowd was, to all intents and purposes, caged in. Kate and Brian joined in with the applause, which occasionally punctuated Lord Coe's speech, but they were unaware of what he was actually saying. They were scrutinising all areas of the arena now and, as in the upper tiers, people in robes now guarded all exits. They looked at one another and their expressions told each other they were thinking the same thing; all they could do was wait.

66

7.45pm

"… All that remains is for me to ask Mr. Hu Jintao to accept the Olympic torches and light the Olympic flame."

Lord Coe held his hand out and Hu Jintao, the president of China (the previous hosts of the Olympics) stood from where he had been sitting with a number of other important dignitaries just below the stage.

The crowd applauded as he walked forward to where the four horsemen now stood holding the torches. They were standing beside a huge, golden, globe-shaped structure. The five Olympic rings wrapped themselves completely around the globe-a symbol of world unity. At the base of the globe and at each of the four compass points were four circular wells. Each well contained oil. Hu Jintao accepted each torch one by one and transferred the flame from each to a different well. When all four were alight, there was a slight pause before the entire globe was engulfed in flame. Once again there was an outburst of cheering and spontaneous applause.

Lord Coe walked forward and down the steps that led off the front of the stage and took a vacant seat with Mr Hu Jintao and the other dignitaries. The crowd grew gradually silent as they waited in anticipation of what was coming next.

A figure dressed in a white robe, holding a golden staff

in his right hand, strode to the front of the stage. The purple light faded and just the light emanating from the Olympic Flame illuminated him.

Kate looked over her shoulder as she overheard a voice behind her saying something about the *bloody Ku Klux Klan*. She squinted her eyes in an effort to see the face of the person on stage but the hood he wore hid his identity. There was total silence in the arena now except for a distant electrical hum. The man leaned forward to address the bank of microphones.

"Good evening ladies and gentlemen. I too welcome all of you to this ceremony. It is an event that will change the lives of billions of people all round the world. Every single person in this building will play a significant part in ensuring that the legacy from this evening will last for eternity."

Kate was looking round at the crowd now, wondering if any of them sensed that the atmosphere in the arena had changed. Most seemed intent on listening to the speech clearly at ease with what was being said.

The person on the stage continued. "A very long time ago, the peoples of the earth began to build. They were the planet's first architects and they used the heavens to guide them in their designs. After all, there were no structures or designs for them to copy. All over the world in remote areas, often thousands of miles from any other civilisations, they built structures; structures which were built to mirror the heavens. The structures were often used to represent stairways that would lead them to the land of the after-life; the heaven that existed amongst the constellations that they could see above them. It is no coincidence that civilisation such as the Incas and the Aztecs and the Egyptians built pyramids and made sacrifices to the Gods they believed in. It is no coincidence that even today architects build structures where they do. Let me show you ladies and gentlemen."

The giant screen behind the stage glowed blue then an image appeared on the screen:

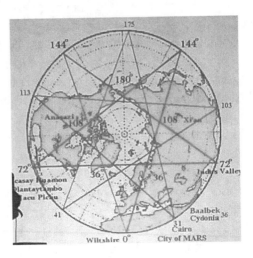

"This diagram, ladies and gentlemen-the megalithic grid as it is known, is part of the celestial design which dictates where some of the major structures have been built on our planet. If you look at the two pentagrams which lie inside the earth's equator you will notice that the first one is anchored at Cairo in Egypt, the site of the Great pyramids at Giza. You will notice that the second pentagram is anchored at the Prime Meridian-You will no doubt be aware that you are currently sitting in a major structure in Greenwich which sits on the prime meridian. Furthermore, notice that both the Indus Valley and the site of Maccu Piccu in Peru also line up with other points on the second pentagram. There are many other such structures which lie on the lines of the two pentagrams, some of which are no longer visible, covered by the sands of time, waiting to be rediscovered by archaeologists if only they knew to use this template as their guide."

Kate noticed one or two people becoming restless now,

a man behind her commenting that he'd come for a night out not a '*bleedin' history lecture.*'

"Why am I sharing this information with you, you might ask. It is very simple, you see; twenty five thousand years ago the stars in the universe were aligned in relation to the earth in such a way that a portal to the underworld was opened and the Great Lord Seth was banished into it by his brother Osiris. Since then all these structures of which I have spoken have been harvesting the souls of mortals so that one day, when the portal reopens, the Master will have enough life force to return and reclaim his rightful place on earth."

Brian prodded Kate in the side, "Kate-he's talking about precession. Do you remember in Australia when we discovered a link between the aboriginal burial sites and the position of the stars? Surely he can't believe that it's anything more than a physical cycle!"

Kate was suddenly distracted and gestured towards one of the exits. One or two of the crowd had apparently heard enough and had already decided it was time to leave. Two men and a woman were remonstrating with four of the robed men 'guarding' the exit. They looked as if they were being told to retake their seats. Turning their attention back to the stage, Kate and Brian also noticed a puzzled-looking Lord Coe whispering to one of the others with whom he was sitting. Clearly, he was perplexed by the nature of the speech that was being delivered.

"That day has finally come. According to the translation of the Seven Seals and as foretold in the Book of Revelations, today is the day of reckoning." The figure raised the staff he was holding and banged it down theatrically. The purple lights came back on again, bathing the arena in an eerie twilight. The four horsemen, who had brought the Olympic flames earlier now cantered forward towards the obelisk. Each rider held something in his hand.

"Shit, Brian, look what they're holding.

Brian recognised the objects from Michael's drawing in his letter. "The keystones!"

"Brian, this is it. This is when it's supposed to happen."

The four riders dismounted simultaneously and took up positions round the obelisk.

The figure on the stage was reaching up to his hood. Suddenly, the electrical hum that thus far had been a distant background noise became louder. The person on stage lifted the hood away from his face.

"Henderson!" both Brian and Kate gasped as they saw his face for the first time.

He raised the staff above his head and closed his eyes. The crowd was clearly puzzled now and their conversations added to the electrical hum that seemed to be filling the room. The vibrations that Kate had felt earlier had also become stronger and her feet felt like they had pins and needles. Others around her could clearly feel it too. She could see people peering down and lifting their feet from the floor.

Behind the noise of the crowd and the humming there was also another sound; a more rhythmic sound, like voices. Brian looked round and noticed that all the robed figures were now linking hands around the periphery of the arena. He strained his ears trying to hear what he thought were words. Lots of people were beginning to stand now, perturbed by what was happening.

Kate's eyes fixed upon the four men standing by the stone. The first one stepped forward and slowly raised the keystone to the obelisk. He appeared to slide the keystone into a slot and as he did so, there was a collective gasp from the crowd. The beam of blue light that had shone from the ceiling of the Dome earlier reappeared. The second man repeated the act with his keystone and as it slid home, there was a definite increase in the intensity of the beam. The vibrations also seemed to get stronger. The sound inside the arena was now uncomfortably loud and people had begun to put their hands over their ears to protect them. The third man approached the stone.

"Brian!" shouted Kate pulling at his arm. "We've got to do something!"

Brian looked scared now as if what Kate had been telling him was finally sinking in. She knew he now believed her. "Come on!" she shouted, scrambling to her feet.

It was at this point, as the third keystone was inserted, that the screaming began. The noise level increased again and a woman in the row in front of them began to wail. Kate looked on aghast as she noticed blood seeping through the woman's fingers that she had covering her ears against the noise.

Panic was starting to ensue and people were trying to get to the exits only to be pushed back by the men in robes. Kate was at the end of the row now but people were streaming down the walkway. Suddenly, there was a loud crack, like static electricity and the floor began to shudder. Kate looked towards the obelisk as the final keystone was placed into its slot.

She turned to make sure that Brian was behind her when she was thrown off her feet by a violent movement beneath them. She fell to her knees along with nearly everyone else on the walkway and she instinctively curled up as bodies rolled down the steps uncontrollably. She felt something slam into her back then strong arms suddenly wrapped round her waist and she was pulled to her feet.

As soon as she had regained her balance, she was pushed forcibly forward towards the arena floor. There was mayhem as the athletes, who minutes earlier had been standing amongst the huge stone and wooden artefacts, now pushed and jostled with each other to get to the back of the building towards the exits.

"We've got to get to the Stone!" Kate screamed.

Brian nodded, lip-reading above the noise.

On the stage, Henderson was gripped by a sudden, violent spasm and it looked as if thousands of volts of electricity were passing through his body. His entire person was floating two or three feet above the stage. He was staring straight ahead, his eyes transfixed on the Stone. Even from her position thirty feet away, Kate could see that he was in some kind of trance. Suddenly, there was a loud grinding sound and Kate looked up to see one of the gigantic aboriginal paintings break loose from the chains from which it had been hanging. The painting fell to the floor crushing twenty or thirty of the athletes beneath it.

Despite having to fight their way forward against the flow of the river of people now panic-stricken and desperate to get out of the arena, they were making progress towards the Stone.

The sound of gunshots momentarily stunned the crowd into silence and then the screaming started again as more shots were fired. The guards had finally called upon the weapons they had concealed beneath their robes, as the crowd grew desperate to escape. Brian felt something whizz by his head and milliseconds later there was a 'ping' as the bullet ricocheted off one of the giant stone Heads to his right. The blue beam of light was now so intense that it was impossible to look directly at it but as he looked up to where it was hitting the ceiling, he realised it didn't stop there but had burned a gaping hole through the fabric of the building. He also noticed that all the way across the ceiling, crack-like tears were appearing. The structure was under such intense pressure it was being pulled apart.

Two more of the paintings crashed to the ground, then a totem pole toppled over pinning several people to the floor. Brian noticed that the four men circling the stone seemed oblivious to what was happening and strangely, there seemed to be a 'space' around them, almost as if there was an invisible force field protecting them.

Kate was still pushing her way forward when she noticed the vast screen behind the stage flicker into life. Henderson still hung mid-air like a puppet performing a macabre show. But there was something different now; his head was thrown back and his arms were spread so that the scene had a crucifixion-like appearance. Kate also thought she could see...*could she be imagining it?* No, she was sure. In the air, immediately above Henderson, Kate could see a kind of interference in the air. It was almost a shimmer, similar to hot air rising from a warm surface. At first, she thought it might be on the screen behind Henderson but it was still flickering as if disturbed by the static. The shimmering was definitely in the air. As she watched, every second or so, there was a pulse of some sort within the shimmer itself giving the impression almost that something had travelled through the air and into Henderson's mouth. Each time it happened, his body gave a small shudder. She watched more closely, and noticed that with each pulse the air lost some of its transparency and gained a translucent quality that misted over momentarily. She turned to indicate what she saw to Brian but he was no longer there. She tried to make out his face amongst the thousands milling round her but all she saw were strangers, mouths open screaming, bloody tears rolling down their cheeks. It was a nightmarish scene.

She turned again to look at Henderson and now she was certain; each pulse seemed to be more powerful and more intense. Each one seemed to originate from somewhere far above Henderson but the misting only manifested itself as the pulse reached him. Then she noticed something else. She tried to look up as far as she could to locate the point where the mist suddenly appeared. After a few seconds, she spotted it, just below the ceiling, beneath a tear in the fabric; almost a wisp at first but then becoming more tangible as it was 'sucked' towards Henderson's hanging form. She realised that beneath every tear in the roof there was a similar misting. Her mind was racing now back to the speech Henderson had delivered a few minutes earlier: '*harvesting souls*' he had said. Brian speaking about Valhalla and the existence of some kind of after-life! It came to her similar to a bomb exploding: *Shit-Henderson's the repository. It's the resurrection. Henderson is becoming the Master!*

67

Outside the Dome, the police officers were looking up river from where they stood on their boats unable to believe what they were witnessing. Apart from a distant hum accompanied by a slight vibration, which had begun some fifteen minutes ago, there had been no warning of what was about to happen. The first sign came when, despite the sky being completely clear of clouds, a huge bolt of lightning had forked down from the sky, striking the Dome exactly at its centre. The sound of static filled the air then there were three more lightning strikes in quick succession, each one hitting the Dome in the same place. Then, incredibly, a bolt of lightning passed between two of the spires that protruded from the roof but instead of dissipating, it continued to spark violently, spanning the two spires like some gigantic TAZAR gun.

The officer in charge was desperately trying to contact his commanding officer on his radio but it was completely dead. He looked round at his colleagues, each completely transfixed by the sight before them. There was yet another ear-splitting crack and the electricity jumped to the next spire along, then another as it leapt across to the next.

In the space of thirty seconds the ring was complete and all twelve spires were connected creating a fiery crown of blue lightning.

The officer could now see along then banks of the Thames people beginning to panic and although they were curious about what was happening self-preservation was more important. They were realising that they were too close for comfort and were trying desperately to move away en masse. The vibrations beneath the ground were becoming more violent with each passing second and the water around the boat was beginning to boil as if thousands of piranha fish were devouring something just below the surface. But the most disconcerting thing was what was happening to the sky above the Dome. Up until this point, the phenomenon might have been accounted for by some kind of freak electrical storm or earthquake. God knows, the scientists had been warning them about the consequences of global warming for the last twenty years. The sky above London had turned a deep crimson in the matter of just a few seconds and out of nowhere, above the Dome itself, a vast, seething mass of clouds seemed to be gathering. The officer's immediate thought was that it was some kind of tornado since, at the base of the cloud, there was a spiral of mist spinning rapidly into the centre of the Dome. But instead of weaving out of control like a normal tornado, this seemed almost *in* control. The cloud above seemed to be running, like sand from an egg timer into the Dome itself.

The boat started to rock violently now and the police officer grabbed hold of the wooden rail that formed the cockpit of the boat to prevent himself from falling. The other men fell to their knees and desperately tried to grasp onto anything solid.

Suddenly, the air was filled with the sound of whirring rotor blades and a police helicopter appeared from behind the Canary Wharf complex. The sight of the scene before him must have taken the pilot by surprise as the nose of the helicopter dipped forward into a steep dive. It swooped to its right towards Westminster desperately trying to avoid being sucked into the maelstrom that lay before it. But it was too late; an arc of electricity from one of the spires leapt out, striking the helicopter's tail rotor. The end of the tail disappeared in a shower of sparks and the helicopter careered into an uncontrollable spin. It dropped from the sky like a wounded dragonfly and crashed in a melee of swirling metal and water into the Thames about two hundred feet from the boat. Within seconds, it had disappeared beneath the bubbling water.

68

Despite the immense effort in trying to fight her way towards the stage past thousands of hysterical people, Kate was now only thirty feet away from Henderson. He was still suspended in the air with his arms outstretched and his eyes staring up at the ceiling of the arena. The disturbance in the air that Kate had noticed earlier had now taken on a new form. It looked to all intents and purposes like an endless swarm of white insects was entering Henderson's mouth.

As she stood, mesmerised by the sight before her, she noticed something else. Henderson's appearance was beginning to change. His limbs were enlarging and becoming more muscular; more sinewy. Thick black hair was beginning to sprout from his skin and the nails on his toes were elongating and taking on the appearance of talons.

The robe that he wore was beginning to tighten round his frame and the seams began to bulge to the point of tearing. His body was now in spasm and the pain he was enduring was apparent in his expression. The eyes were clenched tightly closed and he was throwing his head from side to side violently. Kate was oblivious to everything else around her as she witnessed Henderson's body undergoing the incredible metamorphosis. The hair on his head was now becoming thicker, blacker, and longer. It hung round his face which itself was transforming. The cheekbones were pushing through the skin; skin which was becoming darker and almost vellum-like in texture. The brow bones above his eyes were thickening and the lips were growing larger. Yellow fang-like teeth were now starting to protrude from the snarling mouth. Trickles of blood rolled down the cheeks from the still-closed eyes, mixing with the saliva that was spraying from the mouth as the jerking of his head became more violent.

Suddenly, his head was thrown back with such force that Kate thought it might be torn from his body and at the same time there was a huge intake of breath. His head was raised slowly upright and the eyes opened revealing thin, yellow irises and pupils as black as any night. The countenance was one of pure evil and Kate shuddered involuntarily. His gaze, however, rested not on her but on the seething mass of people in the arena. Henderson, if that's who this creature still was, was no longer suspended in mid air but standing upright on the stage.

Kate stole a glance behind her to see what the Master was staring at. There was hand to hand fighting at the exits between the robed followers and the civilians desperate to escape. The sounds of gunshots rang out across the arena seemingly punctuating the screams and wails of the stricken masses. There were hundreds, maybe thousands, of trampled bodies, bloody and lifeless, littering the arena floor. Her eyes slowly strayed to the obelisk where the four horsemen still stood guarding each keystone. High above, the ceiling of the Dome was now in tatters. She could see a fiery blue halo directly above the Dome and beyond that a sky that seemed alive and threatening. She turned her eyes back to the Master and watched incredulously as he raised his right arm and pointed a long brown index finger toward the obelisk. There was a loud crack of static as the blue beam of light that had thus far been emanating from the stone suddenly enveloped the obelisk, creating a shimmering aura all round it. It was the most bizarre thing that Kate had ever witnessed-almost like a Director shouting 'Cut' on a film set. The screaming cacophony that filled the arena only seconds earlier stopped, and people began to look round them, wondering what would happen next.

Although the eerie silence only lasted a few seconds, it felt like minutes before it was replaced by something different. Kate looked back towards the stage. The Master's mouth was now wide open and from it issued a terrible, haunting screech like the wails of a thousand lost souls. The noise was deafening and once again people began to cover their ears. The Master raised an arm but this time he threw it forward as if he were swatting a fly. Before him in the arena, hundreds of people were plucked from the floor by an invisible force and thrown violently sideways and upwards. Many of them landed in the rows of seating at each side of the arena and Kate watched with horror as their bodies crumpled on impact with the seats. With another wave of the Master's arm, the two remaining gigantic aboriginal pictures still hanging from the ceiling were dragged from their stanchions and hurled into the crowd below, crushing hundreds instantaneously.

Kate's thoughts suddenly turned to Brian. *What had happened to him? Was he still alive?* Before she could consider the answers to her own questions, something caught her eye. Amidst the chaos and carnage that lay all round her, she noticed something that seemed out of place. The four men were still guarding the obelisk, all still in a state of trance, all still apparently protected from everything that was happening round them by an invisible force-field. Something, though, was different. There was something that appeared to be glowing. Round one of the men's neck hung a pendant of some sort, clearly glowing a bright emerald green. For some reason it looked familiar to Kate. *She was sure she had seen it before. Maybe when she was studying for her doctorate?* Kate couldn't fathom why but somehow she felt it had nothing to do with everything else that was happening. Somehow she sensed that it was in fact the antithesis of the madness that was now surrounding her.

She closed her eyes desperately trying to remember the story of Seth and Osiris. Michael had explained in his letter that Henderson believed that the Master was the Egyptian God of Chaos waiting to be resurrected. *What was the story? After Osiris had become Lord of the Underworld, he had appeared to his son Horus who had sworn to avenge his father's death. There followed eighty years of war between Horus and Seth before Seth was defeated and banished. There was something else, she was sure.*

A familiar voice behind her suddenly brought her back to the present and as she turned, Brian threw his arms round her. "Thank God, you're safe," he shouted above the noise.

Kate was aghast at the sight of her husband. Half an hour earlier, he had looked as he always had. Now there was a huge gash across his forehead and blood was caked across his face. His left eye was swollen, bruised, and almost closed. His clothes were torn and covered in blood she hoped wasn't his. Despite his appearance, he was smiling.

"I tried to follow you towards the stage but I just kept getting pushed further backwards," he explained. "Then one of the totem poles fell and I was trapped amongst the debris. Two men pulled me out."

Kate was so relieved to see him that she wasn't listening to the words. She held onto him tightly and sobbed with relief. Then without warning, something sprung into her mind.

"Shit-that's it! I knew I'd seen it before. It's the eye!" Kate was almost hysterical now.

Brian held her away from him. "Eye? What eye? Kate, what are you talking about?"

"The eye of Horus! Egyptian legend has it that when Horus battled with Seth following the murder of his father, one of his eyes was ripped out by Seth. It was later found by another God, healed and then returned to Horus. In many writings it is believed that Seth and Horus have been in continuous battle ever since and it is only Horus that stands in the way of Seth and the evil he represents." She spun herself round to face the obelisk and the horsemen. "That is the eye of Horus!" she screamed pointing towards the pendant.

Brian didn't really understand what she was talking about. He was just relieved that she was okay.

"Brian, I know it sounds crazy but we need to get that pendant. I think it's some kind of portal itself- a bit like the obelisk but connecting Horus directly to the Master. It's our only hope."

"But what do we do when we've got it?" asked Brian.

Kate looked into his eyes and he could see the belief behind the fear. He knew after all she'd been through that whatever happened next, he would be there to help her do whatever she wanted.

"What's the plan?" he mouthed.

69

8.15pm

Kate and Brian were now crouched between what remained of the front and second rows of seats to the left of the stage. In front of them the carnage was relentless. The Master was indiscriminately slaughtering anyone and everyone in the arena. With a wave of his arms he had just brought down two upper tiers of seating, the debris crashing its way onto the people below. Three of the Moai stone heads that had looked so impressive when the ceremony had begun were now the only structures still standing and it was surreal that they seemed to be surveying the destruction all around them.

Kate noted that the 'eye' was still glowing on the man's chest and that he, like the other three men round the obelisk, still remained in the trance they had been in since depositing the keystones. She turned to face Brian. "Right, it's now or never."

They looked at their watches to make sure once again they were perfectly synchronised. In the foot well between them was a fire extinguisher that they'd found hanging on the wall at the end of the row of seats and an axe that had also been hanging on the wall in a glass case with a sticker exclaiming 'break glass in emergency'.

"I love you, Brian. Please be careful," Kate whispered then kissed him gently on the mouth. Suddenly, he was away, bounding up the steps towards the fire exit where he and Kate had entered the building what seemed like a lifetime ago. He only hoped that they were right about the electrical supply. If Michael had been correct in his assumptions that an enormous electrical generator, totally out of proportion to the requirements of the building itself, had been installed beneath the Dome prior to its construction for the sole purpose of powering this whole 'event' then maybe they were in with a shout. The plan was simple, like all the best plans; he would break into the electrical plant (assuming that what they had seen in the stairwell when they'd entered via the fire exits was actually part of the electrical generating system) and either find the emergency cut-off switches or, failing that, cause as much damage as he could. Meanwhile, Kate would stay out of sight and keep an eye on the events unfolding in the hope that, if Brian were successful in knocking out the power supply, something would happen and she could somehow get hold of the 'eye'. What would happen once she had it in her possession was the weak point in their plan.

He wasn't surprised to see the top rows of seats completely empty; they had been some of the first to be vacated when people had begun to panic. Further down, the rows were littered with bodies and debris. He pushed through the doors and jumped down the stairwell. In seconds he was standing in front of the steel doors. The doors looked impenetrable and doubt crept into his mind as to whether he stood any chance of breaching them. He took a step back and swung the axe, aiming for where he thought the weak point might be, in the centre of the doors.

He must have instinctively closed his eyes on impact and when he opened them, he was amazed; firstly, at how bad his aim had proved to be and secondly, because there was a six inch gash in the left hand door. The steel was in fact just cladding and not very thick cladding at that. He could make out some wooden splinters beneath the gash. He swung the axe once more.

Kate looked at her watch for the tenth time since Brian had left; he'd been gone five minutes. The Master was now seemingly growing in strength judging by the fact that he was now pacing the stage and directing his attention to every corner of the arena. Fires had broken out now in some of the recesses behind the main seating areas and the exits at the back were blocked by flames rather than his followers, many of whom had been killed already by the Master's indiscriminate slaughter.

Kate tried to listen for any change to the electrical hum that still filled the air. *Had Brian even managed to get into the generator?*

There was another loud screech from the Master and Kate was sure that the building was vibrating. She held on to the back of the trembling seats. In fact, the floor had now begun to tremble too. She wondered if it was anything to do with Brian. The Master was now staring intently at the man wearing the pendant. She couldn't be certain, but for a second she thought that she saw a flicker of fear in his eyes. Suddenly the vibrations increased in power and frequency and Kate looked down at the floor beneath her feet. It was, she imagined, like an earthquake. Looking up again, the Master was now screaming. He had jumped from the stage and was pacing round the obelisk menacingly. Beyond, further into the main area of the arena, people were struggling to remain on their feet as the ground shook sickeningly beneath them. Kate noticed a long crack snaking its way along the arena floor and once again, she thought about Brian. *If the floor was cracking up here, what was it like in the sub structure below? Had she sent Brian to his death?* She grimaced at the thought of huge chunks of concrete falling down from above. *Come on, Brian!*

With one last enormous effort Brian swung the axe again. The door gave way. He was breathing heavily with exertion but knew he hadn't time to stop for breath. He pushed past the broken door and entered the room. Immediately, his heart sank. Across the far end of the wall was a bank of electrical transformers. They were big but he guessed nowhere big enough to generate the power for the entire Dome. He scanned the small room for any signs of a control box. Suddenly, the ground began to shake, gently at first then the walls in the room began to vibrate. Dust from the ceiling above began to fall round him and he instinctively pushed his back up against one of the transformers to steady himself. It was then that he noticed that the end transformer was slightly different than the others. The front was plain, green steel and had no lights like the others. Set off on one side was a handle. Brian shuffled across the floor to take a closer look. He tried the handle but it only moved a millimetre. *"Shit,"* he cursed before he remembered the axe. He got to his feet and retrieved it from by the door where he had dropped it. *The shaking floor would make it difficult but maybe he could ...*

He steadied himself in front of the door and swung the axe in a high arc above his head. Miraculously, he hit the handle square on top and it dropped to the floor with a metallic clang. The door swung open about a centimetre. As he pulled it open further, he expected to see switches, levers, or some kind of electrical panel but to his amazement, there was nothing but a black hole. He peered inside trying to make out the back of the cupboard and as his eyes adjusted to the darkness he realised that the hole was in fact a chamber. He looked down and realised that there was a ladder attached to the wall, similar to the sort you would find in an average sewer. As his eyes adjusted further, he could just make out some flashing lights below. The vibrations seemed to be getting stronger now and he was aware that the humming that had been present ever since they had entered the building was even louder down below. He knew he couldn't climb and hold the axe at the same time so he took the decision to throw the axe into the chamber. He only hoped it would survive the fall. He dropped the axe and counted in the hope it would give him an idea how far it was to the bottom-*three seconds! Probably fifty feet or so.*

He twisted his body round and planted his feet firmly onto the first rung and began his descent. His breathing was laboured now; the heat and exertion were beginning to take their toll. As he clambered down the shaking rungs, he thought of Kate and only hoped to God that she was still safely tucked between the seats and out of sight of that creature. Suddenly, his feet hit solid ground. His head was throbbing as the humming began to make his skull vibrate. He took a second to look around. What he saw made him gasp. The chamber he was in was vast. It was circular, as far as he could make out, and directly in front of him, about thirty feet away, was what looked like a portakabin with glass walls. It was about fifty feet long and he could now clearly see that this was the source of the lights he had seen from the room above. He realised that the vibrations down at this level were minimal and the floor was no longer shaking. He scanned round looking for the axe. He spotted it quickly and ran across to retrieve it. Thankfully, it was intact. He hurried towards the portakabin and the steps that led up to a doorway. At least this should prove easier to get into being made of glass. To his surprise, the door opened at his first attempt.

Kate was starting to feel sick. The shaking floor wasn't helping matters and for the first time since she'd left home earlier that day, she had begun to reflect on what she had gotten herself and Brian into.

The Master was still pacing round the obelisk and was

clearly perturbed by the glowing stone in the pendant. Now, Kate thought she knew why. *He must know that Horus would not let him go without a fight.*

Several times he had tried to grab the pendant but whatever force field was protecting the obelisk was clearly powerful enough to keep him out. Kate tried to think clearly about what to do next. Even if Brian could somehow kill the power and even if, as they suspected, render the portal impotent, how could she possibly get to the 'eye' with the Master so close? She wriggled uncomfortably as she became aware of the hard steel cylinder of the fire extinguisher digging into her side.

Brian was mesmerised by the myriad of flashing LED lights that lay out in front of him. Running the length of the cabin were about thirty electrical cabinets. Each had a glass door running from the floor to the ceiling of the cabin. Inside each cabinet were hundreds of cables intertwined, completely filling the space inside. He walked quickly along in front of each one desperately hoping for some inspiration. Each cabinet was identical to the next. He finally reached the end of the cabin and looked out through the window and into the huge dark chamber beyond.

It was like looking into deep space and he became aware of a profound sense of destiny that seemed to be seeping into him. Beginning at the soles of his feet, there was the sensation of warmth rising through his legs, up into his torso and finally into his arms. He felt a sudden rush of adrenaline and was immediately overcome with an overwhelming feeling of strength. He lifted the axe above his head and, pivoting round to face the bank of cabinets, swung it heavily in a downwards arc. There was a loud crash as the top of the first cabinet caved in under the weight of the blow. The second blow, if anything, was more devastating as the axe bit through cables. Sparks leapt from the cabinet and the sound of static filled the air. Brian felt another huge rush of adrenaline and he swung the axe once more.

Kate twisted the fire extinguisher round trying to establish what it contained. There was a white label displaying a symbol of some sort. Below the symbol she could just make out the word 'CO_2.' *Not water,* she thought, then almost smiled at the image that had just jumped into her mind; the scene from the film 'The Wizard of Oz' where Dorothy throws water over the wicked witch and she melts. Somehow, she knew it would take more than water to defeat the Master.

At that moment, there was a sudden lull in the noise that had been filling the arena. She wasn't certain that she had imagined it at first but then it happened again-a momentary decrease in the volume. She stared at the obelisk searching for any change in the glow of light that still engulfed it. The four men were still entranced and the eye glowed as fiercely as before. The Master had stopped pacing and was now looking upwards towards the gaping hole in the ceiling of the Dome. He had one pointed ear slightly cocked to one side and it looked as though he were listening for something. *Had he noticed the lull too?*

Kate's hands were still wrapped round the fire extinguisher and without being aware of it, she lifted the cylinder and placed its bulk beneath her armpit and held the hose in front of her with her free hand. In that instant, the sound ceased completely and the blue beam disappeared. Instinctively, she knew that Brian had been successful and, without thinking, she launched herself forward towards the Master. In seconds, she drew level with the obelisk. The four men had all crumpled to their knees as if the life force had been sucked from them. The Master was looking round as if he were searching for something; he seemed taken aback by what was happening.

Kate took this chance and threw herself forward aiming

the hose towards the hideous creature. She timed it perfectly, squeezing the trigger on the extinguisher exactly as the Master turned to face her. The cloud of CO_2 engulfed the Master and she dropped the cylinder and swung herself sideways towards the man with the pendant. She shot out her hand as she fell towards him, losing her footing on the debris that lay on the ground. Her fingers clutched at the chain and she felt resistance but then a snap as she hit the ground heavily. It all seemed to happen in slow motion and only now was she aware of the hissing and screeching of the Master. Looking up, she realised that her assault had thrown him backwards causing him to lose balance. He looked slightly dazed as he tried to regain his feet. Realising there was no time to lose, she looked down at the chain in her hand-there was no pendant! It must have dropped off the free end when the chain snapped.

Frantically, her eyes scanned the debris round her feet. With only the emergency lighting now casting an eerie glow onto the floor of the arena, she knew it would take a miracle to find it. Her chance had gone.

A low groan to her right drew her attention and she turned to face the man who had been wearing the pendant. His eyes were glazed over and he was trembling, but he had somehow found the strength to raise one of his arms. He was pointing towards the ground by his side. Kate looked down and immediately caught sight of the pendant. It was wedged between some remnants of smashed seating. She reached down to pick it up and looked back up at the man. She was certain that for a brief moment a smile crossed his lips before he fell forward, his chest coming to rest on some fallen masonry.

She looked down at the eye. It stared back up at her and she was dismayed not to see some kind of 'life' or 'power' emanating from within. She knew that she had been working on a gut feeling but she had been certain that if only she could get hold of it, what to do next would become apparent.

Suddenly, her ears where filled with a loud whooshing sound, and she was knocked backwards as something very heavy hit her in the chest. Her legs buckled and she toppled backwards once more onto the ground. A spasm of pain shot through her body and she looked down to see a large shard of metal poking up through her side. She was impaled flat on her back. Her left arm was lying at an odd angle, clearly broken as it took the full force of her fall. The pain was intense and her head began to spin. High above she could see the flickering, blue glow of the electricity that still danced between the spires on top of the Dome. She noticed a sudden movement at the periphery of her vision and twisted her head to look. The Master was now towering above her and, for the first time, she appreciated just how incredible the transformation from Henderson had been. At his full height he must have been nine feet tall. His yellow eyes bore deep into her soul and the evil that emanated from him seemed almost tangible. She could smell his foetid breath and there was a musky, damp odour that seemed to permeate the air immediately round him.

He looked down at her, realising that she was pinned to the ground. He seemed to take a deep sigh before reaching down to the ground and picking up a large lump of concrete.

The Master lifted the 'rock' above his head and raised his eyes to the roof of the Dome. He paused for a moment as if he were savouring the moment. Slowly, he looked back down at Kate and as their eyes met for the briefest second she thought she saw something…something human behind the evil. Then it was gone, and she saw the muscles in his upper arms contract slightly and knew that this was the end.

Kate instinctively closed her eyes and threw her right

arm protectively in front of her, preparing for the inevitable when the thought flashed into her mind that she hoped the end would be quick.

70

8.40pm

Brian opened his eyes slowly and groaned. There was only blackness. He tried to lift his hand to rub his eyes but he couldn't move. It took several seconds before he remembered where he was. He tried to move again but the pain in his chest was excruciating and it was only the fact that he could still feel it that convinced him he wasn't dead. He twisted his head to look deeper into the darkness, trying to gain his bearings. A tiny glimmer of light caught his eye. It seemed to be floating in the distance some way above him. Then he realised it was the hatch he had climbed through to enter the basement. He looked around to see where he was in relation to the electrical unit, but he could see nothing. It was then that he noticed the silence...*Shit, Kate!*

71

8.40pm

Kate felt a sudden immense jolt as though something had collided with the hand that she had thrown out to protect herself. The power of the blow took her breath away and she was astounded by the incredible feeling of euphoria that had suddenly engulfed her. *Was this how death was? No pain, just the overwhelming feeling of release? Although she knew her eyes were tightly closed, she was suddenly aware of a blinding light above her and she guessed that this was how it happened, the gates of heaven opening to allow her entry.*

Slowly, she opened her eyes, totally unprepared for what she was saw. The Master, who only seconds ago had been a few feet in front of her was now maybe thirty feet away. He was on his feet but he was bathed in a white light and his head was thrown back as if he were in terrible pain. His long narrow snout-like mouth was open and a high pitched, haunting wail issued forth filling the air so that no other sound in the arena could be heard. Kate looked at the source of the light that was so obviously the cause of his torment-her right hand! It looked to all intents and purposes as if she were directing a laser beam of light directly at the Master. Then she realised that the beam was actually originating from the hole in the ceiling of the Dome and was reflecting off something in her hand. *Of course-the pendant!. She had been holding it when she fell.*

She looked back at the Master who was now quivering uncontrollably as the power of the beam seemed to totally overwhelm him. From his mouth a trail of vapour was rising into the air, but unlike mist which would continue to rise or dissipate, it seemed to hover above him forming a kind of ribbon. It spiralled outwards but not upwards and as it grew thicker, it gained substance and darker, grey patches seemed to be taking shape within it. Then she noticed something else, something she thought she was imagining; faces...she was sure of it...but how? They were becoming clearer now and she realised that the faces belonged to people of different ages, different races, even. Within a few seconds she could make out hundreds of them, young women, old men, children. The mist now began to rise as if some higher intelligence had given it a command. It continued to flow from the mouth of the creature accompanied by the terrible cacophonous screeching. The mist was alive now with hundreds, possibly thousands, of faces. Each one different in every way possible except for one thing-every one of them was smiling!

Kate scanned the faces, confused and still wondering whether or not she was hallucinating or this was actually her descent into hell rather than heaven. *Perhaps she was dead after all and this was payback for all her sins.* Then something inexplicable happened. She heard a voice beyond the wailing-a voice that called her name. *She was sure of it-there it was again, faint but clear....Kate...Kate. So this was it after all-this was her time and now she was being called..*

One of the faces that had just materialised from the mist was now hovering directly above her and she was suddenly startled to realise that she recognised the face-Edward, her brother! He mouthed her name again and she saw him smile. A warm feeling seemed to envelop her whole body and she began to imagine the events unfolding in the next few seconds. She was being guided into the afterlife by those who had gone before. *How could it possibly be any different? It was the way many people who had had near death experiences described the last few seconds before the miracle happened that pulled them back from the brink of death.*

She looked up at Edward's face again and realised that he was rising slowly upwards with the others. Then his mouth began to move again and she tried desperately to lip read what he was saying...*Goodbye...I love you Kate.* The words were like a gunshot to her heart. *Why goodbye? That didn't make sense! What was happening?*

Then a thought occurred to her-perhaps she wasn't dead, perhaps she was still alive, badly wounded, but alive and still breathing. She turned her head to look into the arena at the thousands of people inside still running and screaming, desperate to escape the unholy scenario that was taking place before their eyes. The scene was one of utter devastation. Things could not have been worse if a terrorist bomb had been detonated inside the Dome.

She turned back to look at Edward and was dismayed to see other faces hovering above her instead. These faces looked different from the others though, some wore strange headdresses and colourful face-paint. They looked like people from ancient cultures-Incas or Aztecs, she thought. Her head was spinning now and she felt as if she might pass out. She glanced across at the Master who had now sunk to his knees. Kate sensed that he was weakening and thought she could see a slight change in is appearance. His body looked less muscular and the proportions of his face seemed to have changed. The wolf-like appearance of his mouth and forehead seemed to be shifting as she watched, becoming more human. Still, the mist continued to rise from his mouth.

The mist directly above her began to swirl and another familiar face appeared. Michael smiled down at her and she felt a tear fall down her cheek. He looked exactly as he had on the day he had waved her off at the airport as she left for her expedition. She whispered *'I love you'* to him and he mouthed the words back to her as he began to rise with the others inexorably upwards. Then there was only darkness.

72

Lewisham Hospital, London, three weeks later.

Michael and Edward were waving at her, but they were no longer smiling. They both looked terrified and were screaming something at her. *"Go now-get away from here!"* They kept looking behind them as if they were frightened of something menacing lurking there in the dark.

She wanted desperately to go to them but her legs were useless and wouldn't move. They seemed to be getting further away although neither she nor they were moving. It was like a telescopic camera lens zooming out on a scene. The zoom-out stopped and Kate realised she had been staring into the Master's eyes. The pupils were no longer yellow but black and inky. At their very centre she could see the two figures melting away. She refocused on the Master's face but it was no longer him. Simon Henderson smiled back at her and began to laugh. Kate screamed.

73

Lewisham Hospital, London, a week later

"You mean I've been here for nearly a month?" whispered Kate.

Brian nodded and smiled; his eyes watery with tears. "Four weeks today exactly," he said taking her hand in his. "We thought we'd lost you when you slipped into the coma."

Kate looked a round the hospital room taking in her surroundings. Monitors beeped away at the side of her bed and a tube ran from her nose to a ventilator. More tubes still were attached to drips that fed various types of medication into the veins of her arms.

Brian was smiling at her. There was an angry scar on his forehead and the faint yellowy blue traces of bruising beneath both his eyes.

"What happened at the end?" she asked." I remember sending you off to find the generators and then..." she trailed away.

"Look," he whispered gently, "That can all come later. For now, you need to get some rest." He leaned forward and kissed her forehead. Her eyes closed once more.

74

Richmond, London , October 2012

Brian handed Kate a mug of steaming coffee. She was sitting at the kitchen table in their new house. This was only the second time she had been there. The move seemed like a lifetime ago. Brian was staring out into the garden where a magpie and a squirrel were having a face off over a scrap of bread.

"So, explain to me again," said Kate, "you found out from news reports the identity of the four men who were discovered slumped round the obelisk in the aftermath?"

Brian sat down at the table. "When the authorities eventually reacted and got inside the Dome, you can imagine what greeted them. It took them days to get to everyone and determine whether everyone had been accounted for. Some of the last to be discovered were the four men who were finally found beneath a huge section of the roof that had fallen down into the arena. Miraculously, two of them were still alive."

"And this was why they became such big news?"

"Exactly, the authorities had already declared that, in all probability, no further survivors would be found so after five days, no one could believe it. The coverage was incredible and you can imagine what I thought when the footage showed them being pulled out of the wreckage and I realised that one of them was the man with the pendant."

Kate took a sip of her coffee. "And what was the response of this man...what was his name?"

"Aziz."

"...this Aziz. When you turned up at the hospital, what was his reaction?"

Brian put his mug down, "Well, I was surprised to hear from the Staff Nurse who had become quite friendly with him that he had had no visitors other than the police in the time he had been there. Apparently, the police had questioned him about his role in the proceedings. A lot of witnesses had given statements explaining that the events of the evening only really turned nasty following the offering of the four keys into the stone. After he explained that he was simply a paid employee of the Olympics organising committee doing what he had been told to do as part of the official ceremony and had no memory of what happened after he placed the key into the stone, the police seemed happy with everything. I guess they must have checked everything out."

He paused to take a mouthful of coffee, and then continued. "At first, he was very guarded. He thought I was just another reporter after a scoop. It was only when I mentioned the name Seth and the resurrection that he realised what I knew."

Kate was keen to get to the point, "So how did he react then, did it all come pouring out?"

Brian looked a little put out as he was just getting into his stride and didn't want to omit any important detail. "Well, yes really. He more or less went back to the beginning. As I explained yesterday, it turns out that Aziz was part of a secret society based in the city of Cairo. Apparently, he was originally the assistant curator of the National museum and had, along with several other eminent professors, become obsessed with some ancient scrolls that foretold what was going to happen."

"You mean they already knew about the resurrection and didn't do anything to stop it before it got to the stage it did?"

"Well, yes they knew what it said in the scrolls and they knew of the existence of the keystones. In fact, Aziz told me that there are actually twelve of them. They were scattered all round the globe by the minions of Seth. If the legend is to be believed, he ordered them to be hidden so that the corpse of Osiris could never be resurrected and regain his rightful place as Pharaoh. Because of this, they also realised that it would be impossible to find and destroy all the keystones before the precessional cycle was complete and the portal could be opened. So they came up with a plan of their own."

Kate was rubbing her temple now, a sure sign that she was going to get a migraine. This was a legacy of her experiences in the Dome, the doctors had said. "They had to somehow plant a mole in Henderson's organisation to be certain of being able to sabotage the resurrection?"

"Precisely! And the fact that they had already discovered, through an intricate network of private detective agencies funded by a very wealthy member of their society, that Henderson had been trying to track down the keys for years, made it very easy to make sure one of the keys turned up at exactly the right time. Aziz had been tracking one of the keys for several years and apparently he informed Henderson of the location of it so that he could acquire it. From that point on Aziz became a trusted aide and *'friend'* of Henderson.

"So how did they plan to ensure that the resurrection would not be successful bearing in mind that they were essentially facilitating it?"

Brian walked round the table and stood behind Kate so he could massage her shoulders whilst he talked. It sometimes helped with the migraine.

"Aziz knew that, according to the scrolls, the pendant-the 'eye of Horus'-like the Stone, was also a portal and that if it could also be placed in the correct position at precisely the correct time, there was a chance that Osiris could return and stop the resurrection. What he didn't realise was that once the final key was hooked into place on the Stone, he would be rendered virtually motionless. The pendant was round his neck and he could not move it to line up with the heavens and thus open the portal."

"What did he say when you explained to him that it was you and I that were responsible for shutting off the power and enabling the 'eye' to open the portal?"

"I never studied Arabic so it was a little confusing at first but I got the impression he was very happy!"

Kate slapped his thigh in mock annoyance. "Brian, come on. Help me out here. I want to know everything!"

It was getting dark outside by the time Brian had finished his story and Kate was shaking her head with disbelief. "You know what the most incredible thing is about the whole situation though," Brian said finally.

"What?" Kate asked.

"Well, don't you think it is amazing that you went off on your expedition to Australia with absolutely no knowledge of the fact that Michael was already involved with Henderson? In fact, he actually provided him with one of the keys. And, if that wasn't enough, you then ended up discovering the link between the position of the ceremonial sacrifice sites and the position of the stars. It can't all be coincidence!"

Kate was looking past him as though pondering something in a far off memory. Then she sighed deeply and smiled. "Perhaps it was already written in the stars. Long before our time."

Epilogue

London, July 2013

The murky water lapped round the young boy's ankles. He was staring across at Battersea power station on the other side of the Thames. He was sure his dad had a blue-ray with a picture of it on the cover.

"Come on, Stephen, the tide'll be in soon," shouted an even younger boy who was up to his knees in mud and busily trying to dig something out of the sandbank a few yards behind him.

Stephen turned round to see what his friend was fussing over. "What you got there then? Not another pram wheel is it!"

The boy was trying to lever what looked like a rock out of the sand with a piece of driftwood.

"It's something made of metal I think, might be worth a few quid at Rashid's scrap yard."

"Come here, let me have a go," said Stephen taking hold of the oversized piece of wood. He pushed the wood as far over as it would go then placed his foot on top using his bodyweight for extra leverage. There was no movement at first then, slowly but surely, he felt the stick begin to move.

The younger boy was jumping up and down with excitement. "It's working, Stephen, it's working!"

There was a gurgling sound as air bubbled up

underneath the sand and the object popped out onto the sandbank. Stephen picked the object up and began to wipe it on his shorts.

"What is it, Stephen-let me look!"

"Hang about, Jamie; it's still covered in mud."

Jamie followed the older boy to the water's edge whilst he dipped the object beneath the water to clean off the mud.

As Stephen lifted the object out of the water, his hand became suddenly warm. At first he thought it was his imagination but then his fingers began to tingle. His first thought was that there was something in the water; the local newspapers were always going on about the pollution still being dumped in there.

"Come on Stephen, let me see please. Is it worth anything?" Jamie was desperate to see what he had found.

Stephen was now staring at the object, his mouth open. The object was shaped like a pyramid with two small appendages shaped like stirrups at either side. On one side was an engraving of a woman. Her eyes were open wide and a drop of water dripped from the corner of one them creating the illusion that she was shedding a tear.

Jamie noticed a shudder run through his friend's body and he guessed he was getting cold. He felt a bit chilly himself and he suddenly realised he was hungry. He was also getting a bit fed up of waiting to see *his* object. "Come on, Stephen, let's get going. Mum'll be wondering where I am."

He turned to make his way up the embankment and took the last step of his short life. The keystone hit him on the back of the neck with such force that it severed his spinal column and he fell to the floor, his arms and legs shaking uncontrollably. He had landed face down in the mud and was aware that he was now breathing in sand. He tried to move but his body wouldn't respond. He tried to scream for help but his mouth was full of grit and stones.

Alexander James

Then he felt another blow to the back of his head and the darkness took him…